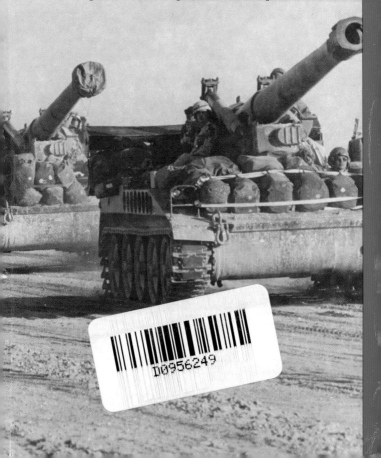

"[A] highly readable book that provides important insights into the general, especially into his origins, character and psychology...fascinating... solid...balanced reporting."
—*The New York Times Book Review*

"Comprehensive...impressive."—*Vanity Fair*

D0956249

In the Eye of the Storm
The Life of General H. Norman Schwarzkopf

Revealed for the first time by prize-winning journalists Roger Cohen of *The New York Times* and Claudio Gatti of *Europeo* . . .

- The inside story on the deep rift the Vietnam War caused in Schwarzkopf's family—including an account of the anti-war activities of his sister Ruth.
- How Schwarzkopf overcame the objections of certain generals to his Desert Storm strategy.
- Exclusive interviews with other key generals in the Desert Storm offensive and their reaction to Bush's decision to halt the Ground War after 100 hours.
- New details from a senior CIA source on the Granada invasion—and how it affected Schwarzkopf's tactics for invading Kuwait.
- Never-before-revealed accounts of Schwarzkopf's leadership in Vietnam from the men who served under him—and nicknamed him "Colonel Nazi."
- Exclusive information on the role Schwarzkopf's father played in the CIA's 1953 coup in Iran—from the CIA agent who orchestrated it.

  And much more . . .

IN THE EYE OF THE STORM

THE LIFE OF GENERAL H. **NORMAN** SCHWARZKOPF

ROGER COHEN & CLAUDIO GATTI

BERKLEY BOOKS, NEW YORK

This Berkley book contains the complete text
of the original hardcover edition. It has been
completely reset in a typeface designed
for easy reading and was printed from new film.

IN THE EYE OF THE STORM

A Berkley Book / published by arrangement with
Farrar, Straus and Giroux

PRINTING HISTORY
Farrar, Straus and Giroux edition published 1991
Published simultaneously in Canada by
Harper Collins*Canada Ltd*.
Berkley edition / December 1992

ISBN: 0-425-13526-8

For Martine, and for Jessica and Daniel
—R. M. C.

For Gail and Aaron
—C. G.

Contents

They taught me that no man could be their leader
except he ate the ranks' food, wore their clothes,
lived level with them, and yet appeared better in
himself.

> —T. E. Lawrence
> *The Seven Pillars of Wisdom*

The success of our lives will be written in your
deeds.

> —H. Norman Schwarzkopf, Sr.,
> in a letter to his son on his tenth
> birthday, August 22, 1944

Introduction

As Only a Soldier Can

The morale of the soldier is the greatest
single factor in war.
—Field Marshal Sir Bernard Law Montgomery

On Friday, June 14, 1985, Major General H. Norman
Schwarzkopf stood before the 16,000 troops of the 24th
Infantry Division on the parade ground at Fort Stewart,
Georgia. Very few people outside the Army had heard of
him. But to his soldiers, this burly and emotional commander, whom they called "the Bear," was already well known
for a style of leadership at once more demanding and more
trusting than was customary. The occasion was a change-
of-command ceremony: Schwarzkopf was about to leave
the 24th Division to take up a job as assistant deputy chief
of staff for Operations and Plans at the Pentagon. In his
two years at Fort Stewart, Schwarzkopf had made many
friends, and he did not forget any of them as he spoke
without notes to the assembled crowd of soldiers, their
families, and local dignitaries. His thirty-minute speech
was eloquent. But in the midst of it he abruptly faltered
and had to fight back tears as he declared to his troops,
"I've loved you as only a soldier can love a soldier."

On the parade ground, bathed in sunshine, soldiers
listened in rapt silence. Joe N. Frazar, then a lieutenant
colonel and battalion commander in the 24th, was among

1

them. He was so struck by the phrase that, as a brigadier general, he would repeat it to U.S. troops during the 1991 Gulf War. Thomas J. Coffey, Jr., an associate editor at the Savannah *Morning News*, was also there and felt moved to write a column about Schwarzkopf's speech. "To hear a general whose presence suggests the total warrior choke back tears as he says, 'I've loved you as only a soldier can love a soldier' is a touching experience," he wrote on June 18, 1985.

Six years later, millions of Americans discovered Schwarzkopf, his tears, and his feelings, and they were touched by him. His swift triumph over Iraq in the 1991 Gulf War came as a shock to a nation that had been battered, by failing industries and festering economic problems, into a sense that the century of its power was at an end, and the mantle of world leadership was passing to others. In a country almost inured to feeling by the drabness of political exchange, and grown unused to leadership from the heart, Schwarzkopf appeared abruptly as an intensely human messenger of hope, however illusory or fragile.

His manner, for many, was a comforting throwback to another time. He had the optimism and the courage of the pioneer. Descended from German immigrants who came to the United States in the mid-nineteenth century and gradually made better lives for themselves, Schwarzkopf stood up for the American Dream just as it seemed most tarnished by spreading poverty and violence.

The general defied the mold. He was overweight and somewhat gauche in his frankness at a time when appearance and measured caution had become the bywords of sound-bite politics. He suggested that words such as "valor" and "glory" were not quaintly old-fashioned but could still have meaning; he urged young Americans to serve their country; and he appeared to demonstrate that character was more important than the astute management of television images.

In a fractured age, Schwarzkopf was a whole man. His wholeness surprised Americans who had come to accept shallowness in their leadership; his success confounded the Cassandras. His impact was particularly strong because he emerged from an institution, the Armed Forces, which had been viewed with skepticism since Vietnam and seemed to many the epitome of unchanging rigidity. Yet the general presented himself as a new kind of leader. He was human, blunt, clear, idealistic, and swiftly effective—shocking qualities in a country accustomed to an apparently mediocre political class more given to obfuscation than clarity, and more inclined to manage the moment than to offer a vision born of personal conviction.

Schwarzkopf's own convictions were slowly formed. If his family provided the basic contours of his outlook, it was the turmoil of Vietnam and the struggle to overcome the consequent disarray of the Army that gave him his mettle.

This long process of revitalizing a degenerate Army was an intensely painful one, which sometimes seemed doomed to failure, and Schwarzkopf's story is also the story of that effort.

At the heart of his credo, always, lay a love of the soldier. That, for him, is what bound an army together and imbued it with nobility of spirit.

His father, Herbert Norman Schwarzkopf, a major general who worked in several countries, first instilled this belief in him. In Iran in the 1940s, Schwarzkopf Sr. was charged with creating a disciplined police force from the ranks of impoverished Iranians. This was impossible without care and courage. As a twelve-year-old child living in Tehran in 1947, Schwarzkopf was able to observe his father's work. At the same time, his imagination was stirred by the great battles of Xerxes and Alexander the Great. The history of these ancient commanders conveyed the glory of soldiering, and it was a hankering for such achievement that Schwarzkopf took with him in 1952 to the United States Military Academy at West Point, where his father had been before him.

When the time came to decide which branch of the Army to enter, Schwarzkopf had little hesitation in choosing the infantry. Although not as prestigious a branch as, for example, the Corps of Engineers, the infantry was at the heart of the battle, where, at no more than a bayonet's length from the enemy, the fight was most intensely human and most given to individual heroism. "He liked the idea of being in the branch that was at the center of the battle. He dreamed of commanding a perfect battle," said a West Point friend, retired Major General Leroy N. Suddath.

But Vietnam, where Schwarzkopf went as a captain in 1965 and again as a lieutenant colonel in 1969, quickly demonstrated that imagined perfection has little to do with the cruelty of war. It was a place in which few illusions could survive. This was a squalid war rather than one of heroic endeavor. Schwarzkopf was appalled by many things. He had grown into manhood in the 1950s, an era of unprecedented prosperity, believing, almost naïvely, in America's ability to do good in the world by defending freedom in places like South Vietnam. Yet he was obliged to be part of an American defeat to the advance of Communism.

Perhaps the most devastating thing to Schwarzkopf in Vietnam was the spectacle of what he perceived to be a lack of leadership among the officer class. Rather than leading by example, he saw, a lot of officers were trying simply to avoid mistakes. Rather than being out at the front with their men, he observed, they were enjoying comfortable headquarters in the rear. Rather than taking the fight to the enemy, he considered, they were opting for passivity. All this contributed in the end to the demoralization and cynicism of the U.S. soldier. When Schwarzkopf tried to drive his men to fight in Vietnam, several of them responded by hating him and nicknaming him "Colonel Nazi."

In the end, after some vacillation during which his military career was in doubt, Schwarzkopf reacted to the trauma of Vietnam by developing his own philosophy of leadership. In posts from Germany to Hawaii, he shook things up. He raged at times, particularly if soldiers were not being looked after. But he also rewarded people generously and gave them real responsibility. He was not vindictive. He was physically warm. If convention was mindless, he flouted it. Above all, he led by passionate example, staying out with his soldiers as much as possible and following the principle first outlined more than two thousand years ago by the Chinese warrior-philosopher Sun Tzu: "The Way means inducing the people to have the same aim as the leadership, so that they will share death and share life, without fear or danger." Like Sun Tzu, he suggested through his example that "invincibility is in oneself, vulnerability is in the opponent."

In the spring of 1984, while he was commanding the 24th Division, Schwarzkopf went to the National Training Center in the Mojave Desert at Fort Irwin, California. There a mock battle pitted a battalion commanded by Lieutenant Colonel Frazar against an opposing force, or OPFOR, trained in Soviet tactics. Frazar's battalion was crushed in just forty-five minutes. "If Schwarzkopf had relieved me on the spot, he would have had a perfect justification. I had failed as a commander," Frazar said.

But after a tough critique in the after-battle review, Schwarzkopf took Frazar aside and put his arm around him. This intimate gesture by a major general to a lieutenant colonel startled Frazar. It was the direct opposite of a martinet's formal distance. Schwarzkopf said, "That's all right, Joe, we're learning by this thing, and it's going to get better. Just keep working on the faults that were revealed. I have every confidence that you will bring it together. *But you must be positive with the young officers who feel they let you down and let themselves down.*"

In Schwarzkopf's vision of the Army, qualities of leadership were passed down by symbiosis. Mutual inspiration replaced the barking of orders. It was essential, therefore, that this chain of values never be broken.

The success of the drive to create such an Army was abruptly revealed to Americans and the world in the Gulf. It was a profound shock. Nobody had paid much attention, but the Armed Forces had reinvented themselves entirely in the two decades since Vietnam.

To compare the stiff style of General William C. Westmoreland in his starched uniform, inspecting troops in Vietnam, with the relaxed manner of Schwarzkopf in his desert fatigues clapping soldiers on the back is to sense the distance traveled by the Army. But its transformation went far deeper than a mere difference of style. It was one of philosophy, doctrine, recruitment, weaponry, and leadership. From a conscript Army in 1972 racked by racial antagonism, drug abuse, violence, indiscipline, desertion, and crime, a new professional force eventually emerged in the 1980s, characterized by its drive, coherence, and dedication. This book is also an account of that slow change. It was one for which Schwarzkopf steadily labored through much of his military career.

In the end, the victory in the Gulf confirmed the Armed Forces' achievement. It was, in many ways, based on the military lessons learned in Vietnam, where the leaders of the Gulf War had been lieutenants, captains, majors, and lieutenant colonels. But many, both at home and abroad, had been skeptical. For the British, Schwarzkopf initially appeared as a troublesome figure, a gung-ho blusterer, while the more sober General Colin L. Powell, the chairman of the Joint Chiefs of Staff, was much more reassuring. But, said Air Vice Marshal Ian Macfadyen, the chief of staff of the British forces in the Gulf, "we quickly discovered that General Schwarzkopf's rudeness was not aimed at people, it was aimed at things. He was a considerable diplomat, even as one sensed that he could overpower people if he wanted. Like all great commanders he could see the big picture."

Lawrence Goldman, a historian and Fellow of St. Peter's College, Oxford, said that "Schwarzkopf's demeanor, his looks, and his fast-talking one-liners initially made everyone worried. He seemed a bit of a hothead. But in the end, there was widespread praise and respect for him. He was a new breed of classless general, a guy to have a beer with, but also a man with a brilliant grasp of his task."

In France, too, Schwarzkopf surprised people with his sensitivity, his political adroitness, and his mastery of the military art. Because the American war effort, involving a thirty-three-nation coalition, was coordinated through the United Nations and conducted with considerable diplomacy, fears of a new era of U.S. military assertiveness were muted. In the end, admiration was widespread, according to French government officials. Brigadier General Daniel Gazeau, the deputy commander of the French forces in Saudi Arabia, kept a journal during his stay in the Saudi capital of Riyadh. On March 1, 1991, he made the following entry:

> What a phenomenal victory of force and intelligence! What good fortune to have been able to live with the Americans in their capacity for courage and determination when it is necessary! Vietnam is at last forgotten.

After the defeat of Saddam Hussein and the recapture of Kuwait, the trauma of Vietnam did indeed seem to be surmounted. It was not that its pain was forgotten by those who had been there or lived those bitterly divisive years in the United States. But many Vietnam veterans spoke of having their pride restored; and the country as a whole appeared to have rallied from an insidious defeatism. There was no longer the sense, evident in the myriad prophecies of doom before the war, that any U.S. foreign policy foray was bound to fail. Optimism and a belief in the ability to overcome, two qualities deeply rooted in the American psyche and eroded in the two decades since Vietnam, appeared to be reasserting themselves.

Schwarzkopf was part of the Vietnamese defeat, and then, sixteen years after Saigon fell, he engineered the victory that laid the "Vietnam syndrome" to rest. Because his sister Ruth became deeply involved in the anti-war movement during the Vietnam years, he suffered, in an intimate way, the divisions that the war caused. Brother and sister, like so many families torn by the war and like the ranks of the Armed Forces themselves, were separated by a deep rift. For many years they did not talk. This book is an account of these family divisions and the way they were finally resolved. It is the story of a society divided from, and then abruptly reunited with, its Armed Forces. It is the tale of a man's healing.

Addressing the House and the Senate on May 8, 1991, Schwarzkopf stressed unity: "We feel a special pride in joining ranks with that special group who served their country in the mountains, jungles, and deltas of Vietnam. They served just as proudly as we served in the Middle East."

The last general to address both Houses of Congress had been Westmoreland, on April 28, 1967, who earned a standing ovation when he declared, "Backed at home by resolve, confidence, patience, determination, and continued support, we will prevail in Vietnam over the Communist aggressor."

In the twenty-four years between those speeches—Schwarzkopf's a statement of triumph, Westmoreland's an expression of vain hope—the world had changed. Schwarzkopf was fortunate in that he fought the first war of the post-cold-war era. As a result, Saddam Hussein was isolated, risks of nuclear escalation reduced almost to zero. Moreover, as Richard W. Murphy, the former assistant secretary of State for Near Eastern and South Asian Affairs, said, "Saddam was a marvelous enemy. He came to Schwarzkopf from Central Casting, and he performed gloriously. We are happier when we fight evil, not different shades of gray, and he was pure black."

Schwarzkopf also proved himself a military leader adept enough to work in this changed world. In the space of a few months, he forged a coalition embracing soldiers from countries as various as France, Bahrain, and Bangladesh. He praised Islam and was sensitive to other cultures. He never gave the sense that the United States was riding roughshod over others. This was reassuring to a world confronting the tremendous technological and military strength of its one remaining superpower.

Schwarzkopf's triumph, of course, was no panacea. America's social, economic, political, and financial problems persisted. Its recession in mid-1991 had not gone away. The battle on the home front promised to be far grimmer.

Some argued that the war had been unnecessary. Kuwait, its oil wells and capital city destroyed, had been dismembered. At the end of the fighting, Saddam Hussein was still in power and the terrible suffering of many Iraqis, particularly the Kurds, was exacerbated. Israel and the Palestinians seemed no closer to peace, although the war had shaken traditional thinking about the Middle East and so perhaps opened the way for innovative solutions. According to a Defense Department estimate, not released until June 4, 1991, over three months after the war ended, as many as 100,000 Iraqis had died, and most of the deaths had been concealed from the U.S. public by sanitized media coverage that distorted the reality of the war. Schwarzkopf was certainly party to this effort at distortion, which he attributed, lamely, to a distaste for "body count"—the practice in Vietnam of estimating, often falsely, the number of enemy dead. "The concealing of the damage of the war led the American public to be indifferent to the casualties," argued Todd Gitlin, a professor of sociology at Berkeley and former president of the radical Students for a Democratic Society in the 1960s. "I assume Schwarzkopf was involved in that, and I think that was vile."

But Schwarzkopf brilliantly accomplished his mission of recapturing Kuwait and destroying the regional threat of a dictator. For the Western world, this was important because the Middle East accounts for 77 percent of the non-Communist world's oil reserves, and Saddam, once he had annexed Kuwait, was moving closer to substantial control of those resources. In crushing the world's fourth-largest army, Schwarzkopf lost just 263 U.S. soldiers, or 0.05 percent of his force of 541,000. This confounded all estimates, both from his own commanders and from outside experts, because it was unprecedented in the annals of military combat. He achieved this overwhelming victory through what may only be called a genius for war. Elaborate deception, inspiration of his men, and superb timing all played a part. Superior technology alone would never have accomplished this. This book tells the story of how the Iraqis were crushed.

In his classic tract *On War*, the Prussian soldier and scholar Karl von Clausewitz distinguished between two forms of courage: "first, physical courage, or courage in the presence of danger to the person; and next, moral courage, or courage before responsibility, whether it be before the judgement-seat of external authority, or of the inner power, the conscience." Both forms of courage, he suggested, were necessary in the military hero.

Before he left for Riyadh on August 26, 1990, Schwarzkopf had already amply illustrated his physical courage during a thirty-four-year military career. In Vietnam, he had walked across a minefield to save a stricken soldier, and he had always insisted on being at the front with his men. But his moral courage—

what Clausewitz characterized as "an act of feeling"—
was most fully revealed in the Gulf War.

When he was commanding the allied Army, his moral
courage was clear to everyone. Schwarzkopf imbued the
men and women in his command with an extraordinary
spirit that carried them to victory. They trusted and identified with him. His style was the fruit of study but, above
all, of experience. It was crucial. As Clausewitz wrote:
"The whole inertia of the mass gradually rests its weight
on the Will of the Commander: by the spark in his breast,
and by the light of his spirit, the spark of his purpose, the
light of hope must be kindled afresh in others: in so far
only as he is equal to this, he stands above the masses
and continues to be their master."

How will these gifts be applied in civilian society?
Schwarzkopf is probably the most conspicuous U.S. hero
since General Dwight D. Eisenhower, who became President seven years after his triumph in the Second World
War. F. Scott Fitzgerald wrote: "Show me a hero and I
will write you a tragedy." After his expected retirement
from the Army in the fall of 1991, Schwarzkopf could
squander his prestige; the potential pitfalls before him
are innumerable. Already, he has shown a susceptibility
to public acclaim and a taste for speaking his mind that
have not endeared him to everybody.

For example, returning to the U.S. Military Academy
at West Point on Wednesday, May 15, 1991, to make
a speech to cadets, Schwarzkopf vehemently criticized
those who had belittled the Army's leadership before the
Gulf campaign. He said: "After Vietnam, we had a whole
cottage industry develop, basically in Washington, D.C.,
that consisted of a bunch of military fairies, that had never
been shot at in anger, who felt fully qualified to comment
on the leadership ability of all the leaders of the United
States Army." After homosexuals complained about the
term "military fairies," a spokesman at Central Command,
John Jendro, had to explain that Schwarzkopf's words

were not meant as "a slight to the gay and lesbian community." The general has much to learn on the perils of public life in America.

But his popularity is enormous and his human qualities conspicuous. From his childhood, he was taught to care for others, no matter what their race or social position; and his concern for the ordinary soldier has been the hallmark of his style of leadership. Raised in several countries, and posted in numerous others during his military career, he is a genuine internationalist in a world growing smaller by the day and an America whose parochialism alarms him. He has the unusual courage to lead from his own moral convictions, and the strength, first learned from his father, to consider that emotional expression is no sign of weakness. His intellect is penetrating, his instinct bold.

Schwarzkopf's life, although solidly rooted in a strong family, has been tempestuous. As this account makes clear, his bristling determination and passionate nature have carried him from storm to storm. It seems inconceivable that for him, at the age of fifty-six, calm will now prevail. Within a year of an anonymous retirement from the Army, fate abruptly placed him in the public gaze. Will he now retreat from it? This seems doubtful. Heroic service has always been his goal. Schwarzkopf is a man who likes to stand squarely in the eye of the storm; and he has now demonstrated that this is a position in which he can serve his country.

His achievement would have pleased his father, who set Schwarzkopf the highest ideals. Indeed, at the age of ten, as a birthday present, Schwarzkopf received from his father an ancient Persian battle-ax, a most unusual gift, offered as a symbol of the magnificence of past civilizations and an augury of his son's future. In an accompanying letter, his father underlined to Schwarzkopf that childhood was now giving way to youth. His words were solemn: he wished his son success in "the battle of life." The letter reflects the steadfast striving, the constant values, and the pursuit of ideals with which the Schwarzkopfs bettered themselves in America, generation after generation.

1

"Honor, Duty, Fidelity"

This above all: to thine own self be true.
—Shakespeare, *Hamlet*

There were plenty of people in New Jersey in 1921 who wished Herbert Norman Schwarzkopf only ill. His mission to establish a state police force threatened too many interests. Bootleggers and casino owners were concerned that the force would prevent them from using bribes to win over local authorities. City mayors did not like the idea of any autonomous group interfering with the way they conducted their police business. Labor unions feared the police would become another instrument of repression. And in the outlying rural areas of the eight-thousand-square-mile state, the robbers who regularly attacked farmers and travelers with virtual impunity had no desire to see anything change. But Schwarzkopf was determined that through the exercise of discipline and authority, a newly created state police should impose order on the unruly state.

His daunting undertaking was announced on July 1, 1921, by the governor of New Jersey, Edward I. Edwards. At the age of just twenty-five, General H. Norman Schwarzkopf's father thus became the youngest head of a statewide police force in the United States. The task before him amounted to the creation from scratch of this organization. All that he had was a budget and a copy of the law establishing the force.

But although he was a young man, Schwarzkopf also had something else: the experience of a tough education at the United States Military Academy at West Point, New York, and of fighting in Europe in World War I. This had given him moral and human values of a strength unusual in a man in his mid-twenties. He intended to apply these standards. Two months after his appointment, Schwarzkopf began the first training course for the police in the New Jersey town of Sea Girt. One hundred and twenty candidates were put through a rigorous semi-military program that lasted three months. On December 5 the new superintendent chose eighty-one of them. They became the first New Jersey state troopers.

Each of the men received a number that he would keep for life. The number 1 was given to H. Norman Schwarzkopf—he preferred not to use his first name, Herbert. At the same time, he was made a colonel. To protect the entire state of New Jersey, Colonel Schwarzkopf acquired the following: one car, one truck, twenty motor-cycles, and sixty-one horses. This was all that his budget would allow.

He also chose the uniform: a light blue jacket, campaign hat of the same color, and dark blue riding breeches adorned with a yellow stripe. More important than the uniform itself, however, was the new force's symbol. Schwarzkopf select-ed a yellow triangle with three words written along its sides. The words he chose betrayed the central role that West Point—with its motto of "Duty, Honor, Country"—had played in his formation. Schwarzkopf adapted this maxim slightly for his state force and had the words "Honor, Duty, Fidelity" printed along the sides of the triangle. In light of this, it is perhaps no wonder that such words came to represent something much greater than abstract notions for his son, General Schwarzkopf: more than general ideals, they became deeply felt personal convictions that could bring him close to tears when he spoke of them because they were a living link to his father.

To underscore his motto, Colonel Schwarzkopf instituted a special two-hour course called "Principles of the Organization." Its purpose was to explain the values embodied by the force's symbol, and to teach trainees how to apply them in their daily routine. "The course is designed to impress upon the Trooper the importance of supporting the ideals and principles of the organization, and to convey to him the true meaning of honor, duty, and fidelity in his work, as well as to emphasize the importance of courtesy, consideration and a sense of fairness to all classes," *The State Police Magazine* wrote.

Schwarzkopf himself, dressed in the new uniform, seemed the image of the officer and the gentleman. Tall and slim, with his blond hair brushed straight back from a strong face marked by a resolute jaw, fine features, and a carefully groomed mustache, he looked effortlessly distinguished. Later, his wife would never tire of saying that he resembled Clark Gable. But this illustrious air was not the fruit of an aristocratic upbringing. Schwarzkopf Sr. was from relatively humble immigrant origins. He had been born in Newark, New Jersey, in 1895, the only child of Julius Schwarzkopf, a jeweler, and his wife, Agnes. He grew up speaking German at home. The house he was raised in—unpretentious, wood-framed, with bay windows—was at 80 West Kinney Street in Newark, in the midst of a neighborhood first settled by German immigrants in the 1840s.

Thus his admission to West Point, the prestigious bastion of U.S. military tradition, represented a social breakthrough for a family that had arrived in the United States just two generations earlier. The young man seized on the Academy's traditions. "Duty, Honor, Country" were values he had already heard from his own parents; but at West Point they were elevated to immortal ideals. Where else, therefore, could he look when establishing the moral framework for his new police force? Such values held out the promise of greatness to come; and they summed up, in their simplicity, the steady, honest endeavor with which the Schwarzkopfs had made something of their lives in America in the sixty-one years since Christian G. Schwarzkopf, the grandfather of the head of the New Jersey State Police, had left Germany to seek fortune and adventure in America.

It was on Monday, September 13, 1852, that Christian G. Schwarzkopf, aged sixteen, caught sight of New York City after six weeks at sea. Frederich Volckmann, the surly captain of the packet ship *Helene*, welcomed the arrival with satisfaction and mild relief Although ships had been making the crossing for centuries, the Atlantic was still dangerous. Just four years earlier, in 1848, a British ship, the *Ocean Monarch*, was swept by a fire in which 176 passengers died. Such accidents were common. But Volckmann had enjoyed a smooth voyage from the port of Bremen in Germany: no deaths and three babies born at sea.

Christian Schwarzkopf had been born on December 26, 1835, in Untersteinbach, a small village in the kingdom of Württemberg. With its capital in Stuttgart, Württemberg was one of the biggest states of the Confederation of the Rhine and was relatively rich, thanks to its textile and precious-metal production. It was there that Christian had said goodbye to his father, a goldsmith named Johannes, and the rest of the family. Although he had chosen not to pay extra for a cabin during the crossing, Christian was better off than many of the passengers: he had 700 talers in his pocket, the equivalent of about $12,000 today. Like Patrick Kennedy, the father of the Kennedy clan, who had arrived in Boston three years earlier, the young Schwarzkopf was not fleeing famine or poverty when he came to the United States. He was merely looking for opportunity in a bigger and richer country.

After docking, the captain of the *Helene* went to the office of the port commissioner to hand over the passenger list. No occupation was ascribed on this list to Christian Schwarzkopf. This may have been because he was a minor, or perhaps it was a reflection of Volckmann's laziness. For the passengers' country of origin, he simply wrote "Germany," rather than the specific state of the German Confederation. And when he mistakenly wrote "Germany" again as the passengers' destination, he opted not to fill out the manifest again. Instead, he simply scrawled the words "United States of America" in big letters over his error.

Christian Schwarzkopf disembarked onto the busy quay in lower Manhattan. It was sixty-two degrees—a balmy late summer's day. There were no customs officials, and no doctors to examine the immigrants, despite the fact that city records show that in the week before the *Helene* docked, 430 people died of cholera, typhus fever, smallpox, and other diseases. Nor was there anybody to welcome him. Christian could only watch as some passengers were greeted joyously by their families.

Although raw and ridden by disease, New York was already a major urban center. Indeed, with over half a million inhabitants, it was the third-largest city in the Western world, trailing only London and Paris. It was unabashed about its opulence. A booklet then in the store windows spelled out the possibilities that awaited Christian Schwarzkopf. Entitled *The Wealth and Biography of the Wealthy Citizens of the City of New York*, it listed the names and incomes of the most prominent New York businessmen. The 32-page booklet included about six hundred people with incomes of over $100,000. The self-avowed aim of the publication was "to hold up to view some of the brightest examples of prosperity in this new land." Among them was another German immigrant, John Jacob Astor, who had crossed the ocean as a penniless young man before making a fortune in the fur trade.

By the time he died, a few years before Christian stepped ashore, Astor had become the richest man in America, with an income of two million dollars a year.

But the young Schwarzkopf did not intend to pursue his fortune in the streets of New York: it was on the other side of the Hudson River, in New Jersey, that he planned to start life in America. So he made his way to Cortlandt Street Terminal, where he boarded the ferry for the fifteen-minute crossing to Jersey City.

The ferry docked at one of the two big quays in front of the New Jersey Railroad Depot. Built on Hudson Street, the depot faced the waterfront. From it the railroad headed out to such cities as Philadelphia and Washington. But Christian was going just eight miles, to Newark. Still, the steam locomotive took one and a half hours to complete this journey, puffing through the Jersey meadows—now known as the Meadowlands—and stopping in front of hotels and taverns. At last the young immigrant got out at Market Street Station in the middle of the town where he would make his new home.

Newark was then a fast-growing community. As the population soared from just 26,000 in 1840 to over 70,000 in 1860, new buildings sprouted every month. The Passaic River was a major center of commerce, crisscrossed by boats serving the four- and five-story factories on its banks. Although the city's streets were hardly paved with gold, it was that precious metal which provided a living for many of the new inhabitants. As the young Schwarzkopf arrived, Newark was earning renown as a center for jewelry.

Indeed, one contemporary account declared that "the eyes of the blind have been opened and dazzled by the brilliancy of Newark's workmanship, as displayed in Tiffany's and other great bazaars of New York and elsewhere." The factories producing these objects were full of German immigrants. They settled on both sides of Springfield Avenue and west of the city's principal thoroughfare, Broad Street.

Among them was Frederick Louis, a goldsmith who also hailed from Württemberg and had come to the United States a few years earlier. He met Christian soon after his arrival, and on April 5, 1853, the young Schwarzkopf made the following application to the judges of the orphans' court in the county of Essex:

> The Petition of Christian Schwarzkopf late from Germany in Europe respectfully showeth that he is of the age of fourteen years or upwards, that he has no parents nor property in the United States of America and that he is desirous of learning a trade and for the purpose of apprenticing to such trade he prays that a guardian may be appointed. He asks that Frederick Louis of the city of Newark may be appointed as such guardian.

Mr. Louis agreed, signing a fifty-dollar bond to the state of New Jersey.

Although the German newcomers were generally better educated than other immigrants, they were also prone to Sunday beer drinking—and singing. This amounted to defiance of the generally puritanical customs of the American Sabbath. A stereotype of the German emerged, portraying him as a noisy, fat, beer-swilling character with a penchant for brawls. People grumbled that "wherever three Germans congregated in the United States, one opened a saloon so that the other two might have a place to argue!"

Sometimes seen, like the Irish, as drunken foreigners, the Germans were natural targets for the Nativism in America movement. The Nativists wanted city life to return to the style of the Founding Fathers. In 1854, two years after Christian settled in Newark, the American Protestant Association Lodge of New Jersey held a parade in the city. They arrived brandishing Bibles and guns. After marching down Broad Street, they turned into William Street, just a couple of blocks from Christian's home, and stopped in front of St. Mary's Catholic Church, which was known for its mainly German congregation. Here fighting erupted. The marchers stormed into the church, breaking the doors, shattering windows, and damaging paintings and statues. Even the organ was destroyed.

But such incidents did not deter the German population from their customs. Between 1850 and 1855, a series of German-language newspapers were started, including *Der Nachbor*, the New Jersey *Volksman*, and *Die Friedensfiefe Zeitung*. The community even tried—unsuccessfully—to get the city of Newark to print its municipal laws in German. In 1855 the first German-American school was founded. As in any other immigrant community, shared origins provided a reassuring bond and a source of strength.

Throughout his long life in the United States—he died in 1916 at the age of eighty—Christian was immersed in this German-American world. Indeed, on his granite tombstone in Fairmont Cemetery in Newark, he had the inscription engraved in German although he had lived in America most of his life: "Ich weiss dass mein Erloeser lebet" (I know that my Redeemer liveth).

What were the values of this German-American community? They certainly included industry, honor, a strong religious sense, and a commitment to the preeminence of the family and to the importance of discipline. These qualities were passed on to all Christian's descendants. It was no coincidence that his grandson Herbert Norman Schwarzkopf, Sr., was a fluent German speaker. "As a boy, my father still lived in a very tight and close German community," said General Schwarzkopf's sister Sally. "It was an environment where one's German heritage was stressed."

While Christian reserved a special affection for his fatherland, he wasted little time establishing himself in America. On November 4, 1856, he stood before the Essex County civil court judge and signed a pledge of allegiance to the United States, renouncing all loyalties to the King of Württemberg. He thus declared his intention of becoming a U.S. citizen. And soon after, he added emotional bonds to such formal ties. He fell in love with his guardian's daughter, Bertha Louis. Like Christian, she had been born in Württemberg, and immigrated with her parents when she was nine.

Although a severe winter and deep depression gripped Newark in the early months of 1857, Christian was already working as a goldsmith and had enough money to consider marriage. On July 5, 1857, the couple was wed by the Reverend Johannes Ulrich Guenter of the German Presbyterian Church of Newark. Christian was twenty-one and his bride just seventeen. They went to live at 38 Baldwin Street in the center of Newark. Within a year, Bertha gave birth to their first child, Henry M. Schwarzkopf.

By this time, Christian was an American. He had applied for citizenship on Columbus Day 1857, after living in the United States for just five years, the minimum time allowed by law. His father-in-law, Frederick Louis, testified to his integrity, moral character, and belief in the principles of the Constitution of the United States.

That Constitution, however, was soon under increasing strain. North and South were riven by bitter differences, which became the focus of the 1860 election campaign. The Newark newspaper the *Evening Journal* declared its opposition to Abraham Lincoln and the abolitionists because of Newark's many commercial ties with the South. The jewelry made by Christian Schwarzkopf and others was widely sold south of the Potomac, so any division of the country threatened to cut off an important market.

"If Lincoln is elected," the paper warned, "many of our artisans will be compelled to face the rigors of winter while being told everywhere: No work! No work!"

So, on November 6, 1860, Newark voted strongly against Lincoln. That, however, did not stop the Republican candidate from winning. On December 20, South Carolina announced its secession. Two days later, the *Evening Journal* weighed in with an editorial entitled "The Southern Cause Is Our Cause." But not everybody agreed. The rival paper, the *Mercury*, promptly poured scorn on the *Journal*, announcing its "contempt for the band of mercenary and unprincipled men engaged in Southern trade."

The German community was divided. But most members showed loyalty to the presidency and sided with Lincoln. They had a chance to demonstrate this in February 1861, when the President-elect came to Newark, riding through town in a horse-drawn carriage. A massive crowd greeted him on Broad Street, less than a block away from the Schwarzkopfs' house.

Two months later, Lincoln called for troops. Alabama, Louisiana, Mississippi, Georgia, Florida, and Texas had joined the Confederacy. Newark was quick to respond. Over three thousand militiamen and volunteers left the city for Washington and, on May 7, were the first uniformed unit to arrive in the capital. Among them was a brigade of German immigrants.

Throughout the early years of the Civil War, Christian's hometown provided many volunteers. Six of the ten companies of the 26th Regiment came from Newark. When they marched through the city in June 1863, they were greeted by what one newspaper called "a grand demonstration."

But at the front, the situation was grim. One month earlier, Confederate troops had won a great victory at Chancellorsville in Virginia over Union Major General Joseph Hooker's Army of the Potomac. While Confederate General Robert E. Lee feigned a frontal attack with a small force, West Point graduate T. J. "Stonewall" Jackson led his II Corps on a surprise fifteen-mile flanking movement before smashing through Hooker's

exposed right side. It was an overwhelming victory—
General Lee's last—won through tactical ingenuity, speed,
and the use of surprise. In conception, it was not dissimi-
lar to the triumph of another West Point graduate 128
years later in the Persian Gulf. Indeed, the battle was
among those studied by the future General H. Norman
Schwarzkopf at West Point.

Success at Chancellorsville led General Lee to invade
the North and move toward Philadelphia, endangering
Newark. Nervousness spread. But on Independence Day,
while the congregation of the Central Methodist Church
gathered, a man burst in with a message. The Southerners
had been defeated at Gettysburg and were in retreat. Outside the Schwarzkopfs' house, a noisy crowd streamed
through the streets in celebration.

That same month, William Tecumseh Sherman was
named brigadier general in the Union Army. Then,
when Ulysses S. Grant assumed supreme command in
the West, Sherman became commander of the Army of the
Tennessee. He went on to direct the Chattanooga campaign,
and to destroy Confederate communications and supplies at
Meridian, Mississippi. His march to the sea, which started
from Atlanta in November 1864 with 60,000 men, brought
the Southern forces to their knees and created a military
legend. It would also provide inspiration to the young
cadet H. Norman Schwarzkopf when he entered West
Point almost a century later.

Sherman believed that "war is cruelty, and you cannot
refine it." But when it could not be avoided, he waged it
with imagination, utter determination, and overwhelming
force. Schwarzkopf's choice of Sherman as a military hero
is therefore not surprising. Traits of candor, enthusiasm,
and eloquence link the two men.

Sherman's blistering campaign led to the surrender of
General Lee on April 9, 1865. The mayor of Newark
ordered a day of celebration. Church bells sounded, factory whistles blew, long-dormant cannons were fired on

Broad Street, and a flag-waving crowd danced in the street. For Christian Schwarzkopf, it was a rare day off. He would work from dawn until sunset every day of the week except Sunday, painfully eking out enough of a living to support a growing family. By 1873, he and Bertha had had five children.

They did not all go into the same field. Henry Gustav and William, the two oldest surviving sons following the death in infancy of Henry M., began their careers selling insurance. It was left to Julius George, General Schwarzkopf's grandfather, to follow Christian as a jeweler. A gifted designer, he opened his own store, which earned renown for its unusual pieces. The Schwarzkopfs still have some of his creations, including an almond-shaped piece that slides open to reveal a Christ Child.

His success marked the point at which the family began to progress from its working-class origins in America and achieved a degree of middle-class comfort. It was not great wealth, but it was a discreet step up the social ladder.

In April 1893, Julius Schwarzkopf married Agnes Sarah Schmidt, the daughter of German immigrants. That same year, Julius A. Lubkuecher, a German-born jewelry maker, became mayor of Newark—an event that marked the growing social esteem and acceptance of the once-derided immigrant community. Two years later, on August 28, 1895, the couple's only child, Herbert Norman, was born. From a young age, he would show a fascination with military uniforms. At the age of nine he went to a military boarding school. And when in 1912 he passed the West Point entrance examination at the age of seventeen, he effectively ushered the Schwarzkopf family into a new and more prominent phase of its American experience: one in which the values of their adoptive land would slowly incorporate and expand those of their tight-knit immigrant world and thrust the Schwarzkopfs onto an ever-wider stage. It would not be long before H. Norman

Schwarzkopf, Sr., was at war in a U.S. uniform against the Fatherland that had been so venerated in his family.

The years of the Great War of 1914–18 were traumatic ones for the Schwarzkopfs. For Schwarzkopf Sr. they brought the shock of West Point discipline. For the family in Newark it was a time of changing values: they were obliged to moderate their German patriotism.

Although the sinking of the *Lusitania* in 1915 by a German U-boat provoked strong anti-German feelings around the country, the initial German victories during the war were still cause for celebration in Newark's German community. On June 10, 1916, as part of the city's 250th anniversary celebration, six thousand Newarkers of German ancestry marched proudly with their German flags.

But by the following year, the flags were being quietly folded and stored in the face of national indignation at German hostility. The Deutsch Club in Newark duly changed its name to the Abraham Lincoln Association. The German Fire Insurance Company became the National Liberty Insurance Company. And one branch of the Schwarzkopf family—headed by General Schwarzkopf's great-aunt—even changed its name to Raymond in reaction to American hostility to Germany.

In the midst of this, Schwarzkopf Sr. completed his degree at West Point. He had been far from a model student. Indeed, he had displayed more of a talent for sports than for academic endeavor and more of a taste for the whimsical than for discipline.

Between 1913 and 1917, he endured hundreds of hours of confinement as his instructors sought to impose their strict order. He was repeatedly made to "walk the area"— West Point jargon for long forced marches in uniform up and down the imposing courtyard. The yearbook of his class mentions Schwarzkopf's prowess at football, boxing, polo, swimming, and basketball. But it is conspicuously silent on the subject of his academic efforts.

He became known to his West Point friends as "Schwarzie"—the nickname that would also be given to his son thirty-nine years later. In the end, he graduated 88th in a class of 139—a passable performance. And in May 1917, one month after the United States entered the war, the young lieutenant from Newark left for France with the 2nd Cavalry Regiment. According to the family, he was not in the least ambivalent about donning an American uniform and fighting the country of his ancestors. The motto of West Point was clear—"Duty, Honor, Country"—and his country was the United States of America.

At the front, Schwarzkopf was promoted to captain and transferred to the 76th Field Artillery. He fought in the Second Battle of the Marne, where, in summer 1918, French, British, and U.S. troops stopped the Germans in their tracks after they had broken through at Chemin des Dames in the spring. During the battle, Schwarzkopf's battalion was the object of a mustard-gas attack by the Germans. This experience haunted him for many years. It was thought by doctors to have been a cause of his ill health in later life.

Undaunted, Captain Schwarzkopf took part in the Allied counteroffensive that led to final victory that November. And, after the Armistice, his command of German influenced the Army to station him in Germany with the Allied occupation force.

Here he had a variety of jobs. But generally he performed duties that gave him an extensive understanding of law enforcement: he was a provisional mayor, a judge, and a provost marshal. After returning to the United States in 1919, he continued in the law-enforcement area. Assigned to the 7th Cavalry Regiment in El Paso, Texas, he worked patrolling the U.S. border with Mexico.

These were important experiences for the young officer. They gave him an early taste of different cultures and led him to hold sensitivity toward them in high esteem.

Later he would insist that his children show interest and respect for the ways of others; he praised eclecticism and criticized the parochialism of many people in the United States. Moreover, confronting the task of restoring order to a defeated country like Germany gave him a firsthand sense of the importance of the very discipline and organization whose application in the name of abstract principles had caused him such grief at West Point.

To Schwarzkopf, the military was the highest form of service. But before all else came family. So when, in late 1919, his father Julius was confined to a wheelchair by an acute attack of arthritis, Norman resigned from the Army and returned home to live with his parents. In addition to helping Julius in the jewelry business, he went to work in the administrative offices of the L. Bamberger Company, which owned one of the three oldest department stores in Newark. Among other things, he was responsible for store security.

For many years, the New Jersey legislature had talked about establishing a state police force. The idea, however, was always strongly opposed by special-interest groups. Nonetheless, the New Jersey Grange and the State Chamber of Commerce of New Jersey continued to put pressure on Governor Edward I. Edwards—better known as Teddy—to approve the state police bill.

It finally became law in 1921. But the arguing did not stop there; in fact, it got worse. Every political boss wanted to ensure his own control over the new department. The two principal contenders were both powerful men. One was Frank Hague, the mayor of Jersey City and boss of the Democratic machine in Hudson County. The other was Harold G. Hoffman, the head of the state's Department of Motor Vehicles and, as such, the controller of a group of state inspectors and a small force of highway police.

The governor decided that he would have to find a man of political independence. One evening, while discussing the situation with his son Irving, he learned about H. Norman Schwarzkopf, the ex–U.S. Army officer who had distinguished himself in Germany by his administrative and organization skills. Schwarzkopf and Irving Edwards had been classmates at West Point and had fought in France together. Edwards told his father that his friend was so non-political that he was not even a registered voter, and urged him to meet with Schwarzkopf.

The meeting took place a few days later in the governor's Trenton office. Schwarzkopf impressed Teddy with his distinguished looks and his enterprising spirit. After the announcement of his appointment in July, Schwarzkopf immediately demonstrated that he had no intention of becoming a mere bureaucrat. He believed, as his son would, in leading by example. Whenever he could, he joined his men in their activities. For example, he never missed an opportunity to join the troopers at the rifle range. He took part in shooting competitions with other police forces and the military. In 1927, armed with his Colt Army Special .38 caliber pistol, he won a medal for hitting the target 98.16 percent of the time. In New Jersey's State Police Museum there are five other Schwarzkopf medals on exhibit.

"Like his son, the colonel was a man's man," said Sergeant Thomas De Feo, the caretaker of the museum. "He loved his troopers, and the feeling was reciprocal. They felt they could joke with him. For example, when he would cut his mustache, they would grow theirs; and when his came back, they trimmed theirs."

By this time, Colonel Schwarzkopf was quite the dapper gentleman about town. He had earned a certain renown as a dashing bachelor. But in November 1928, he abruptly relinquished this reputation, marrying Ruth Alice Bowman of Bluefield, West Virginia. Her father was the superintendent of the county school in Bluefield; her mother, a distant relative of Thomas Jefferson's. They had been divorced when Ruth was seventeen.

Following her parents' divorce, Ruth had moved to Newark, where she entered Mercer Hospital Nursing School. After graduation, she worked for the hospital and also as a private nurse for some of the wealthiest Newark families. At the time that she met Colonel Schwarzkopf, she had become Assistant Superintendent of Nurses at Columbia-Presbyterian Hospital in New York. Thus, in the 1920s, she was in the unusual position of being a single working woman and the daughter of divorced parents.

"She was very much ahead of her time. She took enormous pride in being professional," said her daughter Sally. Her experiences were to be reflected in the way she brought up her children: strictness was never confused with Prussian dogmatism; firm values never precluded open-mindedness.

According to the family, Ruth first set eyes on the colonel at a New Jersey state troopers' parade. She turned to her escort and said, "I'm going to marry that man." From that moment—so the children say—the legend of their father's Clark Gable looks took hold.

The colonel continued to improve the state troopers and, in 1929, despite being a Presbyterian, he selected a Catholic priest of Irish descent to be the force's first chaplain. The Reverend Joseph P. Connor was not merely a religious man. He also impressed Schwarzkopf with his musical abilities. Father Joe had composed music and lyrics for operettas, musicals, and then movies and later contributed to the rise of Frank Sinatra. Under the pseudonym Pierre Norman Connor (chosen in part in honor of his friend Schwarzkopf), Father Joe wrote the music for the song "Head on My Pillow" and for Frank Sinatra's movie *The Miracle of the Bells*. The priest became a close friend of the Schwarzkopfs, performing private concerts for the invalid Julius.

On May 29, 1930, Julius died in a car crash. Before his death, he had closed his jewelry store and started a greeting card business. Designing all the cards himself,

he declared himself the founder of the card business in
America! An innovator throughout his life, he had an
independence of spirit that passed into family legend.
Just five months after his death, on October 13, 1930,
his first grandchild—General Schwarzkopf's sister Ruth
Ann—was born.

It was at about this time that the lives of the Schwarzkopfs
became entangled with that of the legendary aviator
Charles A. Lindbergh, involving them in a complex,
often bitter case that was to leave an indelible mark
on a family for whom honor and honesty are cardinal principles. Tangled up, despite themselves, in a
case where accusations and counteraccusations were
traded for years and the dividing line between fact
and fiction often became blurred, the Schwarzkopfs
came away with a deep mistrust of politics—an art,
unlike that of warfare, in which principle plays little
part. They also came to understand the power of the
press, a power that makes General Schwarzkopf uneasy
to this day.

A few months before Ruth Ann Schwarzkopf was born,
Charles Lindbergh, the aviator famous for his 1927 solo
crossing of the Atlantic in the *Spirit of St. Louis*, and his
wife, the heiress Anne Morrow, celebrated the birth of
their first child, Charles Augustus Lindbergh, Jr. The aviator, like General Schwarzkopf today, was a true American
hero, loved for his single-minded audacity; his wife was
the daughter of a wealthy J. P. Morgan partner. From
the time of their marriage on May 27, 1929, they had
been constantly in the limelight. On Easter Sunday 1930,
they flew together from Los Angeles to New York in
a Lockheed plane, breaking the transcontinental flight
record with a time of 14 hours and 45 minutes. At the
time, Anne was seven months pregnant.

The publicity surrounding their lives was such that the
Lindberghs were anxious to find some privacy. At the

end of September 1930, they bought a piece of land on a wooded hill near the small town of Hopewell, New Jersey. The property was twenty minutes from Princeton and two hours from New York, remote enough to be out of the way of reporters and autograph seekers. While they were building their house there, they kept their main residence at the fifty-acre Next Day Hill estate in Englewood, New Jersey, just across the Hudson from Manhattan. They began using the new house, on weekends only, in 1932.

The last weekend in February of that year, the aviator and his wife were at the house in Hopewell with their twenty-month-old son, Charles; his Scottish nanny, Betty Gow; their English maid, Violet Sharpe; and Ollie and Elsie Whately, the English couple who did the cooking. They had planned to return home to Englewood on Monday morning, but Charles Jr. had a severe cold and so they decided to stay until Tuesday. That day, Charles's cold was still acute, so the departure was put off until the following day. This was the first time that the Lindberghs had been in Hopewell on a Tuesday.

Just after six on that rainy evening of March 1, Betty took Charles upstairs to bed. She gave him a bowl of cereal, administered his drops, and rubbed menthol on his chest. She then put on his flannel undershirt, diaper, rubber underpants, and pajamas before tucking him in and pinning the covers to the bed so that they would not slip down. Once Charles was asleep, she went into the bathroom to wash his dirty clothes. At ten that evening, she returned to the nursery, entering without turning on the lights so as not to awaken him. As she approached the bed, she realized it was empty. Aghast, she rushed through the house asking if anyone had seen Charles. In the end, it was Colonel Lindbergh who noticed a small envelope lying on top of the radiator grille and concluded that the baby had been kidnapped. Assuming that the envelope contained a message from the kidnappers, he left it untouched for the police to examine.

At 10:25 p.m., State Trooper Lieutenant Dunn received a call. "This is Charles Lindbergh," the caller said. "My son has just been kidnapped."

Fifteen minutes later, two policemen arrived at the Lindbergh house. They were officers from the Hopewell sheriff's office. The first New Jersey trooper arrived at 10:55. Superintendent Schwarzkopf was notified at his home and rushed to the scene. He arrived around midnight, followed by a fingerprint expert named Corporal Frank Kelly. Kelly sprinkled the envelope in the nursery with some black powder for fingerprints, but to no avail. The letter was then opened and found to contain a handwritten message in faulty English:

> Dear Sir!
>
> Have 50 000 $ redy 25 000 $ in 20 $ bills 15000 $ in 10 $ bills and 10000 $ in 5 $ bills. After 2–4 days we will inform you were to deliver the Mony.
>
> We warn you for making anyding public or for notify the polise the chld is in gute care. Indication for all letters are signature and 3 holds.

At the end of the note, instead of a signature, there were two interlocking circles with a red ink spot in the center.

Despite an extensive search, no prints were found anywhere in the house. Outside, the policemen noticed footprints in the mud, which led to an unusual, homemade wooden ladder that had apparently been used to get in and out of the window of the baby's room.

News of the kidnapping spread quickly. By midnight it was on the radio and by the next morning on the front page of every single newspaper in the United States. An unprecedented nationwide search for the kidnappers began. One car was stopped at 107 roadblocks on its way from New Jersey to California. The press was in a frenzy. Some journalists disguised themselves as detectives in a bid to get a scoop. When the baby's diet was made known by the family, it was front-page news.

For Colonel Schwarzkopf it was a moment of supreme importance. Franklin D. Roosevelt, then the governor of New York, put his entire state police force at the colonel's disposition. With the eyes of the world on him, Schwarzkopf went to work. By the day after the kidnapping, he had already set up a headquarters with twenty telephone lines in the Lindbergh garage. This impromptu base amounted to Schwarzkopf's War Room.

For the first forty-eight hours, Colonel Schwarzkopf got no sleep. Kidnapping was not then a federal crime, and thus not the responsibility of the FBI. Schwarzkopf nevertheless tried to coordinate his troopers' work with local police forces across the country. He also had to worry about fending off an army of journalists. On March 2 he advised the Lindberghs to state that they were prepared to negotiate with the kidnappers. The next day the announcement was in the press, and on March 4 a note arrived expressing the kidnappers' anger that the police had been notified. They would not negotiate further or give instructions on delivering the money "until the Police is out of ths case and the Pappers are quiet."

It had been mailed from Brooklyn, New York. In place of a signature, it had the two interlocking circles with the red spot.

But the note led nowhere. Nor did a minute examination of the ladder. Ten days after the kidnapping, Colonel Schwarzkopf was moved to make a nationwide appeal for help. Running out of money, he also had to appeal to the State Finance Committee for more funds.

By the end of the second week of the investigation, the country's mood turned against him. The press accused Schwarzkopf of withholding information. Rumors had spread about the existence of a ransom note, which the New Jersey State Police had strongly denied. A reporter had been told by Lindbergh's attorney that, in fact, a message had been found, but Schwarzkopf was still denying it. The superintendent was also attacked by the press for not cooperating with the New York City police, with whom he had also refused to share any information about the second note, although it had been mailed from Brooklyn.

In April the case took a turn for the worse, placing Schwarzkopf in a still more delicate position. At a pre-arranged meeting in a cemetery, an intermediary for the Lindberghs, Dr. John F. Condon, gave an envelope containing $50,000 in bank notes and gold certificates to a man the police believed to be a messenger from the kidnappers. In exchange, he received a letter saying the baby was hidden in a boat off Martha's Vineyard. Lindbergh himself rushed to Massachusetts—to find nothing. The money was gone, but there were no new leads.

A month later, the baby's body was found by a truck driver in woods not far from the Lindberghs' house. The boy was face down, half-hidden by leaves. The corpse had been ravaged by animals and was missing its left leg, right arm, left hand, and all its organs except the heart and liver. The autopsy revealed that the death had occurred soon after the kidnapping and had been caused by a blow to the skull. It was Colonel Schwarzkopf who delivered the news to Mrs. Lindbergh.

Immediately afterward he called a press conference and announced, "Apparently the body of the Lindbergh baby was found at 3:15 p.m. today by William Allen, negro, from Trenton, who was riding on the Mount Rose Road toward Hopewell." The press went wild. In a report sent to J. Edgar Hoover of the FBI, an agent wrote: "According to the newspapers, some diapers were found near the body. But the State Police has conclusive proof that these were planted by a newspaper reporter."

Hoover responded to the crisis by ordering the FBI to help Schwarzkopf. A fifteen-man FBI team under special agent Thomas Sisk was later set up. But the superintendent, who was already having difficulty cooperating with the New York City police, showed little enthusiasm and denied the FBI access to the Lindbergh files. Both the FBI and the New York City Police Department complained publicly, and the press weighed in with articles calling for Schwarzkopf's resignation. "The behavior of the press in the Lindbergh case was appalling," recalled his daughter Sally. "And there was strong rivalry between my father's force and the police in New York and the FBI. I remember my father's bitterness toward Hoover and the FBI."

On June 10 another piece was added to the puzzle: Violet Sharpe, the Lindberghs' maid, committed suicide. Because nobody but the servants had known that the Lindberghs would be in Hopewell that Tuesday, Schwarzkopf had long suspected the possibility of an accomplice among the household staff. But there was still no proof. And the press took the opportunity to attack the superintendent again, accusing him of pushing Violet to the edge with his persistent questioning.

Faced by this barrage of pressures and criticism, Schwarzkopf reacted with a dogged determination that verged on obstinacy. It was not only his competence that was being tested. Early on in the case, according to family members, the superintendent formed a friendship with Lindbergh. As the investigation dragged on, the aviator would come regularly to the Schwarzkopfs' house. Their second daughter, Sally, had been born the year of the kidnapping, on Charles Lindbergh's birthday, February 4, and her birthday became an occasion to celebrate his as well. Emotion and professional honor thus became intertwined. "It was almost as if they had kidnapped my father's son," said Sally. In an interview with the *New York Journal*, the superintendent publicly expressed this feeling: "I have made a friend. There is nothing I would not do for Colonel Lindbergh. There is no oath I would not break if it would materially help his well-being. There is not a single man in my outfit who would not lay down his life for Colonel Lindbergh."

Time passed without any breakthrough. But in November 1933 a wood expert from the Forest Service Laboratory in Madison, Wisconsin, brought into the investigation by Schwarzkopf, established that a piece of wood used to build the ladder had been bought three months before the kidnapping at the National Lumber and Millwork Company in the Bronx. This—along with the fact that some of the bills in the ransom money had begun to show up in Manhattan—centered the investigation on New York City. Schwarzkopf was unhappy about this because of his rivalry with the city police. For him, solving the case had become a personal crusade.

The next year, on September 18, 1934, FBI agent Sisk received a call from a bank executive saying he had received one of the gold certificates from the ransom payment. Sisk went to the bank immediately and discovered that there was a license plate number written by hand on the back of the certificate. The plate was for a 1931 Dodge sedan, registered under the name of Bruno Richard Hauptmann, a German immigrant and a carpenter by trade. Investigators had already determined that the ransom notes were probably written by someone of German descent; and a carpenter could easily have built the odd makeshift ladder used by the kidnappers.

In the morning of September 19 Hauptmann was arrested in the Bronx by a team of police from the FBI and the New York and New Jersey police forces. A twenty-dollar gold note was found in his wallet. Schwarzkopf immediately notified the Lindberghs.

The next day, in Hauptmann's garage, the police found more than $13,000 of the ransom payment. Hauptmann, who had denied having any more notes, said he was given the money by Isidor Fisch, a friend and partner who had returned to Germany. But Fisch had since died.

The carpenter continued with a trail of unconvincing stories or outright lies. He said he did not have a gun, but one was later found in his garage. It also transpired that he bought his wood from the same Bronx company that sold the piece found in the ladder. All of this convinced Schwarzkopf that he had found his murderer. He had him extradited to New Jersey and arrested for homicide.

The evidence linking Hauptmann to the crime proved contradictory and controversial. A farmer who had previously said he had not seen anyone now claimed to have seen the accused in the vicinity. An expert said Hauptmann's handwriting did not match that in the note, and then changed his mind. Nobody saw Hauptmann kidnap the baby and nobody could place him inside the house that evening. Hauptmann himself never wavered in declaring his innocence.

He had his supporters. Schwarzkopf's FBI rival Sisk telegraphed Hoover: "The New Jersey authorities do not have one single reliable witness who can place Hauptmann in the vicinity of Hopewell prior to or on the date of the crime." Moreover, even if Hauptmann was the kidnapper, nothing proved that he was also the murderer.

On February 13, 1935, at 11:25 a.m., the jury of eight men and four women retired to deliberate. It took them eleven hours to reach a verdict, which found Bruno Hauptmann guilty of murder in the first degree. He was sentenced to death.

While the judge announced the sentence, one of the jurors, Mrs. Verna Snyder, was seen biting her lips, her eyes wet with tears. It was later reported that she had been one of two female jurors who held out to the last ballot for a verdict of guilty with a recommendation for life imprisonment.

Her emotion was apparently not shared by Colonel Schwarzkopf. At the end of the trial, he spoke tersely to the press: "I feel that the verdict is in accordance with the evidence and that the ends of justice have been served. The people of Hunterdon County have thoroughly justified the confidence we had in them. The presentation of the case by the Attorney General was not only masterful and resourceful but inspired, and the preparation was unquestionably the most thorough and competent that I have ever heard of."

Then he diplomatically went on to praise the very forces he had clashed with so bitterly: "I have said that this case is a triumph for coordinated and cooperative police work, and full credit should go to the New York City police and to the federal agencies for their unfailing and comprehensive cooperation."

But this attempt at diplomacy did not end the acrimony. Harold G. Hoffman, the former commissioner of motor vehicles, whom Schwarzkopf had beaten for the job of state police superintendent, had just become governor of the state of New Jersey. He still harbored a deep grudge against Schwarzkopf. Dissatisfied with the trial, he hired a detective who had been denied access to the Lindbergh files and hated Schwarzkopf. The detective then secretly visited Hauptmann in prison. Newspapers got wind of this and trumpeted headlines like "Lindbergh Case Reopened."

Colonel Schwarzkopf was enraged. So, too, were the Lindberghs, who left the country. But the fight went on, and Hoffman humiliated Schwarzkopf by instructing him to continue investigating the case and to report to him on a weekly basis. He then called in some other investigators to reopen the case. As the feud escalated, Schwarzkopf accused Hoffman of trying to convince some troopers to admit they had framed Hauptmann. The colonel's dislike of Hoffman was, according to the Schwarzkopf family, accentuated by his belief that Hoffman was a bootlegger. Hoffman fired back, calling the Lindbergh investigation "the most bungled case in police history."

But in the end, nothing could stop the execution. On Friday, April 3, 1936—four years after the kidnapping—

Bruno Hauptmann died in the electric chair.

Even after this, Hoffman and Schwarzkopf continued to spar. The governor called for an investigation of the New Jersey State Police. And a few months later, when Schwarzkopf's third term as superintendent ended, it was no surprise that Hoffman named the colonel's deputy to succeed him.

The last word, however, belonged to Schwarzkopf. Eighteen years after the Lindbergh investigation, he led an investigation into the financial activities of state officials. It resulted in the forced resignation of Hoffman from the position he then held in the Division of Public Security. The investigation found that he had taken $300,000 of government funds.

Of course, this did not change any of the murky facts of the Lindbergh case. For four years it became an obsession—a personal point of pride—for General Schwarzkopf's father. For him it was inconceivable that dedication and hard work would not get him to the bottom of the case. He was prickly because he felt that he could not rest until he had solved the mystery of the kidnapping of his friend's son; and he did not see how others might succeed where he had not made headway. In the end, he seemed tranquil in his certitude. If he had a doubt, he did not betray it.

The case was unquestionably traumatic. Schwarzkopf was attacked by Hoffman on something his family stands by with a fervid conviction: his integrity. This attack left him with a lasting disdain for politics—a disdain he consistently expressed to his children. Although often asked to run for the Senate, he repeatedly declined.

In the midst of this long furor, in the summer of 1934, the colonel's only son—Herbert Norman Schwarzkopf, Jr.—was born. The future general joined a family that had gained a notoriety that was a far cry from the humble anonymity of the immigrant community in which his great-grandfather started life in America. But was his father permanently troubled by the Lindbergh case? "Lindbergh was totally satisfied with the results of the investigation and wrote to my father thanking him for all he had done," said Sally. "I know that my father never doubted Lindbergh's belief that Hauptmann was guilty. Never."

2

The Battle of Life

Example is the best precept.
—Aesop

The birth of a boy in the Schwarzkopf family had been anxiously awaited for some time. "A German woman would have had a son first!" Agnes grumbled when her thoroughly American daughter-in-law, Ruth, gave birth to Ruth Ann. Then came Sally. But at last, after the two girls, a boy was born on August 22, 1934. H. Norman Sr., who was determined to pass on his name, was delighted. His one dilemma was that he loathed his own first name, Herbert. But family pride prevailed, and the boy was called Herbert Norman Schwarzkopf, Jr. In time, he would grow to dislike the name Herbert more passionately than his father had; indeed, it would cause him such grief that he would formally change his name eighteen years later.

With the baby's arrival, their house in Pennington was too small. Colonel Schwarzkopf found a larger home in the nearby town of Lawrenceville, midway between Trenton and Princeton. Lawrenceville dated back to before the American Revolution, but it did not consist of much more than Main Street. It was on Main Street, at number 2549, that the Schwarzkopfs set up residence. The Green House, as their home was called, was not quite an estate;

but it was certainly one of the most stately houses in town. Built in 1815 of dressed stone taken from a local quarry, it represented, in the view of local historian Donald Tyler, "the finest example of Colonial architecture." It was a marked step up from Pennington.

On the lawn stretching in front of the two-story house there was a Camperdown elm with strong, low, outstretched branches. Ideal for climbing, it soon became the children's favorite tree. Even more impressive, however, was a huge European purple beech that was centuries old. It had probably been there at the end of December 1776, when George Washington marched down Main Street after defeating the British at Trenton. The beech stood in front and to the left of the house and made a big impression on the children's imagination. In summer it would cast a shadow as big as a basketball court; in winter its stark branches would stand out against the clear sky like an immense sculpture creaking ominously in the wind.

In the back yard the colonel built a large stone grill in the shape of a huge armchair where, at dusk, under Japanese lanterns, he would cook steaks so enormous they became legendary. When not used by the colonel, the grill became a stone throne where big sister Ruth would sit and play princess. Sally was her valet and little Norm her slave. He had to show absolute servility and address her as "Your Majesty." This was difficult for a child, and the best he could manage was "Your Majesqueak"—a family joke to this day.

His mother, Ruth, was an excellent cook. In the new house she had an enormous kitchen in which she prepared her specialties. Everybody loved to eat, but Norm—a chubby little boy with a very full, round face—stole the show. For Christmas he would always get a pound of his favorite food—bacon—stashed in his stocking along with his other gifts. He also loved his mother's homemade Swedish sand tart cookies. Indeed, Ruth would even send them to him years later when he was in Vietnam.

When the family moved to Lawrenceville, H. Norman Sr. was still superintendent of the State Police. Ruth had stopped working after their first child was born, but she did charitable work and served as president of the parent-teacher association of the local grammar school.

In 1936, however, after Governor Hoffman failed to reappoint him as superintendent of the troopers, H. Norman Schwarzkopf, Sr., became executive vice president and later president of Middlesex Trucking Company, a subsidiary of Johnson & Johnson. He also became a radio personality on a cops-and-robbers show called "Gangbusters."

The children loved the show, but when it started, Ruth and Sally had been too young to stay up to listen. Later, when they were finally given permission, so, too, was Norm, even though he was much younger. The girls called this discrimination and claimed that their brother was the pet of the family. As a boy and the baby, he probably was pampered. Certainly he was his father's favorite. The first thing H. Norman Sr. always did when he came home from work was to ask, "Where is little H.?"

From the beginning, "little H." showed a great deal of curiosity and independence. At three years old he started walking around town by himself. Since the Schwarzkopfs were new to the neighborhood, his mother told him to mention the name of their neighbors, the Satterthwaites, should he ever get lost. They were well known in town even if their name was quite a mouthful for a three-year-old. One Sunday, while Mr. Satterthwaite was sitting in the garden reading, Norm suddenly appeared. Not knowing the instructions the child had been given and having seen him only a couple of times, he was dumbfounded when the tiny boy walked up to him and politely said, "Hello, Mr. Satterthwaite."

Norm's mother was an accomplished horseback rider. She liked to say that her experience offered her a model for raising the children. She had always been told to keep the reins firm but slightly slack. In the same way, she tried to teach the children the importance of discipline without being too strict. Sally summed up the feeling in the household with this phrase: "We were allowed to cultivate our own garden."

The children had rules and were punished when they disobeyed them. Their allowance might be taken away; and sometimes they were grounded. Occasionally they were sent to bed without dinner—but then Ruth invariably felt pangs of sympathy and brought some food upstairs to them. The worst that could happen was a mild spanking from their father, but this was rare.

H. Norman Schwarzkopf, Sr., did not believe in a puritanical education; his nature was more that of the German romantic than that of the Prussian, and this, too, he passed on to his son. Emotion, he taught him, should be expressed, not suppressed. He was surprisingly affectionate and emotional for a military man. He was strict with his men. He made surprise visits to their posts to test their preparedness. But at home with his children he was openly tender. It was completely in character for his eyes to fill with tears when his older daughter gave short piano recitals for the family at Christmas.

Even though the Germanness of the family had been strongly emphasized by his parents, Colonel Schwarzkopf did not impose it on his wife or children. While speaking German to his mother, Agnes—often to the point of driving his wife crazy—he never taught it to the children. And the Germanness eventually lost its meaning for them, almost a century after Christian's arrival in the United States from Württemberg.

The children were sent to Sunday school, but religion was not forced on them. Their parents were not regular churchgoers; they just wanted their children to have a religious education and then decide for themselves. Ruth liked Sunday school and kept going for years, becoming very involved in the church choir. Norm and Sally did not have a great love for it, and after a while stopped going.

Ruth Schwarzkopf came from the South, even retaining a slight Southern accent, and she had seen racism there that appalled her. A woman of liberal views and a rigorous morality, she taught her children that skin color makes no difference. "Remember this," she once told Norman, "you were born white. You were born Protestant. You were born an American. Therefore, you are going to be spared prejudices other people will not be spared. But you should never forget one thing: you had absolutely nothing to do with the fact that you were born that way. It was an accident of birth that spared you this prejudice."

The Schwarzkopf children were taught to give up their seats on the bus to the elderly—white or black. At school, they learned not to discriminate among their classmates. The best student in Sally's class was black. When she came home with Sally to play, she was as welcome as anyone else. One of Norm's classmates came from an extremely poor family. Knowing that the boy did not have much to eat at home, Ruth invited him to almost every Sunday dinner.

The family thus practiced the values H. Norman Sr. had instilled in the state troopers: "the importance of courtesy, consideration and a sense of fairness to all classes."

Norm got along well with both his sisters. But he did not have much in common with Ruth—except that they were both left-handed, a trait that Schwarzkopf also shares with one of his heroes, Alexander the Great. It was with Sally that Norm developed an enduring relationship of special intimacy. General Schwarzkopf would later call her "this sister I dearly love." Sally was a tomboy, so for Norman it was like having an older brother. They played the same games, loved the same things, and spoke the same language.

Paul Mott, who was a friend of the Schwarzkopf children, remembered all the kids in town getting together in the Schwarzkopfs' yard to play hide-and-seek, cowboys and Indians, or cops and robbers. Ross Bevis, another boy from the neighborhood, said, "There were those among us who liked to be Indians, but Norman wasn't one of them. He always wanted to be the cowboy—the good guy!"

When the children were little, they lived close to their grandmother and frequently visited her. To the children, Agnes was a typical grandmother—gentle, loving, and always ready to make them their favorite foods. But Ruth never particularly liked her mother-in-law. She found her cold. There was always an underlying tension between them, which mounted in the late 1930s, when Ruth was angered by Agnes's views on the Nazis and the Jews. As World War II raged in Europe, Agnes tended to endorse the German line, talking about the "Jewish conspiracy" to control the world.

Her son harbored no such feelings. When he reenlisted in the Army, H. Norman Sr. was ready to fight the Germans again. He returned as a lieutenant colonel in the New Jersey National Guard and then became colonel in command of the 113th Infantry Regiment. Before he could fight in Europe, however, he was given a different mission.

In August 1942 he began a four-year assignment that would change the Schwarzkopfs' lives. This period would open the children's hearts and minds to different cultures and religions in a way that is still rare for American children. The experience would serve General Schwarzkopf well during the Gulf War when dealing with a thirty-three-nation coalition in a strictly Muslim land.

The unusual assignment H. Norman Sr. received took him to the Iranian capital, Tehran, to train and reorganize the Imperial Iranian Gendarmerie, a rural police force that would play an important role in stabilizing the country.

From its conception, the gendarmerie was an American creation. In 1911, W. Morgan Shuster, a U.S. economist, was invited to Iran—then still called Persia—by the Shah to reorganize state finances. He found that widespread tribal banditry had made the collection of state revenues in the countryside almost impossible. Shuster recommended that the Shah establish a constabulary of about 8,400 men to serve as rural police under the Ministry of Finance.

Soon after World War I, with the assistance of Swedish Army advisers, the imperial gendarmerie was created as part of the Ministry of the Interior.

In 1921, Reza Khan Pahlavi, an army officer, established a military dictatorship. Four years later he was elected "hereditary shah," ending the Kajar Dynasty that had reigned since 1794. During the 1920s and 1930s, Reza Shah modernized the Army and partially industrialized the country.

Early in World War II, the Third Reich moved east toward the Caucasus Mountains, posing a threat to Iran and to the so-called southern route, otherwise known as the Persian Corridor—the Allied supply line essential to the survival of the Soviet Union. In August 1941, to avoid the risk of Germany's overrunning Iran (it had invaded the U.S.S.R. in June), British and Soviet troops occupied the country. A month later, on September 16, 1941, the Allies coerced the pro-German Reza Shah to abdicate in favor of his son, Mohammed Reza Pahlavi.

In January 1942, to increase the stability of his regime, the new Shah formally asked the U.S. State Department for military advisers to help reorganize the Army and the gendarmerie. The State Department suggested that H. Norman Schwarzkopf "take charge of the reorganization of the Iranian national police force." The War Department accepted the request and in a letter to the U.S. Minister in Tehran, Louis Dreyfus, the State Department introduced the colonel as "exceptionally qualified for the job."

Schwarzkopf spent June and July of 1942 in Washington, preparing for his mission. Then, on August 29, 1942, with a staff of half a dozen officers, he left for Tehran.

Iran, a country three times the size of France, had a badly organized central government, few serviceable roads, and many different tribal clans. In the first few months the colonel visited the outposts of the gendarmerie to familiarize himself with the problems and the personnel, and in March of 1943 he submitted a 200-page plan to the Minister of the Interior and the Prime Minister. He wanted to reorganize the gendarmerie completely, but his mission and his status in Iran had not yet been formally recognized.

It was not until November 27, 1943, that the Iranian Foreign Minister signed an agreement retroactive to October 2, 1942, which established the GENMISH, or Gendarmerie Military Mission. The letter of instructions defined the goal of the mission as "to advise and assist the Ministry of the Interior in the reorganization of the Imperial Iranian Gendarmerie . . . thus facilitating Russian supply." It was decided that the U.S. officers would have "precedence over all Iranian Gendarmerie officers of the same rank" and that the chief of the mission (Schwarzkopf) would have "rank precedence over all officers of the Imperial Iranian Gendarmerie." With Article 20 of the agreement, Schwarzkopf was also granted the right to recommend to the ministry "the appointment, promotion, demotion or dismissal of any employee of the Gendarmerie."

It was by no means an easy mission. In a series of long letters to his family—remarkable for their acute observation, humor, stylistic elegance, and deeply felt emotion—the colonel painted a picture of a country in disarray, racked by poverty and unused to any form of strict organization. At the same time, he conveyed his fascination with an ancient culture and his rapture at the extraordinary beauty of gardens stumbled upon in the midst of arid expanses and untended ruins just distinct enough for the imagination to build again the great cities of Xerxes, Darius, and Alexander the Great.

Recruiting suitable people for the gendarmerie was one of the colonel's biggest problems. Barefoot and unshaven, most candidates, he noted, looked more like bandits than enforcement officers. Precision, he found, was rare in the Middle East. In a long letter in April 1943, he explained that one gendarme who was clearly over sixty seemed to have no idea how long he had been in the service and even less idea how old he was.

Punctuality was also a problem. The colonel noted that delays of an hour or two or even more meant absolutely nothing to the people he was working with. Ordering a nine o'clock departure usually meant leaving closer to eleven o'clock because, invariably, the vehicles had not yet been filled with gasoline; nor had their tires been fully inflated; nor the oil level checked; nor an appropriate escort found for traveling through sometimes treacherous passes frequented by an assortment of bandits. Once the destination was reached, such irritations did not abate. A dinner ordered for seven-thirty would often arrive after ten o'clock.

But H. Norman Sr. never let his occasional irritation show to his Iranian hosts. Indeed, it is clear from his letters that he went to great lengths to ensure that any anger was directed solely at his own officers. He was scrupulously polite, even consuming every course of elaborate lunches that constantly delayed his journeys through the country. A typical "light" lunch, he observed, might consist of bread, fried eggs, an omelet, mashed potatoes, chicken and rice, "a doughnut sort of affair with meat inside," and several varieties of cookies.

From the letters—some illustrated with fine sketches of things he had seen—an image of a man of scrupulous honesty, humor, deep feeling, and considerable culture emerges. He marveled at Persepolis and recounted stories of Alexander the Great; he told of countless blind beggars with whitened eyes in oozing, diseased sockets; worried by censorship, he called the Russians "Harvards" (crimson, after all), the British "Yalies," and the Persians "Dartmouths"; and he unflinchingly described to his family how opium was grown and harvested.

But it is his longing for his family which—even beside other passages of unusual beauty—is most arresting in the letters. In one dated May 15, 1944, he described Persian gardens in great detail to his wife, who was about to address the local garden club in New Jersey. The gardens seemed remarkable, but in the end they paled beside his feelings. The colonel wrote that none of them could compare with the garden of his memories.

On August 22, 1944, Schwarzkopf Sr. wrote to his son for his tenth birthday. It is an inspiring letter expressing pride in his son and conveying ideas and ideals more advanced than most ten-year-old children could assimilate. He saw this birthday as the point of transition from childhood to youth. He went on to say that he and Norm's mother were confident in the knowledge that "the success of our lives will be written in your deeds."

His present to the young Norman was an ancient Persian battle-ax, dated by inscriptions on the shaft as about three hundred years old. Of this gift, H. Norman Sr. wrote to his son: "I find joy and significance in giving you this for your tenth birthday and consider it a prediction of your worthy success in the 'Battle of Life.' "

Reflecting the warmth of his emotions, the father went on to say that he intended to walk out into the streets of Tehran in search of a boy with the appearance of a ten-year-old. He would stop him, give him ten taumans, and inform him that this was a gift to celebrate his son's tenth birthday.

The letter is profoundly illustrative of this crucial father-son relationship. It reveals a boy raised to aspire to achievements comparable to any in the panoply of human history and heroism; it shows a father determined to instill a sense of the successive stages in a man's life and the aspiration to advance as they unfold; above all, it reflects the character of a man unafraid to express his ardent affection for his son.

By the end of August 1944, two years after his arrival, Schwarzkopf had acquired equipment and supplies from Washington including 1,200 motor vehicles, 23,000 pairs of shoes, and 15,000 yards of woolen cloth for new uniforms for the gendarmerie to wear to the Shah's birthday celebration in November 1944. He had also established training schools and communication systems for the outposts. He had worked quickly, considering that he had to deal with eleven different Ministers of the Interior and an uncooperative Iranian military. The military had campaigned against him and had, at times, refused to provide vital information. According to the OSS, the forerunner of the CIA, even the Shah, a personal supporter of Schwarzkopf's efforts, had shown misgivings about his "very broad powers."

Notwithstanding this opposition, and despite personnel problems such as illiteracy and opium addiction, by the end of 1944 the colonel had made great progress toward establishing a more disciplined, honest, and efficient force.

In December 1944 the military attaché to the U.S. embassy in Tehran reported that "rebellious tribesmen in various remote sections of the country" no longer threatened the government's stability because of the "greatly improved Gendarmerie." He continued by saying that "the mission has a definite effect in discouraging brigandage and in promoting security along the routes" and it was "a decided strength factor in maintaining stability and law and order . . . The Army and Gendarmerie are capable of eventually putting down any tribal disorders or rebellions." Schwarzkopf had achieved what he set out to do.

It was not just letters that the colonel sent home to his family. Untold quantities of bric-a-brac would arrive from Iran: watercolors bought in the streets of Tehran, hand-crafted silver objects, bags of pistachios, and Russian cigarettes. Ruth thought the Russian cigarettes were terrible, but since American brands were rationed, they were better than nothing. Sally remembered the letters and packages being a cause for celebration and dread:

"In his typically methodical way, my father chose specially picked presents, specifying what was for whom. For example, I was crazy about pistachio nuts, so they were always for me. Norm, on the other hand, went crazy over hats, so my father would send him all kinds of hats. Every package would arrive with a long letter inside, which we always had to read out loud. My father inherited his dad's artistic talents. He made drawings and caricatures, and in his letters he would include drawings of people, animals, and local scenery. Once he even made a caricature of Norm from a picture that he used to carry in his wallet. My sister, Ruth, recently found it and sent it to him in Saudi Arabia. He was also very prolific, and since he was interested in Iranian culture, he would write pages and pages about local history and customs. Given our age, reading these letters was like doing homework. We dreaded them."

But for the children's mother these letters were clearly a comfort. It was a difficult time. With her husband in Iran, the Green House became too big and expensive to maintain. She and the children moved to a smaller place on Hibben Street in Princeton.

Occasionally H. Norman Sr. did return for visits, and he then took an active role in the children's upbringing. For example, Sally started smoking secretly when she was thirteen. Her mother, herself a chain-smoker, would find traces of ash in the bedroom. She was worried about Sally ruining her health—or setting the house on fire. One day, after dinner, H. Norman Sr. took his pack of Kents and offered his wife one. He then turned to Sally and offered her one. Mortified, she ran up to her room crying. He continued doing this for days. Before returning to Iran, he told her, "If you want to smoke, we can't stop you; you would do it secretly anyway. So I would prefer that you do it downstairs where there are ashtrays." This was the way in the Schwarzkopf family: reason and openness prevailed over punishment and subterfuge.

With the war, Ruth returned to nursing. There was a shortage of doctors and nurses, so she organized accelerated courses in home nursing where she taught small groups of lay people how to feed and care for the sick. Betsy Bevis, a neighbor of the Schwarzkopfs at the time, said that "when people talk about the organizational skills of the Schwarzkopf family, they automatically think of the colonel. But as head nurse at Columbia-Presbyterian Hospital, Ruth was an outstanding leader."

Norm's life changed considerably during this period. His mother was worried about the absence of a male role model and at the end of the summer of 1945, after talking it over with her husband, enrolled him in a military boarding school near Trenton. He was just eleven when he began school at the Bordentown Military Institute, and although the school was only fourteen miles away, during the school year he came home only for Christmas and major holidays.

Norm showed a taste for leadership. Pretending to be a general, he proudly donned his very first military uniform—his school dress. "He was in heaven in a military environment," his sister Sally said of the school he attended. "It was very natural for him." Posing for yearbook pictures at the end of the sixth grade, Norman already seemed to have his future mapped out. Two pictures were taken: in one he was smiling, in the other extremely serious. His mother wanted him to use the smiling one for the yearbook, but Norman insisted on the one with his chin jutting out in a pose of stern military authority. He said, "When I become a general, I want people to know that I am serious."

When it came to sending his father a photograph, Norman demonstrated the same concern for detail, as well as the whimsical side of his nature. He posed in front of an impressive convertible in his uniform—this time with a big smile on his face.

The school year that ended in June 1946 was his last in Princeton. That August, at the age of twelve, he left for Iran on an army aircraft, accompanied by a new member of his father's mission. His mother and sisters followed in the fall. They traveled by boat to Alexandria, Egypt, and took a plane from there to Tehran, arriving in November of 1946. In the few months they were separated, Norm had gone from a short, chubby boy to a taller, thinner young man.

With his family now in Tehran, the colonel had to find a new house. The Schwarzkopfs moved to one of the nicest neighborhoods in the center of the city, just a few minutes from the U.S. embassy and not far from the royal palace. Almost overnight the family had gone from a relatively small house in America to a Persian palace in Tehran. In Princeton, the family did not have a housekeeper; in Tehran, they had a butler, chef, gardener, Russian laundress, chauffeur, and a number of maids.

However, any grandiose ideas the children might have had were immediately put to rest by their parents. They were told never to give orders to the servants. One day Sally's dog went out and ate a melon from the garden and then threw up all over a beautiful Persian rug. Sally was so worried that the rug had been ruined that she told the butler to clean it. But when Ruth came home, it was the fact that Sally had been giving instructions to the butler, rather than the stained rug, that made her angry.

Although the Schwarzkopfs were strict about some things, they were lenient about others. The children were free to spend their allowances as they pleased. They would buy pistachio nuts and sometimes dried-up candy bars from old street vendors. Only ice cream was forbidden, because a member of the American mission had died from a tainted batch. But the children would sometimes buy some secretly anyway. When the Schwarzkopfs had people over for dinner, they would allow the girls to have a light vodka and orange juice with the guests. Ruth Ann and Sally, sixteen and fifteen respectively, could go out with their Iranian friends as long as they did not come home too late. One night when they came back long after curfew they found an angry father, standing at the door in his pajamas, waiting for them. After a stern lecture, he grounded them and took their allowances away for a while.

Adventures like this brought the two sisters closer. Sally was becoming a young woman with different interests from those she had shared with Norman. Her relationship with her brother became more distant as she changed, and Norman began to spend more time with his father.

For Norman Jr., life in Iran was fascinating. His father tried to make up for lost time by taking him out often, particularly hunting. On gazelle-hunting expeditions into the mountains and the highlands of Iran, Norm learned to shoot a rifle for the first time. These experiences instilled in him a lasting love for hunting and an awareness of different customs. In the interior of the country he witnessed the tremendous poverty of the rural people. At the same time his father taught him to appreciate the genuine warmth of the Iranians and introduced him to the beauty of their art.

One evening the boy found himself in the middle of the desert being entertained by the chief of a local tribe. The main dish was sheep; and the greatest delicacy, in the view of the Schwarzkopfs' hosts, the sheep's eyeballs.

Confronted by this, the young Norman turned to his father with an expression that was a mixture of nausea and desperate entreaty. But he found Colonel Schwarzkopf unmoved. The interpreter explained that the dish was a local delicacy, and his father made it clear to his son that he could not give offense. Norman was obliged to swallow the soft, round offering.

His mother's lifestyle changed, too: she had to become a diplomat's wife, which meant attending endless bridge games and parties. But Ruth did not confine herself to these activities and often ventured out. One day she and her driver found themselves in the middle of a Shiite religious procession. It was at the height of a religious holiday, and when the emotionally charged crowd saw the car with a Westerner inside, they surrounded it and started pounding on the hood and roof. It was a terrifying moment for Ruth, as she helplessly confronted the frenzied expression of a religious fervor wholly foreign to her experience. But fortunately the driver managed to calm the crowd and drive back to Tehran. It was the only incident in which the family felt any kind of ostracism or antagonism from the local population. Their experience, however, was greatly influenced by their spending most of their time in the more modern and relatively cosmopolitan capital. In primitive rural villages, many mullahs of nomadic and semi-nomadic tribes shared a xenophobic sentiment directed at Western infidels.

This exotic sojourn ended for the children at the beginning of the new school year, in the fall of 1947. They had gone to an American-run Presbyterian missionary school in Tehran that only went through the second year of high school. Ruth had already completed that class in Princeton and was forced to repeat the grade. At the end of the 1946–47 school year, Sally, too, had completed the grade, but there was no higher school for them in Tehran, American or English. The Schwarzkopfs therefore decided to send their children to the Ecole Internationale, a boarding school in Geneva, Switzerland.

The Ecole was a private school attended by the children of diplomats, American officers, and war refugees. Here Norman became more Europeanized. He learned to speak some French, ski, and play soccer and tennis.

A year later, in the summer of 1948, Norman Sr. was posted to Frankfurt, Germany, as deputy provost marshal of the army police. His mission in Iran was completed; the gendarmerie had been recognized and modernized.

In spite of his considerable achievements, the War Department had been slow in granting Schwarzkopf a promotion. He remained a colonel until June 1946, when the new American ambassador to Tehran, George V. Allen, sent a message to the Secretary of State underlining the importance of the gendarmerie and recommending that Schwarzkopf be promoted. "Iranian Gendarmerie constitutes an important deterrent to governmental overthrow. This organization, by its promptness last month in establishing security in Caspian area as Soviet troops evacuated, deserves large degree of credit in preventing rebellion."

The War Department initially refused the proposal because of its policy of capping the number of generals. But the chief of staff, General Dwight D. Eisenhower, decided to make an exception. On July 12, 1946, H. Norman Schwarzkopf was made a brigadier general.

In the fall of 1948, after only one year at boarding school in Geneva, Norman Jr. joined his parents in Frankfurt, where he was enrolled in a U.S. Army dependents' school. His sisters, who were preparing to enter college back home, remained at the Ecole in Geneva.

At the end of the school year, Norman moved again, this time to Heidelberg, Germany, where his father had become provost marshal of the army police. In the fall he began attending Heidelberg High, another American school for military dependents, where he played for the football team and helped it win the European Command Championship.

Norm immediately took to a group of youngsters called the Hoods and joined them in their practical jokes. He had always been an extrovert, but it seems that he was never a problem child. The only thing he ever did to anger his parents was to come home late. He was allowed to go out on Saturday nights, even to bars, but he had to be home by midnight. One weekend he was grounded for having come home in the early hours of the morning. He was so angry that he went to the music room and played "Home, Sweet Home" on his accordion over and over again. In the end, this broken record drove his mother so crazy she let him go out.

The Schwarzkopfs, like many others in their situation, continued moving around the world, taking their children with them. In 1950 Brigadier General Schwarzkopf was sent to Rome to head the Military Assistance Advisory Group (MAAG), the military assistance program to Italy. The family went to live in a beautiful neighborhood of Rome, near the American embassy. When his son was still very young, H. Norman Sr. had told him that he, too, would go to West Point and have a military career. So, with this vision in mind, he sent his son home to the States that year to Valley Forge Military Academy, where he was accepted on an athletic scholarship.

Valley Forge Military Academy, situated on a hundred acres of rolling countryside near Philadelphia, is famous for grooming students for West Point. It is also the school described by Holden Caulfield in J. D. Salinger's *Catcher in the Rye* as a place that advertises "in about a thousand magazines, always showing some hotshot guy on a horse jumping over a fence . . . And underneath the guy on the horse's picture, it always says: 'Since 1888 we have been molding boys into splendid, clear-thinking young men.' Strictly for the birds. They don't do any

damn more *mold*ing at Pencey than they do at any other school. And I didn't know anybody there that was
splendid and clear-thinking and all. Maybe two guys.
If that many. And they probably *came* to Pencey that
way."

H. Norman Schwarzkopf saw the institution differently.
In 1989, making the commencement address given every
year by an alumnus on the third weekend of May in the
chapel of the school, he expressed his gratitude: "Valley
Forge taught me to be proud to be an American . . . to
choose the harder right rather than the easier wrong . . .
West Point prepared me for the military; Valley Forge
prepared me for life."

Salinger's Holden Caulfield was not impressed by such
speeches by visiting dignitaries or former cadets who
had become successful. He found them patronizing and
self-congratulatory.

General Schwarzkopf, however, was humble: "What
should I tell you? How to live your lives? I would not
pretend to have the wisdom to do so. You are the future
of Valley Forge, I am the past, and the world has turned
over at least three times since I graduated."

He then read a poem:

You may give them your love but not your thoughts,
For they have their own thoughts.
You may house their bodies but not their souls,
For their souls dwell in the house of tomorrow,
    which you cannot visit, not even in your dreams.

The poem is by the Lebanese poet Kahlil Gibran, whose
book *The Prophet* would lie by Schwarzkopf's bed in
Riyadh next to the Bible and the memoirs of General
William T. Sherman.

J. D. Salinger created a fictional young rebel very different in temperament from Norman Schwarzkopf. But he
would not have disagreed with General Schwarzkopf's

assessment of the school. Salinger, who attended the academy fourteen years before Schwarzkopf, had great respect for the school. General Milton H. Medenbach, the cadet commander, remembered him as a well-disciplined, academically able cadet and said that "despite what he says in *The Catcher in the Rye*, he wrote me a letter twenty years after graduating saying how grateful he was for the training he received."

The general also remembered Norman. "He was a solid teenager from a good family with great values. Already then I could see that he had the potential to be an outstanding officer."

Norman got into trouble only once. There is still written documentation of his transgression in the school records: "It is hoped that you have had time to think this over and understand that we never throw any article of food in the mess hall at Valley Forge." Catapulting a pat of butter off one's spoon at another cadet is the type of thing that did not go down well at the academy.

Norman followed a strictly disciplined schedule in which every hour—from six in the morning to nine-thirty at night—was accounted for. This included obligatory Sunday chapel service and weekend parades. Any cadet who did not maintain good grades was put on the "deficiency list." But Norman's grades were always too good for that. "Among other things," said one of his classmates, James R. Bower, "we had to know how to debate. And Norman was a master debater. Even then he could dominate the stage." In his senior year, Norman won the Dunaway Debate Award.

It was at VFMA that Schwarzkopf's IQ was first measured. The day after the test, a teacher burst into his room, saying, "Norman, you scored 168 on the IQ test!" And then, in reaction to his expression of bewilderment, exclaimed, "Don't you realize you have the IQ of a genius!"

Norman was now a brawny young six-foot three-inch, 220-pound cadet who excelled in sports. His football coach,

Maitland Blank, remembered that with Norman as tackle he had a powerful team. But he had trouble turning Norman into an aggressive player.

To play football well, it helps to get angry, which Norman then had difficulty doing. Fortunately, his teammates developed a system to stir him up. In the first tackle or scrimmage of the game they would punch him, pull his leg, or kick him and then tell him that the other team had done it. This would put him in the right state of indignation for the game.

But what really upset him was someone making fun of his name. "What is the 'H.' for?" cadets would ask him. He would always say, "Nothing." So they would joke and call him "Hugo." He would get annoyed, but not lose his temper. Colonel Stuart Mulkerns, his tactical officer, said, "He was too even-tempered to take advantage of his size. When some other cadets would call him Hugo, he would simply say, 'Knock it off!' But it was evident that he was hurt. That 'H.' was his affliction."

"H." for Herbert became such an obsession for Norman that he decided to do something about it. In January 1952, during the Christmas vacation, Norman sent his parents, who were now living in the United States, to Trenton to legally change his name to H. Norman Schwarzkopf. New Jersey records reveal that the future general's birth certificate reads "Herbert Norman Schwarzkopf, Jr." But above that has been typed the name H. Norman Schwarzkopf. Not only has "Herbert" been changed to "H." but, to underscore that fact, the "Jr." has been dropped as well. At the bottom of the form is a notice that this change is the result of a "correction form filed on January 2, 1952."

The cadet's decision suggests a still-raw sensitivity over a rather old-fashioned name. Even today the name change is not something General Schwarzkopf likes to talk about. During the Gulf War, he would explain to one reporter that he was not really a "Jr." because his father's name was Herbert. He left it at that.

But his torment at Valley Forge was not over. His friends managed to have the last laugh: they slipped in a line in the yearbook under his class picture: "Nickname: Hugo." They pulled the joke off right under his nose. Norman was in charge of the yearbook that year.

Norman's father was now back in New Jersey, working for the state as coordinator of public safety and law enforcement activities. But in Iran the gendarmerie that he had trained was suddenly confronting widespread popular unrest fomented by a strong opposition movement.

Even though the Shah held vast powers, such as the appointment of the Prime Minister and the dissolution of the Parliament, Iran was a constitutional monarchy with a parliamentary form of government. The Parliament was composed of an elected assembly, the majlis, and a Senate, with half of the members elected and the other half appointed by the Shah. Since the end of the Second World War, the opposition had been weak and the Shah had managed to run the government almost single-handedly.

But in reaction to an agreement made by the government in 1949 which was considered too favorable to the British-owned Anglo-Iranian Oil Company (AIOC), a strong, although divided, opposition movement emerged. The new movement, which became known as the National Front, was led by Muhammad Mossadegh, a lawyer and landowner. His was a coalition of most of the main opposition groups, with the exception of the local Communist Party, the Tudeh.

Support for the National Front grew, and bowing to popular demand, the Shah appointed Mossadegh Prime Minister on April 29, 1951. The new head of the government had two main objectives: the transfer of power from the Shah to Parliament and the reinforcement of Iranian control over its oil production. The appointment of Mossadegh as Prime Minister alarmed Britain, which called for an oil embargo against Iran in 1952 and sent four destroyers and the cruiser *Mauritius* with a brigade of British parachutists to the Gulf. Supported by a cross section of the population, including businessmen, politicians, and military officers, the British tried to destabilize the government and oust Mossadegh. According to Professor Mark Gasiorowski, a political scientist and expert on Iranian affairs at the University of Louisiana, the idea of a coup against Mossadegh was first suggested by Winston Churchill and Anthony Eden, the two leaders of the Conservative opposition in Britain. Among their allies in Iran was Senator Faziollah Zahedi, a former general whom the British had arrested during the war for being a Nazi sympathizer. With British support, Zahedi began plotting against Mossadegh, but the Prime Minister became aware of this maneuvering. On November 1, 1952, he broke off diplomatic relations with Great Britain and expelled the British ambassador and his staff. Now, without a local base, the British looked to the United States for help.

At that time, the Truman Administration officially backed Mossadegh and had repeatedly advised London that Mossadegh was in fact willing to negotiate and that Britain should do so. The British, therefore, decided to turn to the CIA, which since 1948 had independently started meddling in Iranian affairs. The Agency had a secret propaganda operation, code-named BEDAMN, to weaken the Communist Tudeh Party and, to some extent, Mossadegh's National Front because of its nationalistic policy.

In November of 1952 the head of the British Secret Service in Iran, Christopher Montague Woodhouse, met with the CIA Middle East chief Kermit (Kim) Roosevelt, grandson of President Theodore Roosevelt, and agreed to pursue the goal of a coup d'état to restore power to the royal family and guarantee foreign oil interests.

Three months later, after Dwight D. Eisenhower became President, the United States government became sympathetic to the views of the CIA and the British. The Secretary of State, John Foster Dulles, and his brother Allen, the new director of the CIA, decided to oust Mossadegh and replace him with the former Nazi sympathizer Zahedi. The operation, headed by the CIA's Middle East Division chief, Roosevelt, became known as AJAX and was undoubtedly economic in nature: the fact that the Dulles brothers' law firm had many American oil companies as clients certainly played a role. But Professor Gasiorowski said that the leading motive for ousting Mossadegh was probably fear of a Communist takeover. The Eisenhower Administration was convinced that the Prime Minister was just a weak figurehead who under internal pressure would end up giving control of the country to the Tudeh and, therefore, to Moscow.

Once the decision was made, the United States had to inform the Shah. This was difficult because Mossadegh kept Reza Pahlavi in virtual isolation inside the royal palace. Kermit Roosevelt was sent to Tehran to coordinate the operation. In order to conceal the CIA's involvement, he flew to Rome and then Beirut and from there continued by car to Tehran. But the Agency wanted somebody other than its local division chief to communicate the plan to the Shahanshah—the "King of Kings." And having unsuccessfully tried the Shah's twin sister as a messenger, the CIA turned to Brigadier General H. Norman Schwarzkopf.

Schwarzkopf, as the former commander of the Imperial Iranian Gendarmerie, knew the Shah personally and appreciated the nuances of Iran's delicate political situation. He immediately accepted the mission and, armed only with a diplomatic passport, left for the Middle East under the pretense of making a trip to visit old friends.

In Tehran, Schwarzkopf was briefed by Roosevelt. "The general thought the coup was a good idea," the division chief, now retired in Washington, recalled. "He agreed with the need to change the government, and I got the feeling that he enjoyed playing a part in it. But Schwarzkopf had no operational role of any sort, and he was not briefed on the details of the plan. He was simply supposed to relate our intentions to the Shah. He was strictly a messenger."

Schwarzkopf was duly granted an audience with the Shah. He went to the palace and the two men walked in the garden to avoid being overheard. The King of Kings was visibly nervous. He appreciated the American offer but feared that it would provoke uncontrollable internal unrest that might lead to a civil war. He refused to accept the U.S. proposal. They talked for about half an hour, but the general could not coax the Shah into changing his mind. Schwarzkopf then drove to Tajrish, a town near the capital, where he had secretly arranged a meeting with Roosevelt. The CIA man was staying at the home of Jake Goodwin, the local chief of station and a former Associated Press reporter whom Schwarzkopf knew from his days in Iran.

Goodwin lived in a two-story house surrounded by a ten-foot wall that he rented from a member of the royal family. That afternoon, in late July 1953, Schwarzkopf and Roosevelt sat outside on the patio overlooking the pool and garden, drinking beer under the hot sun.

"Kim," said Schwarzkopf, "you are not going to be able to deal with the Shah through any intermediary. Arrangements cannot be made that way. Somehow or other I am convinced that you will have to meet with him personally."

Schwarzkopf knew that the State Department feared that Roosevelt's personal involvement might expose the role of the CIA, but he did not think the Administration had any choice. He looked at Roosevelt with what the agent described as a "comically gloomy face" and added, "If this undertaking fails, we'll all be in such hot soup that I don't really think disclosure of your name would make much difference."

Roosevelt nodded. He, too, realized at last that he had to act himself. In the early hours of August 2—thirty-seven years to the day before Saddam Hussein unleashed another upheaval in the Middle East—Roosevelt had a secret nocturnal meeting with the Shah that laid the groundwork for the coup. The meeting, Roosevelt said, took place inside a car in the driveway of the royal palace. As Schwarzkopf had anticipated, the Shah was much more responsive to a direct contact. After a few more secret meetings, the deal was struck.

On Monday, August 17, the CIA paid a large crowd $50,000 to stage a so-called Communist demonstration in downtown Tehran, aiming to provoke a reaction among forces loyal to the Shah. The demonstrators, joined by unsuspecting Communist supporters, attacked the royal mausoleum and smashed the statue of the Shah's father. This secured the desired reaction. On August 18 the streets of Tehran filled with pro-Zahedi crowds. The day after, an anti-Mossadegh demonstration, again sponsored by the CIA, was joined by army and police units. Pro-Zahedi military forces took control of radio stations and started broadcasting anti-Mossadegh appeals. The demonstrators marched to the Prime Minister's residence and attacked it with tanks and artillery fire. The battle ended, after nine hours and three hundred deaths, with the Prime Minister escaping from the roof. The next day, August 20, Mossadegh surrendered to Zahedi, who was later appointed Prime Minister by the Shah. At the time, one of the CIA agents in Tehran, Howard "Rocky" Stone, was buttoning the jacket of Zahedi's uniform; the Iranian was too nervous to do it himself. As with the coup, he had to ask for CIA help.

The previous summer, H. Norman Schwarzkopf, Jr., had been accepted at West Point. These were exciting years to attend the Academy. A general and former West Point cadet, Eisenhower, became President; moreover, the war in Korea ended in 1953, and many of the officers, with their medals and stories of the battlefield, returned to the Academy to teach. Alexander M. Haig, Jr., was one of them.

Cadets were then assigned by height. Schwarzkopf went to Al—Company A of the 1st Regiment. It was the company of the tallest cadets; no one under six foot two could be in it. With great anticipation, he walked into his new room—to find Leroy N. Suddath and David Horton, two cadets who would be his roommates and friends over the next three years.

Leroy and Dave immediately decided to call Norman "Schwarzie," the nickname also given to his father by the cadets of the class of '17.

To the older cadets, Norm was just a plebe, a cadet who had to do the bidding of every upperclassman. But to his roommates, he was a man of the world—almost a Renaissance man. Leroy and Dave had not ventured much beyond their own states of Georgia and North Carolina, while Norm had lived in faraway places such as Iran and had traveled through Europe. His roommates did not know another language. Norm spoke German, a little French, and knew a few select but graphic swear words in Farsi. He already had an understanding of different cultures at a time when Americans were still adjusting to their new postwar role of superpower and were relatively uneducated about the world around them.

"Whenever I needed him he was there to help me," said Dave Horton. "He didn't have trouble with any subject, although he never studied more than necessary." Leroy Suddath was even more effusive about Schwarzie's intelligence: "Norm seldom studied hard. He would glance over something and know it pretty well. In that sense he was the most brilliant student I knew, the only Einstein in the class."

Norman was very busy in his free time. He sang in, and later conducted, the choir; he wrestled, boxed, lifted weights, and played tennis, football, and soccer. In sports, as in his academic subjects, he was good but never the best in the class. "He didn't have what it took to be a champion. There were many cadets who were better than he," said his classmate Colonel James L. Anderson, who is now head of the Physical Education Department at West Point. "He even had trouble doing pull-ups."

Brigadier General John "Doc" Bahnsen, a classmate, now retired, remembered the same thing. "Because of his weight, he had trouble getting airborne. More than three pull-ups were difficult for him."

Naturally, his friends made the most of this, telling him to go on a diet. But despite all his running and marching, Schwarzie never managed to lose weight. "He wasn't fat—he was just big. And because of it he had to watch what he ate," said Dave Horton. "His weight was a sore point. For us, on the other hand, it was a good way to poke fun at him."

The three roommates spent much of their time together. In the evenings they listened to music, read, or talked. Norm's favorite record was Beethoven's *Emperor* Concerto—until, that is, Leroy Suddath developed an obsession with the record and started playing it all the time.

"I played that thing nonstop—it was pretty steady stuff for a couple of months," Suddath recalls. "And Norm got real tired of listening to it."

One day Schwarzie approached him with the record, handed it to him, and said, "Here, take it, it's yours, a present from me. But there's one condition."

"What's that?" asked Suddath.

"That you only play it when I'm not here. You've overdone it, Leroy!"

The young men would also recite poetry, particularly these lines by an unknown poet:

> Here dead lie we because we did not choose
> To live and shame the land from which we sprung.
> Life, to be sure, is nothing much to lose:
> And young men think it is, we were young.

They were not particularly interested in politics except when a major event such as the McCarthy hearings was widely covered in newspapers and on the radio. They were unanimous in their distaste for McCarthyism, but, inevitably, three young men living in such close proximity were bound to have their disagreements. On no occasion, however, did any of these clashes lead to physical violence. Highly colored accounts of General Schwarzkopf's supposedly explosive temper are not supported by the testimony of Dave Horton, who described him as someone who could control his temper and had respect for others.

This respect did not confer immunity from Schwarzie's love for practical joking, and Horton, particularly when he wanted to study, was a frequent victim. Leroy Suddath still enjoys relating the story of how he and Schwarzie opened the window to a freezing gale while Dave was trying to work. They insisted that this was part of an experiment on the mechanics of fluids and that the window could not be closed, because they were trying to calculate the ratio at which a certain number of leaves would come through an aperture of such and such dimensions with the wind blowing at a speed of x for a duration of one hour. Leroy and Schwarzie added further experimental details as they went along until even Dave dissolved into laughter.

Schwarzie was expansive, extroverted, energetic, and enthusiastic. With these characteristics, and a mischievous streak in addition, it is hard to imagine that he would not have transgressed the strict rules of a place like West Point. Yet somehow he avoided a single blot on his record during four years at the Academy. Unlike his father, he was not punished even once: never confined to barracks and never made to "walk the area." Colonel Anderson disclosed that this immaculate record was in fact besmirched in 1954 when Schwarzie missed his train on returning from New York and the officer on guard issued a punishment. But, before this took effect, supernatural intervention, in the form of the Emperor of Ethiopia, came to the rescue. Emperor Haile Selassie came to West Point on a state visit and, as was the custom for a foreign head of state, was given the privilege of granting amnesty to cadets. As Haile Selassie waved to the cadets from the balcony, he granted pardons to those awaiting punishment. Loud cheers, not least from Schwarzie, greeted the announcement.

Even if he liked a good time, Schwarzie was quiet and serious compared to Dave Horton. He chose to stay in on weekends or go to plays with Leroy rather than chase women with Dave. "Schwarzie didn't think about women, only about passing his exams," said Doc Bahnsen. Horton, by contrast, thought only about women.

He would spend infamous nights at the Piccadilly Hotel in Manhattan. "They weren't prostitutes, just girls or women who liked horny cadets," said Doc Bahnsen. "We passed their names around, and the only thing we had to worry about was not getting them pregnant." On one of these nights at the Piccadilly, Dave Horton acquired a nickname. The woman he was with left long red scratch marks all over his back. The next day, in gym, his classmates saw them and nicknamed him Tiger. The name stuck.

If Norman had no great passion for a woman, he was certainly passionate about military history. He read voraciously about General George S. Patton and General William T. Sherman. But two other commanders really fired his imagination: Hannibal and Alexander the Great. Leroy Suddath remembered how they would spend hours reading about the great battles of the past, and how the one that most fascinated Norman was the battle of Cannae in 216 B.C. It was the classic battle of annihilation, in which Hannibal led the Carthaginians to a crushing defeat of the Romans, even though his army of 50,000 was outnumbered by the more than 80,000 Roman soldiers. Under commander Gaius Terentius Varro, a vain man with little military skill or experience, the Romans hoped to overwhelm the

Carthaginians by sheer force of numbers. Varro set up his formation in three to four times the usual depth, but Hannibal fell back at the center of his line to lure the Romans forward. As the Romans advanced, Hannibal, with the help of his more numerous cavalry, brilliantly managed to encircle and then destroy the entire force. Three-fourths of the Roman army was captured or killed, in one of the greatest military disasters in history.

"Norm admired Hannibal for his near-perfect plans and execution, and he could see himself commanding a battle as perfect as that," said Suddath. Years later, in the Gulf War, he almost did; and he referred specifically to the way his rout of the Iraqis might have turned into a battle of annihilation like Cannae if orders had not come from Washington to stop the slaughter.

But even more than Hannibal, his model was Alexander the Great, who by the age of thirty-three had conquered much of Asia, from the Black Sea to the Indian Ocean. In Iran, he had read about Alexander's formidable march through Persia in the fourth century B.C., conquering one city after another—Babylon, then Persepolis, then all of the Persian Empire. Since Schwarzie had seen the terrain as a young boy, all this was vivid to him. And having witnessed his father playing a role in events of historic importance, he dreamed of doing great things himself. The Persian ax he had been given as a ten-year-old boy was not intended as a gift to a young man who would be satisfied with mediocrity.

"More than anyone else, he wanted to be able to change the course of the nation, to have a great impact on the United States and humanity," said Suddath. "He had real hopes of doing that. He could see himself accomplishing every bit as much as those great leaders of the past. And he wanted to be prepared in case the opportunity came." Although General Schwarzkopf has denied expressing these aspirations, Suddath recalled them vividly. Dave Horton preferred to be on the safe side: "I don't remember him wanting to follow in the footsteps of Alexander the Great, but I wouldn't exclude the possibility."

In the summer of 1955, as a future senior, Schwarzie was part of a committee in a training camp where sophomores were taught outdoor tactics. The cadets were transported by army trucks to Camp Buckner in upstate New York to train, engage in field maneuvers, and learn to patrol. Schwarzie and five other classmates were assigned to now-retired Lieutenant General Harold Moore, a Korean War veteran who taught tactics at the Academy. "Young Schwarzkopf had been in my class for years, but until that summer I had not noticed him," said Moore. "In Camp Buckner, I was struck right off by his potential in leadership. He was an exceptionally fine young man, smart, very quick to learn."

The future chief of staff of the Air Force, General Michael J. Dugan, who was fired early in the Kuwaiti campaign for what Defense Secretary Dick Cheney called some injudicious remarks about allied bombing plans, was at this camp. Schwarzkopf was two years ahead of him and was, for a time, his supervisor. He recalled Schwarzkopf as "a memorable figure, a big healthy character who made a considerable physical impression. He had an idea that he wanted to be an infantryman, and talked about this ambition a lot. It's like the coal-miner syndrome—the infantryman believes with pride that not many are tough enough to do this job. Schwarzkopf had that toughness. He was demanding, never wishy-washy, balanced, and had a sense of humor. When it rained, he was out there with the troops."

At the beginning of the senior year, each cadet was graded by the officers for his military potential. Leroy and Dave were made platoon leaders and Schwarzkopf, thanks in part to Moore's enthusiastic report, was picked as a company commander. He was given the rank of cadet captain—a good rank, but not the best. Above him were battalion commander and regimental commander, and above everyone was the first captain, a position that had been held by men like General John J. Pershing, General Douglas MacArthur, and General William C. Westmoreland.

As a cadet captain, Schwarzkopf was in a position of command for the first time. He took it very seriously, but never went overboard with his "men." If he saw someone becoming abusive in the hazing of first-year cadets, he would intervene to stop it. "He was always very sure of himself, very confident, but never to the point of arrogance," said Suddath.

In that last year, as a senior, Schwarzkopf kept up his relationship with then Major Harold Moore, an airborne infantry officer very proud of his branch. Schwarzkopf had the privilege of being invited to dinner by the major's wife and had long, after-hours conversations about the Army and its various branches. "Artillery might be the king of the battle, but Infantry is the queen. It is also the heart of the Army. In other words, it is the place to be," the major told Schwarzkopf one night.

Those conversations helped confirm Schwarzkopf in his desire to be an infantryman. The fact that one of his heroes, General Sherman, shared the same opinion might also have helped. "Modern wars have not materially changed the relative values or proportions of the several arms of service: infantry, artillery, cavalry and engineering. If anything, the infantry has been increased in value," Sherman wrote in his memoirs.

In the winter of '55, Schwarzkopf decided on the infantry. He was not deterred by the fact that he would be called "ground pounder" by the Air Force cadets or that at West Point the infantry had always been considered the least attractive of the combat arms branches of the U.S. Army.

Aware of the need for engineers, in 1817 Superintendent Sylvanus Thayer, the "Father of the Military Academy," made engineering the heart of the curriculum at

West Point. Since then the Corps of Engineers had always been considered the most prestigious branch, traditionally attracting the brightest students. After the engineers came Armor, Artillery, Signal Corps, and finally Infantry. Not many people liked the idea of the Spartan, tough life of the infantryman; and the great tank battles of World War II and the heroism of George S. Patton had made Armor very popular, especially the cavalry.

Dwight D. Eisenhower and Omar N. Bradley were in the infantry. "It is the infantry that ejects the enemy, gains ground, and holds it," Schwarzie started telling people. "Without the infantry it is impossible to win a war."

It seems likely that his fascination with historical battles attracted Schwarzkopf to a branch of the Army that he could trace all the way back through time to Alexander the Great. The Corps of Engineers certainly did not have the same historic appeal.

From then on, Schwarzkopf actively tried to recruit his friends. He succeeded so well that in March 1956, when it was time to pick a branch, many of his classmates followed his lead. The Army had designated a specific number of slots for each of the branches. The cadets were asked to list their first three choices in preferential order. Each cadet, in order of rank, starting with the top-ranked man, turned in his paper and was assigned a branch. Little by little the branches would be filled, so that the lower-ranked cadets would have to accept their second or third choices. Schwarzie was in the top 10 percent of his class (42nd out of 485) and was given his first choice, Infantry. Many others who followed him also went to Infantry. And when it was the turn of Jack Sloan, the "class goat," or last-ranked he, too, wanted Infantry, but there was no more room.

Following in Major Harold Moore's footsteps, Schwarzie decided not to become a regular infantryman—a "straight leg," a term derived from the regulation thirty-inch step with which the infantryman marches. Norman picked Airborne Infantry, as had Moore. So, immediately after West Point, he went to the Airborne School at Fort Benning, Georgia, to learn parachuting skills. He graduated in the spring of 1957 and became a platoon leader with Company E, 2nd Airborne Battle Group, 187th Infantry Regiment, at Fort Campbell, Kentucky. Here his enthusiasm and exuberance were immediately tested by a much harsher reality, as he later told the writer C. D. B. Bryan:

> I had an alcoholic commander. I had an executive officer who was a coward. I saw terrible things going on around me and I said, "Who needs it? When my three years are up, I am getting out!" But a very sage guy sat me down and said, "Young man, you know, if all the guys who see these bad things happening quit, then all the guys who don't think these things are so bad are going to be doing them later on. If you really think it's that bad, why don't you stick around until someday you get into a position to do something about it?"

It was a difficult time in his personal life, too. His father had been in poor health for years. He had an ulcer and stomach problems that some doctors attributed to the mustard gas of World War I. A chain-smoker, he had developed lung cancer, for which he underwent surgery and chemotherapy. But not even that convinced him to stop smoking his Kents.

In November 1958, Sally, who was then living in Washington and working for the Defense Department, received a call from her mother. Her father's ulcer had started bleeding and her mother needed help. Sally arrived just in time to see her father before he died, on Tuesday, November 25. Still perfectly coherent, he knew how sick he was, and was as practical as ever. He told Sally that she must use his ticket for the Army–Navy football game on the following Saturday, November 29. Later, he dozed off as Sally watched him, and never awoke.

The day after his death, Norman arrived from Fort Campbell. His father's end had come more abruptly than expected, and Norman had been unable to see him. It was certainly terribly painful for him not to be able to say a last goodbye to this man whom he loved and respected, a father whose influence on his life and values was decisive.

Norman's mother insisted that he accompany Sally to the Army–Navy game, saying to him, "Dad would have wanted you to go." The game relieved the tension to some extent. By the time they returned home, their sister, Ruth, had arrived. The following day, their father's funeral was held in West Orange, New Jersey. He was buried in the West Point Cemetery.

Schwarzkopf returned to Fort Campbell and spent the next eighteen months there. But it was his transfer to Germany and the Berlin Command in July 1960 that really gave him renewed enthusiasm for army life. He was appointed aide de camp to Brigadier General Charles Johnson. It was a job he loved, in a city that inspired him, and he became an immediate star. He was a young, athletic, good-looking lieutenant, in direct contact with a powerful general.

"The Berlin American community was small. We would all meet at Harnack House, the officers' club," recalled Jill McCaffrey, now wife of the 24th Infantry Division commander, Major General Barry R. McCaffrey. "I was at the Berlin American High School, and my good friend Pat was the daughter of Brigadier General Charlie Johnson. Lieutenant Schwarzkopf was his dashing aide. We were all interested in whom he was dating, always watchful of the girls he was seeing—all these beautiful, sophisticated older women."

But the political situation in Berlin was grim. While in Germany, Norman witnessed the massive defection of Germans from the Communist East to the West. At the same time, he heard John F. Kennedy's 1961 Inaugural Address—and the words now engraved on the President's tomb at Arlington: "Let every nation know, whether it wishes us well or ill, that we shall pay any price, bear any burden, meet any hardship, support any friend, oppose any foe to assure the survival and the success of liberty." With nearly a thousand refugees a day fleeing into West Germany from the East, these words had a particular impact on Schwarzkopf.

The oppression of Communism was no longer an abstract concept; it was a reality he witnessed day to day. And it was shortly after Schwarzkopf's departure, in August of that year, that East German leader Walter Ulbricht, unable to stem the tide, ordered the building of the Berlin Wall.

Schwarzkopf returned to the United States to take the career officer course at the Infantry School at Fort Benning. There he joined his old West Point friend Leroy Suddath. He brought back many pleasant memories from Germany, as well as a German shepherd named Troll. To reinforce his image of the flashy bachelor, he bought a new Oldsmobile convertible.

"He obviously thought of himself as quite the young man about town—always with a new girlfriend," commented Suddath, adding, however, that Schwarzkopf never seemed to have serious involvements with any of these women. By that time, Suddath was already married and had a child, Leroy Jr., also known as Baba. Baba, who was two at the time, could not pronounce "Schwarzie," so he called Norman "Sportsy." Given Norman's lifestyle and his love for tennis, the name was quite appropriate. "Baba just set it all off with that name. Norman was delighted," said Suddath.

At the U.S. Army Infantry School, Schwarzkopf's attitude toward studying was the same as at West Point. That year, he and Leroy had to write a paper. "We sat next to each other and I saw him write his paper. At least 75 percent of it was done as the lectures were going on—

while the teachers were droning on. He just glibly wrote it out without having to give up any of his nonacademic activity," said Suddath. Schwarzkopf won the award for best paper.

West Point had decided to call Schwarzkopf back to teach in the Department of Civil and Mechanical Engineering, but in order to do that, he needed a master's degree. He enrolled at the University of Southern California, in Los Angeles, for a master's in Mechanical and Aerospace Engineering. As always, studying did not take away from Norman's enjoyment, and at USC he was able to take advantage of the hot weather to improve his tennis game. In June 1964, after the completion of his degree, he went back to West Point for a three-year teaching appointment. But this did not last long.

The Vietnam War was slowly escalating. In 1961 the United States and South Vietnam had signed a military aid treaty that led to the arrival, in that year, of the first U.S. troops. U.S. military aid kept increasing. So, too, did the number of U.S. advisers sent to help the South Vietnamese Army. Throughout the early sixties, the intention was to send the best possible U.S. advisers and trainers and let the Vietnamese fight the war.

Schwarzkopf's classmate Ward Le Hardy was one of those sent. He went in 1962 to replace one of the first U.S. officers killed in Vietnam, and stayed for a year as an adviser to the Vietnamese Infantry Battalion. Once back, Le Hardy made it clear to all of his friends that Vietnam was the place to be for a professional soldier. There was a real war to be fought, and that was the job they had been trained to do. Charles Prather, another West Point graduate of the class of '56 who followed Le Hardy's call to Vietnam, explained it this way: "We were all young lieutenants out of West Point; war for us was like fire for firemen. Our life gravitated around it, not because we yearned for it but because we wanted to contribute to get it over."

On August 7, 1964, at the request of President Lyndon B. Johnson, the U.S. Congress passed the Tonkin Gulf Resolution, which provided the legal basis for an escalation of U.S. military involvement in Vietnam. Then, in early 1965, Johnson ordered Operation Rolling Thunder, the first air-raid campaign on North Vietnam and Viet Cong–controlled areas of the South. Among the young officers who taught at West Point, nobody had the slightest doubt about the outcome of the war. The United States was sending its best officers, and the South Vietnamese Army was bound to profit from their knowledge. "There was no doubt then. We were going to win that war," said Prather. "And we were eager to carry out that mission." At West Point the spirit was high, and so was the enthusiasm of young instructors and cadets alike. For its summer camp, in a training area in upstate New York, the Academy had even built a mock Viet Cong village to train and orient the cadets toward that kind of fighting. It was a village of bamboo huts with straw roofs and defense positions along the trails approaching the village. Even the ambush sites were exactly like those of the Viet Cong.

Vietnam was all the cadets and young instructors talked about. And Schwarzkopf could not bear the thought of having to stand in front of a blackboard, teaching scientific theories to cadets, when he could be in Vietnam advising people on how to fight a war.

"In those days he was the type of person who would move to the sound of the guns," explained Le Hardy. "If there was a war, he wanted to be in it. He wanted to be with the troops. That was why he had gone to West Point."

In the spring of 1965 H. Norman Schwarzkopf requested that the Department of the Army send him to Vietnam as an adviser. There his gung-ho military enthusiasm would be severely tested—and forever changed.

3

Booby Trap

Send me off to a foreign land, to go and
kill the Yellow Man. Born in the U.S.A., I
was born in the U.S.A.

—Bruce Springsteen

1970, Near My Lai

In Vietnam, nobody used real names. His was Paul
Deer, but he was known as "Buck." He was a platoon sergeant in Charlie Company of the 1st Battalion, 6th Infantry
Regiment, 198th Infantry Brigade, Americal Division—the
1st of the 6th for short.

On that day in February, Buck was particularly nervous.
He knew the area was *bad*. He was in a valley of rice
paddies that had dried up when the monsoons ended. It
was open, flat terrain, exposed to enemy fire. Rumor had
it that there was an old Australian minefield, or maybe
it was French. Vietnam was a place of rumors, none of
them ever verified. There were old, spooky foxholes, dug
who knows when. The men did not like it.

Buck called his captain by radio and told him he was
uncomfortable moving forward. But the officer ordered
him to keep going. Night was approaching, so they set
up a defensive perimeter, digging holes in the shape of
a big circle and filling sandbags with the dirt to form
a protective wall in front of the foxholes. Outside the

perimeter, Buck set up four-man posts to guard against enemy attack. They were still digging when an explosion ripped through the air: a mine. Perfect and Coconut were blown up. Two great guys. Perfect and Coconut. Nobody in the platoon knew their real names. They were always together; and they died together.

The next day, while the platoon was preparing to move out, another explosion shattered the silence. This time it was Pauly, a radio operator. Six foot tall, and a terrific basketball player. Just the day before, he had told Buck, "I'd rather be dead then lose my legs." And there he lay, with both legs torn to bits. He looked down and saw both feet were missing. Then he looked up at Buck in open-mouthed terror. Then he got his wish. He died. Damn mines! They were old, but they worked.

The guys began to panic. Buck called the captain and asked permission to ride the tanks and armored personnel carriers. "They are anti-personnel mines," he explained. "They can't do much damage to tanks." The captain gave his okay. With a sense of relief, the men clambered into the armored vehicles. They moved off.

A few minutes later a helicopter swirled overhead. The captain got a frantic radio call from the battalion commander, who had seen them from his helicopter. "Are you crazy? Get them off immediately! *Now!*" screamed the commander. His name was Schwarzkopf, Lieutenant Colonel H. Norman Schwarzkopf.

The captain ordered everybody off the vehicles. The men couldn't believe it. Here they were, in the middle of a goddamn minefield that their maps did not even mention, and the commander was asking them to get off their APCs and get maimed. Vietnam—the land that God forgot—was a place where even saints would swear. "Fucking Colonel Nazi," a few grumbled. That was the name some used for this burly, unstinting commander with a German-sounding name who had descended on them a few months earlier.

That time it was not just soldiers like Bill Savage who complained bitterly. Everybody called Savage the platoon bitcher. Not even the sergeant liked it, or understood what Schwarzkopf was so upset about. But orders were orders. With the colonel up there in his helicopter, there was no way of ignoring them. The soldiers climbed down and started following the tank tracks. Back at the fire base, Schwarzkopf abruptly relieved the captain of his duty.

The incident was too much for Buck. Enough. One after the other, he had lost most of his platoon. Out of the original thirty men, only four were left. The others had all died or been badly wounded. That February he decided to apply to the sniper school the division was setting up in the rear, at the headquarters near Chu Lai. The intention was to train snipers to be on call with their respective line unit—a combat unit in the field—so that whenever a field commander needed a sniper, they could move one up to the front to set up an ambush and shoot at the enemy. To do this, the Army had brought its ten best marksmen over to teach the course. Or so it claimed. Vietnam was a place of rumors and unverifiable assertions.

The future snipers set up a firing range and spent days using their XM21 rifles with 3×9 variable scopes. They learned to hit a target at six hundred meters in the dark with a starlight scope and nine hundred meters in daylight. Buck was one of the best of the twenty students. He graduated easily and was ordered back to his company along with another sniper, Larry. Nobody knew Larry's last name. Nobody cared.

Buck had no intention of going back to a line unit. He had become convinced that moving in large, noisy groups was a damn stupid way of fighting guerrillas. All it did was advertise your presence. Buck had a different plan. He decided to go to the battalion commander and tell him about it.

Between Buck and the commander there were scores of lieutenants, captains, and majors. He was a platoon sergeant, not even a first sergeant. He had never talked to Schwarzkopf before. The colonel had no reason even to know of his existence.

But that did not deter Buck. Danger had a way of concentrating the mind and cutting through hierarchy. Coming back from the graduation ceremony at the sniper school, he went to see the commander. Schwarzkopf received him. After introducing himself, Buck explained what he had in mind.

"Why can't we fight like they do? Instead of being their target, why don't we reverse the roles for once? I just got out of sniper school. Instead of doing what the other battalions are doing, assigning the snipers to the line units, I would like to form an independent sniper team with the other sniper and the survivors in my platoon. We could have two snipers and four men for security. We would go out at night and work independently of the line unit—search-and-destroy missions directly under your command."

This was unheard of in the regular Army. It was what Special Forces did, and Schwarzkopf shared the infantryman's skepticism of special-operations forces. He did not like the fact that they did not play by the rules of the regular Army, and he thought that their freedom to act differently sometimes caused more problems than it solved. But Schwarzkopf had realized by then that Vietnam was not a regular war. They weren't fighting another army. There was no front line, no visible enemy battalion. It was no damn good lining up to confront an enemy that shifted like a shadow in the foliage, and pretending that you were back in Flanders fields facing a visible target.

Schwarzkopf liked Sergeant Deer's idea. It was unconventional, creative, and appropriate. He approved it on the spot.

"Anything you want you'll get. Just ask me. You'll always report to me," he told Buck. The sergeant was happy. With the heavy casualties, anything was better

than going back to a field unit. Unofficial statistics reported nine Americans killed for every dead gook, that is,
Viet Cong or North Vietnamese Army regular. The sniper
team was no joyride—they were six men with very little
firepower and no protection—but it was better than being
a walking target for booby traps and mines. It was a crazy
way to stay alive: risking more to increase the chances of
surviving. But it was a crazy war. Buck knew it. His men
knew it. Even Schwarzkopf probably knew it.

That was why Schwarzkopf let Buck have anything
he wanted. The thirty-five-year-old lieutenant colonel, a
stickler for discipline, always insisted that every soldier
wear his steel pot and flak jacket (helmet and bulletproof
vest). But when Buck told him they were too bulky and
noisy for the sniper missions, Schwarzkopf allowed him
to break the rule. The entire division had green army
uniforms. But Buck wanted camouflage fatigues like the
Marines', and Schwarzkopf granted this request, too. Buck
asked for silencers for the M16. He got them. And every
time he requested a chopper, the colonel found one for
him, even though the Americal Division was renowned
for its shortage of helicopters.

Bill Savage, the platoon bitcher, was also happy to
get out of the line unit. But he was not planning to
stop bitching. He would become the sniper team bitcher.
He disliked Schwarzkopf. He disliked any career man.
Schwarzkopf was not only a career man, he was a gung-ho
career man, and that was about as bad as you could get.
To Savage, things had been much better with the previous
battalion commander. There were almost no casualties.
Everything had been safer then. He missed what now
seemed like the good old days.

Mike Filben and Bill Chupp, two other members of the
team, were not thrilled about Schwarzkopf either. They
did not understand how he could think of winning the
war. Winning the war! This war was a sick joke; nobody
could remember the beginning or imagine an end. Then

there was K.Y., short for his home state of Kentucky. His real name was Karl McDowell. He had a wife and a one-year-old baby daughter waiting for him at home. Maybe he liked Schwarzkopf; maybe not. It was difficult to say because he hardly ever spoke. His buddies could count on the fingers of one hand the number of times he actually uttered something. Buck had chosen K.Y. for the team after noticing that the soldiers in his platoon were picking on him. The last member was Larry. The guy with no last name.

The procedure was always the same. Buck flew to Landing Zone Dotty, in the Batangan Peninsula, near My Lai, where the 1st Battalion had its headquarters at that time. He met with Schwarzkopf to get his instructions and took a reconnaissance flight with him to check the ground. Then he went back to his team and prepared. At the same time, Schwarzkopf moved a company—about one hundred men—into the area where the sniper team would operate.

Before nightfall the company "circled up," forming a defensive ring the size of a football field in which Buck's team could land. Every day helicopters brought supplies to the units in the field, so, for any Viet Cong spies, the sniper team's arrival looked like a regular supply operation.

When it was dark, the sniper team sneaked out of the circle into the jungle, moving toward a ridge or other high ground. The next morning the company moved out of its position. Thinking that all the Americans had gone, the Viet Cong then came out of their hideouts. Buck and the others observed without moving. Then they closed in. No other U.S. Army unit in Vietnam did this sort of thing, so the enemy had no reason to be suspicious. The Viet Cong regrouped and went to work laying mines, setting booby traps, or firing rockets at an American base. On the second day, Buck watched them from a closer position. On the third, he made his move.

At dawn he set up at about a thousand meters. Larry started from the back, while Buck worked the front of the Viet Cong group. Four or five seconds and a few, almost noiseless XM21 shots later, the VC were down. Probably they never knew what hit them. The snipers then ran down from their vantage point to pilfer any rifles or documents they could find.

Buck radioed the line unit that their mission was accomplished, and stated the sniper team's position. The message was relayed to Schwarzkopf, who sent a helicopter to observe the team's handiwork. Buck started walking toward the line unit, while they walked toward him and his men. At that point they were separated by a distance of three to five clicks (jargon for kilometers). At night the line unit circled up again, and in the dark the sniper team sneaked in. The next morning a helicopter came to take them back to the base, so the sergeant could brief Schwarzkopf.

It was a successful start. But the sniper team lasted barely three months. Its last mission was in May 1970. It was coming down off a hill. Mike Filben was in the rear, sick with hepatitis, and Larry had a high fever, probably from malaria. As usual, Buck was in front, leading the team. He was known for his eagle eyes and sixth sense for booby traps and mines. He was looking down as he walked, scanning the terrain, checking it for any signs of ground disturbance.

Bill Chupp followed two steps behind. Suddenly Buck realized that he had tripped on a wire; it was a delayed-reaction mechanism. He just had time to shout, *"Booby trap! Booby trap!"*

They all hit the deck. When the grenade exploded they were already on the ground. Buck came out of it with only an arm wound. Chupp was hit in the leg, but nothing too serious.

That was the end of the sniper team. Buck, who had been the driving force behind the operation, was sent home because of his injury, and no other platoon sergeant was crazy enough to want to roam the jungle with a bunch of snipers and no fire support. So Chupp was sent to the rear and Larry somewhere else. Filben, Savage, and K.Y. went back to the line unit—back to more mines and more booby traps, back to being moving targets for gooks.

In the end they all came out of Vietnam. However, none of them was ever the same. After a year in the jungle, seeing all those maimed bodies, the corpses, they had problems readjusting to American life. But they managed to recover, except K.Y., the silent one. He was last seen on the base in Washington State where all the soldiers went at the end of their tour. He never made it back to Lexington, Kentucky. His wife and parents never heard from him again, and his daughter, now twenty-two, knows him only from pictures. Vietnam did that to people.

"Want to know what Vietnam was like?" Paul "Buck" Deer asked. "I'll tell you. It was as if someone came to your home and said, 'You are going to be killed in the next few months, but before that, everybody else in your family will be killed. You will all be killed.' Initially, it doesn't hit you. Then one day, right in front of your eyes, you see your wife being blown to pieces while opening a package she got in the mail. A few days later, while your daughter is playing in the back yard, a shot is fired from a passing car. You see her lying in the grass, moaning, asking for help while she's bleeding to death. You are her father, you want to help; you *have* to help. But there is nothing you can do. Not a damn thing. Then you start to feel really shaken, and try to protect your son and yourself better. But one day the telephone rings and he answers it. He picks up the receiver and an explosion tears him apart. Your son is badly mutilated, gasping for air, dying in front of you. He, too, asks for help, but you have none to offer. He, too, dies in front of your eyes. At that point you are alone. Your entire family has been decimated by invisible enemies. And you know that you are going to be next.

You get a machine gun, put a helmet on, get rid of all the light bulbs, and start living in the dark, barricaded in your house. You always have your finger on the trigger, ready to shoot. One day the mailman comes with a package. You don't answer the door. He keeps buzzing. The noise of the bell makes you crazy. You want to scream but you can't because he would know you are there. You hear a long, loud imaginary scream in your head. You know that this is *it*. They are coming to get you. All of a sudden you see the mailman knocking on the window. You turn abruptly, roll over on the floor, and start shooting—a long, crazy burst of fire. It lasts only a few seconds, but those seconds seem endless. The mailman is dead. But there is nothing to celebrate. Someone comes and says that he was just a plain, harmless, innocent mailman. *That* was Vietnam."

Everything happened very quickly. All of a sudden a soldier burst in. He was blond—a typical American-looking kid with green army fatigues, boots, and a rifle. The girl was dressed like any other Vietnamese peasant—conical hat, light shirt, and ankle-length pants. He started screaming and swearing at her, accusing her of being a "fucking gook." But she was just a plain, harmless, innocent Vietnamese woman. The soldier started shooting—shooting and swearing. She was hit many times. Every blow sent her jerking farther backward until she finally went down. She remained there motionless. The American soldier left.

They called it "guerrilla theater." In that spring of 1970, while Lieutenant Colonel Schwarzkopf struggled to make headway with his battalion near My Lai, this sort of theater became one of the tactics used by the anti-war movement at Oberlin College, a small liberal-arts college in Ohio with a progressive reputation. The scene of the soldier killing the peasant girl was part of an "act" that anti-war students performed in front of a class to stir things up and bring the war home, as they used to say.

What was happening at Oberlin was happening on campuses throughout America. The bombing of North Vietnam and the deaths of tens of thousands of U.S. soldiers stirred emotions everywhere. Atrocities such as the My Lai massacre on March 16, 1968, when members of the 11th Infantry Brigade of the Americal Division slaughtered several hundred South Vietnamese villagers, made matters worse. President Richard M. Nixon talked about a "silent majority" who supported his policies, and Vice President Spiro T. Agnew dismissed the students as "an effete corps of impudent snobs." But the war divided America. It pitted children against parents, friends against friends, students against college administrators, and youth against the Establishment. In the Schwarzkopf family, it created havoc, pitting sibling against sibling in a bitter rift.

Ruth Schwarzkopf, the then lieutenant colonel's older sister, was one of the most active participants in the protests at Oberlin. Every Tuesday at noon—Tuesday after Tuesday for months—people would gather for silent vigils in Tappan Square, the main square in Oberlin. They would stand there for half an hour in absolute silence, wearing "practice non-violence" tags and black armbands. The fact that Ruth's own brother was there in Vietnam, directly involved in that senseless war, made her anguish particularly intense. Like her younger brother, Norman, Ruth was a very emotional, caring person. But the war brought out their differences. He had dreamed of becoming a great military leader. She had dreamed of becoming a great educator. He dreamed of winning the most decisive battle in history. She dreamed of a world without wars.

In the mid-fifties, Ruth had married Simon Barenbaum, a European intellectual. It was because Simon had been offered a tenured position in the French Department at Oberlin that Ruth found herself on that campus during the anti-war movement. Simon Barenbaum, a Latvian Jew, had lived in France from the age of one. He had managed to escape death when Hitler turned Europe into a vast battlefield, and later emigrated to the United States. But he was no stranger to the pain and atrocities of war. He did not have a brother in Vietnam; his brother had been killed in a Nazi concentration camp. That was one reason why Professor Barenbaum hated war even more passionately than Ruth.

For Simon Barenbaum, war could not be just. Certainly the one in Vietnam was not. Simon's opposition to the Vietnam War was not so much political as moral. Professor Barenbaum was a radical, but not a Marxist or even a socialist. He was a "moral radical," even in his teaching. He never dwelled at length on Jean-Paul Sartre in class; he preferred spending time on Albert Camus's *The Plague*, with its overpowering metaphor of moral pestilence destroying man. He, like Ruth, was gentle and spiritual, a humanitarian to whom war was anathema. In the late sixties, as the war ripped college campuses apart, many were forced to choose sides. Simon and his wife chose the only side possible for them.

When faculty members at Oberlin started to argue that military recruiters should not be allowed on campus, Simon was in the forefront of the fight. Ruth, who taught a class in French pedagogy, was as committed to peace as he was. She would attend the vigils on Tuesdays and talk about peace with students. Nothing too radical: Oberlin was not Columbia or Berkeley. Most protests were peaceful; classes were rarely disrupted and confrontations were avoided. That is, until May 1970, the same month that Schwarzkopf's experimental sniper team broke up in Vietnam.

On April 30, 1970, a warm evening in Oberlin, President Nixon announced his decision to send American troops to Cambodia. For years the Pentagon had complained about enemy sanctuaries and support bases in Cambodia, and Nixon had finally decided to send U.S. troops in to destroy them. But this was an escalation of the war that many Americans found totally unacceptable.

Three hundred students took to the streets, moving to the main intersection of College and Main. They sat on the sidewalk, chanting and listening to anti-war speeches, before proceeding toward the administration building for a symbolic takeover. They wanted to push for an "institutional stand against the war." The then acting provost talked to them and promised to call a special session of the General Faculty Council for the following day. On Saturday, May 2, hundreds of faculty members packed into an auditorium. The students crowded together outside the room, effectively taking the professors hostage. Tension mounted, with some professors accusing the students of kidnapping.

Finally one of the most militant professors successfully appealed to the students. The area was cleared. Inside, a motion to send a letter from the faculty to President Nixon demanding the immediate withdrawal of American troops from Vietnam and the rest of Indochina was put to a vote. It passed 88 to 2. Simon Barenbaum cast his vote in favor of the resolution.

The situation started to get out of hand the following Monday, May 4, when news spread through the campus that students at nearby Kent State University had been shot. More than twenty National Guardsmen had fired about thirty-five rounds into a crowd of students, leaving four of them sprawled dead on the ground. From Hamburger Hill, the war had reached the hills of northeastern Ohio. It was brought home to young, middle-class kids who until then had never really felt threatened. Only sixty miles away from Oberlin, students just like themselves had been killed. Everybody was in shock—students, professors, employees. More than ever, people felt that the war was destroying the country. For Simon Barenbaum and Ruth Schwarzkopf, the period following Kent State would be one of the most intense of their lives.

On Tuesday, May 5, the General Faculty Council held its best-attended meeting in Oberlin's history and voted almost unanimously in favor of "emergency educational measures," including the suspension of all classes, in order to discuss the war. The students proclaimed a symbolic general strike. The rest of May was dedicated to the fight against the war. Art professors and students produced anti-war posters with mottoes such as "How many more must die?" The corridors were plastered with notices and petitions announcing teach-ins and think-ins. The local radio station, WOBC, canceled all regular programming and served as a general strike information center. The student weekly paper started publishing daily to keep students up to date on the events. A strike steering committee was formed, and many ad hoc subcommittees soon followed. A "liberation school" sprang up from nowhere. Law professors led forums on "The Legal Aspects of War," professors of religion on "Western Religion and the War," and biology professors on "Napalm and Biological Weapons in the Vietnam War." Students talked about revolution in the Third World, wars of liberation, capitalism and imperialism, peace and equality.

Schwarzkopf's brother-in-law, Simon Barenbaum, was asked to address the Senior Assembly. He decided to approach the war-peace issue in a non-ideological but radical way. Instead of a lecture he gave a mime performance, including the symbolic release of a dove for peace. Some students were moved to tears. His brother-in-law would have reacted differently had he been there.

But H. Norman Schwarzkopf was in Vietnam, doing what the U.S. government had asked him to do, commanding American troops in the name of democracy and freedom. And after a total of twenty-two months in Vietnam he was still among the "silent" millions who believed that the United States was involved in a just war.

In early 1965, at the age of thirty, H. Norman Schwarzkopf had volunteered to go to Vietnam. That year, U.S. involvement escalated rapidly. In March 1965 the U.S.

Marines were deployed at Da Nang, and by May, President Johnson had increased the number of the U.S. troops to 46,000. Schwarzkopf was made an adviser to the Vietnamese Airborne Division, one of the elite troops of the South Vietnamese Army. It was a choice assignment and a feather in his cap. Ecstatic about it, he immediately went to Washington to tell his sister Sally the good news. Her reaction was one of dismay.

"The thought of volunteering to go to war blows my mind," she told him. "I will never understand why you did it." He tried to explain: "Sally, this is what I've been training for, and this will give me a chance to see if it has paid off. You know that I'm going there with one objective above all others: to save as many lives as I can."

In June 1965 he left for his first tour in Vietnam, as a captain. In that month the number of U.S. troops in Vietnam was already 75,000, and a month later it grew to 125,000. However, H. Norman Schwarzkopf had no combat role with the American soldiers. He was to use his military and tactical knowledge to advise the top officers of the Vietnamese Airborne Division.

He remained true to his word. He reduced the casualties to a minimum and planned operations that would not require troops to go directly into the shooting.

Later, he explained in an interview, in *U.S. News and World Report*, what he had seen:

I was in Vietnam—three days short of being promoted major, advising the Vietnamese. We were getting ready to go into a military operation during the Ia Drang Valley Campaign in 1965 and had been given this wonderful operations order, written in total Leavenworth style by the senior Vietnamese HQ. Then, suddenly, I discovered that (contrary to the order) we had no fire support nor any advance air strikes. I'd been told we'd have a Ranger battalion as our reserve and I suddenly found out that they were all on leave. So I went back and advised my Vietnamese counterpart not to go. Three or four hours later, I was hauled in before an array of colonels. "Captain," one of them said, "how dare you say not to go. Who are you to decide what adequate air support is?" "Sir, with all due respect," I answered, "when I'm the senior man on the ground, and it's my ass hanging out, adequate support is about 100 sorties of B-52s circling my head all in direct support of me . . . that's just barely adequate when it's my butt on the line." Of course he got furious. But that's my approach to military operations. You are talking about human lives, and my responsibility is to accomplish my objective with a minimum loss of the troops under my command. That's my job, not just accomplishing the mission.

Schwarzkopf was there as an adviser, and he could have done as many others did: remain in the rear administering, powwowing, and watching the war from afar. But he was not that type. He had to be where the action and troops were, no matter how deep in the jungle or how close to the front, in order to give proper advice. In August of '65 he was in the Duc Co Special Forces camp in the Vietnamese highlands, near the Cambodian border, when the enemy attacked unexpectedly. He found himself with two battalions of airborne troops surrounded by thousands of Viet Cong and North Vietnamese. For days, the enemy pounded their position with shells, mortar and heavy machine-gun fire. They could not get out or get any new supplies in. Their rations dwindled; they had only rice and fish sauce to eat until a relief unit broke through. "I smelled, I stank, I was awful," recalled the general. But he helped those who were in worse shape.

While other officers were attending visiting American VIPs and letting them use the few available helicopters, Schwarzkopf was doing his best to care for the wounded. Indeed, he was immortalized in that role, supporting a wounded paratrooper, in a photograph taken by a young

Associated Press reporter called Peter Arnett. The rest of his tour of duty was as hectic. He ended it with two Silver Stars, both earned for attending to or saving lives while wounded or under intense fire. He received his first Silver Star on August 5, 1965, for reorganizing the unit he was advising, which had been split into three parts during a fierce battle. While under intense fire, he treated injured soldiers in one element and led them to safety. He then went through enemy fire to locate the other elements, leading them back through the shooting to reunite the unit. He received the other Silver Star (with a first oak leaf cluster) on February 14, 1966. During an assault on a heavily defended Viet Cong position, Schwarzkopf exposed himself to intense enemy fire. He was wounded four times but refused to take cover or be evacuated until he could consolidate his position and be sure that all the wounded were taken care of.

"We fought almost every day of every month for thirteen months," Schwarzkopf said later. "I really thought we had done something good, just like George Washington. I had gone and fought for freedom."

He expected a hero's welcome. But when he arrived in New York, he found instead an empty terminal and a totally uninterested cab driver. Schwarzkopf could not understand the indifference. It infuriated him. There was no reason to be ashamed or even modest about what they had done.

His friend Ward Le Hardy, now a retired brigadier general, described that first tour in Vietnam as "a wonderful experience for Norman and me. We both felt proud to serve in combat, proud to have taught the Vietnamese what we knew. There was a sense of accomplishment for having helped some wonderful people defend themselves." Norm himself told his sister Sally that it had been "one of the best years of my life." He had proven to himself that he could apply what he had learned at

West Point. He was confident of having made a difference and optimistic about the future of the war and South Vietnam.

He was thus still enthusiastic. But he lost something in that first encounter with war. It shook his basic optimism, as it shook the optimism of America. He had known that war could be devastating, but deep in his heart he had had a romantic vision of a war that would be thrilling, not dreadful. "He lost his youth in Vietnam, his ebullience. He came back different. He came back a very serious person," said Sally. He had left as a young captain yearning for the adventure of war and came back as an experienced major for whom fighting a war was a professional responsibility.

As planned, Schwarzkopf went back to West Point after Vietnam to complete his three-year teaching assignment. He found an old classmate there, Charles Prather, who had also gone to Vietnam as an adviser and had come back to teach at West Point. Schwarzkopf dated Charlie's sister for a while, but it did not last. He had remained a bachelor for a long time and, like his father, had not felt in a hurry to settle down.

His father had married at thirty-three. Schwarzkopf followed him in most things and, sure enough, at the age of thirty-three he met Brenda Holsinger. She was waiting for him at the officers' club at West Point. Actually, she was with a faculty member she had been dating, but Norm soon wrested her away. Brenda, then twenty-seven, was from Timberville, Virginia, but at the time was living in New York City and working for TWA as a flight attendant. She had dark hair and a lovely smile. She was much smaller than Schwarzkopf—she hardly reached his shoulder—but that did not bother them. Soon after their encounter at West Point, they began meeting in New York for walks in Central Park, movies, and plays.

Brenda's upbringing was very different from Norman's. The only child of Jesse and Elsie Holsinger, she was raised on an apple and chicken farm. Her father was a simple man, utterly unlike the sophisticated and worldly former superintendent of the New Jersey State Police. But Mr. Holsinger was friendly and witty, and Norman liked him immediately. The two men also shared a love for hunting and would often go off together into the Virginia countryside.

Brenda was very attached to her family. She was a small-town girl. And although she had moved to New York City and had found a job that required traveling, she was still thinking of building a house on her family's land and living next door to them. That was certainly what her parents would have wanted. These homespun values attracted Norman, whose peripatetic army life had, if anything, increased his deep sense of the importance of the family.

"Wait until you see Timberville," he told his sister Sally. "It's really just like old-fashioned America. There is only one main street, and the people sit in their rockers on the porch waiting for neighbors to pass by."

It was quaint; but there was never much doubt that small-town America was too small for a man like Schwarzkopf. It was clear from the outset that building a house on the Holsinger farm was never a serious option.

On July 6, 1968, eight months after they had met, Brenda and Major Schwarzkopf were married at West Point. H. Norman wore a white dress uniform, and Brenda a traditional wedding gown with a short train.

Brenda's congeniality and gentleness made her an instant success with the family. "Everyone agreed: Brenda was perfect for him," Sally said. "She was the only girlfriend that Norm had brought home that my mother said she would like to have as a daughter-in-law."

Her only fault was that she never managed to learn how to make the family treat, the sand tart cookies. But she would soon become "a great army wife." Brenda was supportive, patient about the changes and disruptions of military life, and willing to deal with a husband who was used to giving orders. Norman has been the dominant figure at home. But Brenda, according to those who know the family well, has never let him walk over her. In her own quiet way she would set him straight. "Oh, Norman!" she would say when one of his outlandish moods took him—and that was usually enough.

Shortly after their marriage, Norman ended the serenity of their new life together by volunteering for war again. He was promoted to lieutenant colonel, well ahead of most of his contemporaries, and in the spring of '69 he asked to be reassigned to Vietnam. As a lieutenant colonel, he had the necessary rank to command a battalion. He was eager to prove himself a leader.

In June of 1969 he returned to Saigon, where he was assigned to U.S. Army Vietnam headquarters. But Norman quickly rediscovered how much he disliked working at a desk next to officers who lived a life of luxury and tranquillity.

"I hated it in the rear," he said. "It was a cesspool . . . You saw the worst there; the commander was living in luxury and his focus was on things like the re-enlistment rate." It was another blow to his idealistic view of the military. They were in the middle of a war, but his superiors had an army of servants, ate with silverware at tables covered with white cloths, and had tea parties and dances with Red Cross girls. For Schwarzkopf it was no way to fight, and certainly not the right example to set for American and Vietnamese soldiers while Vietnam was being blown apart.

By October 1969, Schwarzkopf had lost respect for many of his commanding officers. He was disgusted. There were over 500,000 men in Vietnam—troop strength peaked in March of that year at 541,500—but they were not being directed to do anything. What Schwarzkopf wanted was to command a battalion in the field because he was convinced he could save lives there while taking the fight to the enemy.

In November, Lieutenant Colonel H. Norman Schwarzkopf got what he wanted: command of a battalion. He was given the 1st of the 6th in the 198th Brigade of the Americal Division. It was not a prime assignment. The Americal was not a standing division, and had been hastily put together for the Vietnam War. It therefore lacked the cohesiveness of other divisions. In addition, it was particularly tainted by the My Lai massacre, because the unit responsible was part of the Americal.

Before the transfer, Lieutenant Colonel Schwarzkopf was given the only R & R (rest and relaxation break) of his entire second tour in Vietnam. He called Brenda, who was still working as a flight attendant, and arranged to meet her in Hong Kong. Gregarious as ever, Norman made friends with the in-house tailor at the Presidential Hotel, who invited the couple to dinner and for a tour of the city. Colonel Schwarzkopf reciprocated by ordering a couple of suits. It was in Hong Kong that the Schwarzkopfs conceived their first child, Cynthia.

At that time the headquarters for the 198th Brigade was near the town of Chu Lai in a place called Landing Zone (LZ) Bayonet. The area had been filled with rice paddies, but the Army Corps of Engineers brought tons of sand over and transformed it into a huge beach. Every helicopter taking off, every tank moving into position created a desert-like sandstorm.

The buildings at the headquarters were constructed of 4 × 5 sheets of plywood, with screens for ventilation and tin roofs. Three or four feet of sandbags protected them against explosions. Schwarzkopf had a one-room structure, called "the hootch," sparsely furnished with a footlocker, a metal-framed bed, a lamp, a small refrigerator, and a wooden brace for clothes. It was cozy but primitive, a far cry from the opulent villas in which the top officials in Saigon lived. There was no air conditioning, no bar, no servants—not even a bathroom. Toilets were outside. There was also an operations building made up of a big room with fifteen to twenty chairs around a large table and a smaller room in the back with a desk for the commander.

Schwarzkopf's predecessor had been a much older man with very little combat experience. He had spent most of his time in Vietnam as a staff officer in the rear. The situation at LZ Bayonet reflected his relaxed character. The place was not exactly humming when Schwarzkopf took over. There were very few marches, scant training sessions, and hardly any missions. Few missions also meant few casualties. Discipline was lax. The soldiers used to say, "What can they do? Court-martial me? It'd be better than being here, risking being blown apart for nothing."

Marijuana was everywhere. So, too, was moo juice, a sort of liquid amphetamine that soldiers found in Vietnamese villages. A former soldier recalled one scene: "There was a young lieutenant, fresh from the Academy, who went to the platoon sergeant, saying, 'I think we have a problem. I think people here smoke marijuana!' The sergeant almost laughed in his face."

The motivation level was about zero. "We used to have a lot of arguments," said another soldier. "Nobody wanted to carry the M60 machine gun because it was heavy and was a target for snipers. There were also people who refused to dig foxholes. I remember a guy from California called Wild Billy. He would never dig a foxhole. Never. He would just sit there smoking pot, watching the others dig."

At the fire base, there were soldiers sunbathing in hammocks all day. They never wore flak jackets or steel pots because these were considered superfluous and annoying. Over the entrance to the mess hall there was a sign that said: "Through this door passes the best damn soldier in the world." It was a lie.

"When I first landed there, I thought I was in the wrong place," recalled Paul Deer. "There was so little activity that the rear would have seemed hectic in comparison. The VC could come in, fire a few rockets, and leave totally undisturbed. We didn't even respond. There was no security, no interest in tracking them down or following them into the jungle. I was shocked."

The impact on Lieutenant Colonel Schwarzkopf was even stronger when he arrived at the beginning of the second week of December 1969. He was astounded by the lack of training and discipline. "When I took over my battalion, it was totally unprepared for battle, yet it had been in battle. All they were doing was taking casualties, not inflicting them. It was a nightmare," he said later.

After quickly assessing the situation at the fire base, Schwarzkopf set off to get to know his officers in the field. Around the middle of December, Captain Tom Cameron got a call from his new commander, saying he was on his way to meet him. The captain was told to secure an area for landing. It was not a great place, but he had no time to find anything better. Schwarzkopf arrived on a cold, misty day in the early afternoon. For a five-foot-nine, 145-pound man like Cameron, he was intimidating. The colonel immediately expressed doubts about the security of the landing area, but was put at ease when the captain explained how he had positioned his men. Schwarzkopf then started firing questions about the tactical situation. Where were they going? How far was it? Had they met the enemy? What was the status of the unit? How many men were there? How well trained were they? Were they getting the needed support? Did they have enough food? Captain Cameron was not used to this kind of interest; in fact, he was not used to any interest at all from the previous commander. Schwarzkopf then spoke to each platoon leader, all the sergeants, and a few enlisted men.

In all, he stayed about three-quarters of an hour.

It was evident that Schwarzkopf would be a different kind of commander, the type who takes charge. Rumor had it that he was smart and effective and that he had the potential to become a general. His reputation had preceded him: Captain Cameron realized there was something to it.

Schwarzkopf spent the first few weeks trying to change habits and routines. The soldiers of the 1st of the 6th were dying more from overlooked details and unpreparedness than from combat. The colonel briskly set a battalion policy that the troops had to wear steel pots and flak vests any time they were out of the fire base. He started new training activities and imposed new security rules, which were all carried out and enforced with rigor. One evening, while flying over Cameron's unit, he noticed the captain digging a foxhole without his protective vest. It was a hot day, and digging was more difficult with the vest on. But those were not sufficient justifications for the commander, who radioed Cameron and gave him hell. It was the only time in Cameron's career that anybody had ever chewed him out—and for a reason.

This concern for the safety of his men explains the incident that drove Buck and others crazy: the occasion when Schwarzkopf, circling in his helicopter, saw the men on the tanks and made them climb down and walk through a minefield. One of the times, that is, when they muttered "Colonel Nazi" under their breaths.

Schwarzkopf knew that a tank with a dozen soldiers on it would be a prime target for special anti-tank devices that were operated by the enemy from a distance. On a tank a dozen infantrymen would have been lost, compared to only a few lives if the soldiers had been on foot, following the tracks at the appropriate distance from one another. Allowing the men on the tanks was a gross violation, serious enough for him to relieve the captain of his duties. It was a measure he had never taken before and would never take again.

Even Buck later understood why Schwarzkopf did it. "At the time, I did not like having to walk through a minefield," he said. "But if I had been in his shoes, I would have done the same."

All these changes increased the survival rate. But they also led to a lot of moaning. The soldiers did not want to wear heavy flak jackets, and they did not like to train for a war they could not understand. Most of them were nineteen or twenty years old. What they thought about was getting through their one-year tour and getting home. They missed those days lounging in their hammocks, under their former commander.

"If they could have had their way, they wouldn't have done anything or shot anybody," said Bill Chupp, one of the members of the sniper team. "Everybody just wanted out—with all their limbs intact if possible. And the best way of getting out safely was by doing nothing." By trying to make "real soldiers" out of the grunts and draftees and by imposing unheard-of rules and discipline, Schwarzkopf earned the nickname of "Colonel Nazi." Others preferred calling him "Stormin' Norman."

But to the officers he was known mostly as "Black Smoke 6." The "6" came from the number designating the commander of a battalion, and "Black Smoke" from the first speech he gave to his officers: "I am here to help you and to work with you. I'll do everything I can to support you. But if you mess up, wherever you are, I'll spot you and arrive in a black Chinook helicopter. I'll pop a black-smoke grenade and under that black cloud I'll hook you and take you with me. Nobody will ever hear from you again. On the other hand, if you do a good job, when the time comes for you to go home, I'll give you my very special black-smoke grenade as a memento and a sign of gratitude."

Black-smoke grenades did not exist. There were grenades that produced white, yellow, or red smoke—but not black. However, when it came time to go, the officers got a discarded canister, painted black, with the inscription: "Thank you for a job well done. Black Smoke 6."

This was typical Schwarzkopf. Even at his age of thirty-five, his main traits were clear: a tough demeanor often leavened by humor; and a twin commitment to waging war because "some things are worth fighting for" and to saving as many lives as possible in the achievement of victory.

Despite the flak vest incident, Captain Cameron was one of many who left Vietnam with a black-smoke grenade. But the executive officer, a major Schwarzkopf inherited with the command, did not get one. This major had come from Special Forces and was, in Schwarzkopf's view, typical Special Forces material—a swaggering fellow who fancied himself John Wayne. His nickname was Major Roger Roger, a name given to him by the radio operators because of his habit of ending a conversation with "Roger, Roger."

The major was very aggressive with his subordinates, and even with other officers. One night he went out on an ambush with a group of soldiers and a young second lieutenant, nicknamed Tricky Dicky, from Charlie Company. The lieutenant was asked to look for a safe spot to spend the night, but when the major got there he found it was too wet. Roger Roger was furious and started screaming at the young lieutenant. Then, to everyone's dismay, he grabbed him by the collar, picked him up, and threw him into a rice paddy.

Roger Roger's behavior was not any more diplomatic with enlisted men. Most of them hated him for being so belligerent. Someone even tried to shoot him down one day while he was flying a small helicopter. A few rounds of 50 mm ammunition were shot from a tank, but missed the major—or so the story went.

Roger Roger had taken advantage of the previous commander's lassitude, assuming de facto leadership in the field. With Schwarzkopf in charge, officers had someone to whom they could gripe about the major. Captain

Cameron remembered calling Schwarzkopf on at least one occasion to complain about an order. The colonel heard his argument and decided to allow him to ignore Roger Roger's instructions.

Christmas came soon after Schwarzkopf's arrival at LZ Bayonet. He could have decided to spend the day with his staff in the rear, eating at a table with a white tablecloth. But he was not that type of man. He radioed Captain Cameron in the middle of the jungle and told him to find a position for the next twenty-four hours and wait for him. He was going to spend Christmas Day with his company. Schwarzkopf had already spent a Christmas in Vietnam, in 1965, but for many of the enlisted men it would be the first Christmas away from their families. He wanted to show his personal commitment, as he would two decades later in similar circumstances in Saudi Arabia.

It had been a particularly wet month, even for the monsoon season, and some sixty-five or seventy inches of rain had fallen. But that Christmas Day the sky had cleared and it was warmer. The company had dug in on the side of a large river, setting up defensive positions all around the area. They had also dug some shallow sleeping positions.

Footage shot on a Super 8 camera by a young lieutenant from Charlie Company captures the feeling of that Christmas. The camera scans the area, showing jungle trees primitively decorated for the occasion with odds and ends that each soldier has contributed. There are Christmas balls, white strings of paper, Christmas cards, a hat, a soda can, a peace sign, and even a bullet cartridge. The camera moves to the men in the camp, zooming in on smiling faces. The men look relaxed and seem to be enjoying the warm sun. They are in army T-shirts or regular army shirts with the sleeves rolled up—no flak vests or helmets. They start waving to the camera; some clown around. One soldier is cleaning his rifle. The camera scans the camp, showing many small low tents and sandbags. Most of the men are around the tents, completing last-minute preparations. The camera cuts to the sky and an arriving helicopter. It follows the chopper as it descends, kicking up a cloud of dust in the camp. Now the camera switches to the bush, showing about half a dozen men walking toward the camp, carrying cartons. As the men walk toward the camera, a smiling Colonel Schwarzkopf with packages under each arm approaches. One of the men is dressed up like a G.I. Santa Claus with a red helmet. He's walking toward the camp in a jolly, swaggering style.

Now there is a cut back to the camp, to men on guard duty with rifles, helmets, and flak vests, then back to the middle of the camp, where the cartons of food are lined up. The men move around getting turkey from one carton and the trimmings from others. They are sitting on sandbags, happily eating. There is a cut to Colonel Schwarzkopf wearing his flak vest, unlike the other men, and drinking a soda next to a tree. He is already a heavyset, bearish man, unlike the tall young fellow caught in photographs of him during the 1965 tour. Then the film cuts to a well-decorated artificial Christmas tree—an unexpected present from Cameron's wife.

The next scene is of the chaplain, with a camouflage poncho over his white robe, performing a short Christmas service. And then the camera cuts to Schwarzkopf's helicopter again, this time taking off.

That day, Schwarzkopf and Cameron talked about their wives back home—they were the only married men. They also conferred about knives, which both men loved. Schwarzkopf had been a knife enthusiast since his tenth birthday, when his father's Iranian interpreter sent him one as a present. In Vietnam, the colonel always carried a survival knife with a screw-on cap. Inside the knife were survival necessities, including a fishing line. The captain carried three different knives: a bayonet, an air force survival knife, and an army demolition knife.

After talking for a while, the colonel retired to one of the foxholes for a short nap before returning to LZ Bayonet.

Officers like Captain Cameron never had any doubts about Schwarzkopf's concern for his men. They saw his roughness at times in dealing with soldiers who did not follow orders. They saw his short temper when someone did something foolish or careless. Some even used the nickname "Stormin' Norman" in those cases. But they all knew that his behavior came from his relentless zeal. "The only time he would get upset was when someone did something stupid," said Cameron. "I never heard him raise his voice, though. He would merely get a very intense look in his eyes. And that would be more effective than a scream."

In mid-January 1970, Captain Cameron had another opportunity to experience Schwarzkopf's intensity in person. He was standing with his company at the helicopter pickup zone, a large flattened area adjacent to LZ Bayonet. Some of his men had started burning trash in a metal barrel to keep warm, and suddenly there was an explosion. Someone had accidentally dropped a 40 mm grenade in the barrel. Cameron and one of the soldiers were injured, but not seriously, because both of them had protective vests and helmets on. The radio operator immediately called HQ for an evacuation helicopter. Schwarzkopf got word of the incident, but somehow was told that Cameron and the soldier had been badly hurt. He grabbed the battalion surgeon and flew to the scene. When he got there, he was visibly upset: Cameron was walking around, giving orders.

"Are you all right?" Schwarzkopf asked in disbelief. It was quite clear that the captain's injuries were not as serious as Schwarzkopf had heard. Still, the colonel insisted that he go back with him and check into the hospital. "Get into my helicopter," he said.

Thinking this was friendly advice, Cameron said that he was all right and did not need to go to the hospital.

Schwarzkopf got so upset that he grabbed Cameron, lifted him up in the air, and said, "Captain, I said to get in my helicopter, *now!*"

"Yes, sir! I'm going."

Schwarzkopf brought qualitative changes to the 1st of the 6th, but he could not perform miracles. It was still Vietnam and still the Americal Division, a weaker division than others. Many of the soldiers were draftees, and many of the career men had little training or combat experience. Mistakes were unavoidable, and a particularly grave one occurred on February 17, 1970.

Charlie Company, one hundred men strong, under the command of Captain Cameron, moved onto a horseshoe-shaped ridge. They were too far away for their fire base at Landing Zone Bayonet to support them, so they arranged for artillery to be flown in closer. The men set up a night defense position on the ridge and designated targets all around. As a precautionary measure, Cameron had asked the artillery to shoot in the direction of the three most likely avenues of approach that he thought the enemy would use to attack them. The first marking round, the white phosphorus-filled round used to identify the target, was successfully fired. But the next, the high-explosive round intended to strike the enemy, fell about four hundred meters short, hitting the tops of the trees above Charlie Company's position. The shells exploded right above one of the platoons, killing Sergeant Michael E. Mullen and another soldier and wounding six men.

It was later discovered that the Fire Direction Center had miscalculated; it had not taken into account the height of the trees for the heavier high-explosive round. Captain Cameron radioed to stop the shelling and ask for evacuation helicopters. As soon as Schwarzkopf was informed, he got on the radio. "He was terribly upset," recalled Tom Cameron, "and got even more upset when I left the radio to try to coordinate the emergency operation. I had lost a good part of my platoon; I had wounded and dead soldiers. I was concerned about reestablishing security and calming my men, but Colonel Schwarzkopf wanted to continue talking to me. He wanted to know who was wounded, exactly what had happened, and he wanted to make sure I was doing all the right things."

From the fire base, Schwarzkopf coordinated the arrival of the choppers, and a few hours later, with the early light, he flew to the area himself. Later this event would become the subject of a book, *Friendly Fire* by C. D. B. Bryan, and a TV movie, which tell the story of the Mullen family's long and difficult search for the truth about the death of their son. Michael's parents were convinced that Schwarzkopf somehow covered up the incident. But Bryan fully exonerated the colonel, who said to him that it was "a tragedy typical of a profane thing called war."

Schwarzkopf was struck by the lack of motivation of some of his soldiers. He could not accept the idea that they did not want to be there. He could change their training schedules and impose stricter routines, but he could not give them the will to fight. Under his command, discipline did get much better, but was still not very rigorous. One soldier was notorious for having tried every possible way of getting out of the field. He had fired at civilians, refused orders, and been insubordinate. One day he got into a fight with a staff sergeant at the fire base. A young lieutenant by the name of Paul Cullinane heard the altercation and intervened. When the lieutenant turned to leave, the grunt tried to stab him. The lieutenant might have been killed if a soldier standing nearby had not hit the assailant on the head with a pipe.

Lieutenant Colonel Schwarzkopf did not have time to clear the battalion of shirkers and make all the draftees real fighters. He was sent there to confront the enemy, and that was what he tried to do. This made him very unpopular with many of his troops. Why, they wondered, did their colonel want to fight an unwinnable war? When the 198th Brigade switched positions with the 11th, moving to a much more dangerous area in the Batangan Peninsula, Schwarzkopf decided to step up the frequency of missions, patrols, and ambushes. None of this was appreciated by his soldiers. As soon as the move to LZ Dotty was completed, casualties rose.

The area was more heavily infiltrated by the Viet Cong than the previous one and was filled with mines and booby traps. "Schwarzkopf kept repeating that he worried about us, that he would always look out for us, but we didn't get that impression," said Bill Savage. "When something went wrong and someone got hurt he would get upset and make it sound like it was our fault. He would always say, 'You guys are messing up; that's why you get hurt.' So to us all his worrying just sounded like public relations."

Savage continued: "I don't know if the previous colonel cared about us. I don't remember ever seeing him in the field or briefing the soldiers. All I know is that when he was there, casualties were relatively low, and when Schwarzkopf ordered us to LZ Dotty, they increased dramatically. We couldn't understand that move. We didn't want to be in Vietnam, so you can imagine how we liked being sent into an area referred to as a killing field."

Savage was not alone in feeling that way. "Schwarzkopf was a career man. He wanted more Killing in Action; he wanted the KIAs to increase, and he wasn't happy because we weren't living up to his expectations," said Bill Chupp. "I had volunteered after high school mostly to take advantage of the G.I. Bill, and I wanted to go back to my small town in Michigan as a hero. When I got there I was so chickenshit, so unheroic. There were so many people dying so fast, without even seeing the enemy, that I soon realized what the others before me had grasped: that the only important thing was to get out of there alive and in one piece. Most of us were looking at it from the point of view of survival, possibly with some kind of dignity."

Schwarzkopf had a totally different perspective. He was looking at Vietnam as a war to be won, like the wars he had read about at West Point. He was determined to win what he saw as a battle against Communism. His disgust with Vietnam would come when he realized, in the end, that there was no overall point to these missions, that he was laboring to advance in pursuit of a goal that was never defined.

He was willing to spend as much time as needed in the field. His commitment was unquestionable, even to Savage. "For a battalion commander in Vietnam it was unusual to be with his troops in the field so much," Savage said. "But he was gung-ho, and I felt at the time that he was doing it for his own career. He wanted the action; he wanted those KIAs. That's why he accepted the idea of the sniper team to begin with. It was a great way to improve the numbers. The six of us were killing more VC than entire companies."

Tom Cameron, now a lieutenant colonel in the U.S. Army, did not agree. "I know that Colonel Schwarzkopf was *not* interested in body count. That was not an objective of his. Sheer numbers didn't mean a thing to him. He told us this loud and clear: your responsibility is to accomplish your mission and do it as carefully as possible. Just going out there counting bodies is a poor measure of the success of an operation."

Cameron added, "Keeping that in mind, it is possible that he wanted to increase the number of engagements with the enemy. But isn't engaging the enemy what any officer should do?"

Sergeant "Buck" Deer, now a real estate agent near Las Vegas, was in the unusual position of being intimate with both the colonel and the enlisted men. He offered this explanation:

"Between a drafted sergeant and a lieutenant colonel there is a big gap. But Schwarzkopf made it feel almost like we were the same rank. He went over things in a very friendly way, making me feel at ease. He was always very concerned and always asked me if anybody had been uncooperative or difficult. He was determined to make things as easy as possible for us. But all my men usually knew was that they were going on a mission to kill some Viet Cong. They didn't know why, they didn't know how carefully it had been prepared or how much planning was put into reducing the risks. In the meantime, all around them—in the My Lai 4 area—their friends were being killed. That was enough to make them think that Schwarzkopf cared only about killing VC and didn't give a whit about us. But one thing is for sure: if the battalion had been sent to My Lai 4 with the previous colonel, we would all have been killed the first week. Schwarzkopf asked a lot, but he also got a lot. And he saved many lives by making everybody work harder."

Schwarzkopf's reaction after the tragic death of Michael Mullen and his help in the evacuation when Captain Cameron was wounded demonstrated his commitment to men of all ranks. On March 17, 1970, he exhibited the same concern for a general. That day, a helicopter carrying the commanding general of the American Division, Major General Lloyd B. Ramsey, crashed into a mountainside in the middle of a thick jungle area. Schwarzkopf immediately directed his units in the vicinity to start a hunt for the downed aircraft. HQ then sent a Chinook to pick up Lieutenant Paul Cullinane and fly him closer to the area where they thought the helicopter had gone down. The lieutenant started the rescue operation and at dusk asked Lieutenant Colonel Schwarzkopf to order the firing of illumination shells. Cullinane and his men continued the search all night, marching through the steep mountain terrain without food or water, in constant radio contact with Lieutenant Colonel Schwarzkopf.

At daybreak they found the chopper. Cullinane and his men were the first to arrive from the ground, but a rescue helicopter had located the downed aircraft, too, and radioed its coordinates to Schwarzkopf. Although he had not slept all night, the colonel flew to the site with the company doctor. It was foggy, and the victims were down on the side of a ridge. Schwarzkopf took a rope, tied it around himself, and lowered the surgeon to the crash site to administer first aid to the survivors. The survivors, including Major General Ramsey, were then picked up in the early hours of the morning by rescue helicopters. By that time the fog was dense and the jungle impenetrable, so the dead were left there. The next day, after spending another night without food or water, Lieutenant Cullinane and his men brought the bodies up, an act that earned them Army Commendation Medals.

Schwarzkopf received medals for similar acts of courage. The most celebrated incident occured on May 28, 1970, when Bravo Company got stuck in a minefield during a patrol mission. Both the captain and the lieutenant were badly wounded, and the men were left without leadership. Schwarzkopf flew in with his artillery liaison officer, Captain Bob Trabbert. He moved closer to the nervous soldiers, who were still trapped in the minefield, and tried to restore their confidence and instruct them on how to get out of the field. But as soon as they started moving, one of them hit a mine, which tore his leg apart and slightly wounded Captain Trabbert and Lieutenant Colonel Schwarzkopf. In *Friendly Fire*, C. D. B. Bryan describes the incident:

> "My leg! Somebody help me!" the kid was screaming . . . Schwarzkopf began inching across the minefield to reach him.
> "Somebody help me, HELP ME!" The private was still flailing about.
> "Don't move!" Schwarzkopf yelled at him . . . "You're going to be all right, just hang on." Schwarzkopf was maybe thirty feet from the wounded private. He carefully,

slowly, slid one foot forward, testing the ground beneath his boot before placing his weight on that foot. There was absolute silence now except for Trabbert talking on the radio to the med-evac helicopter, telling them where Bravo Company was and what they would need. Schwarzkopf still had twenty feet of minefield to cross when the wounded soldier started panicking again: "I'm going to die! We're all going to die!"

Schwarzkopf's legs suddenly began to shake uncontrollably; his knees were so watery he had to reach down and grip them until they stilled. The perspiration was stinging his eyes. He straightened up and saw the men were watching him, waiting for him to move forward again. Schwarzkopf, to his astonishment, suddenly thought of the sign on Harry Truman's White House desk: "The buck stops here."

Finally Schwarzkopf reached the young private. He lowered himself across his body to keep him still. Then he called back to Trabbert to get a splint. As a man next to Trabbert moved, another mine exploded, killing two people and seriously wounding Trabbert. That mine exploded in the place where Schwarzkopf had been standing before he set off across the field.

In June 1970, adding another Silver Star Medal with a second oak leaf cluster to his two Purple Hearts, three Bronze Stars, and variety of other medals, he ended his second tour of duty in Vietnam. His predecessor had left the battalion the same way he had ruled it: unnoticed. The soldiers had been informed of his departure only by word of mouth. Schwarzkopf was different even in his manner of leaving. He took his chopper and went into the field to say goodbye to every single unit. After positioning each unit in a safe spot, he flew in, gathered the soldiers and officers together, and told them, "My time is up. I am going back to the States. I tried my best. I tried to save as many lives as possible."

The men of Charlie Company listened with skepticism. To some of them, all he had done was to guide them into that huge, deadly trap called My Lai 4. That was not saving lives. Mike Filben of the sniper team summed it up for everyone: "We sure didn't think much of him then. But maybe we were just looking for someone to blame for a war we didn't want to be a part of."

By the time Lieutenant Colonel H. Norman Schwarzkopf left in July 1970, more than 50,000 Americans had lost their lives in Vietnam. Three years later, the last American troops would leave. And on April 30, 1975, South Vietnam surrendered to the Communists.

4

Wilderness

Where have all the soldiers gone?
—From Pete Seeger's "Where Have All the Flowers Gone?"

When, in July 1970, H. Norman Schwarzkopf returned home from his second tour in Vietnam, he found a country in the midst of violent upheaval. The Kent State killings of May were still fresh in people's minds; protest marches and demonstrations were daily occurrences; Vietnam and the military were dirty words. He did not expect a hero's welcome and he did not get one. In fact, the situation was worse than he had expected.

For it was not just Vietnam that had shaken America over the previous years, although the war certainly acted as a catalyst to all forms of protest. After the placid prosperity of the Eisenhower years, the 1960s were a period of turmoil. Tensions between blacks and whites built to a crescendo. The 1967 Detroit race riots were among the worst in American history, prompting President Lyndon B. Johnson to call in army paratroopers. Student protest was unprecedented in scope and violence. The women's movement began to gain momentum. At the same time, among many young people, a culture of drugs and nonviolence spread across the nation, from San Francisco to the village of Woodstock in New York State.

All this upheaval was acutely reflected in the Armed Forces. Testing of soldiers in Vietnam found that at least 5 percent had used heroin. By 1970 desertion rates were at a record high. According to one 1972 Army report, "Drug abuse among soldiers increased steadily from 1968 to 1971, when it approached epidemic proportions in Southeast Asia. It flourished in Vietnam, where soldiers seeking release from hardship, danger, boredom and fatigue found a steady supply of powerful drugs at low prices."

In short, as Lieutenant Colonel Schwarzkopf returned to his country and his heavily pregnant wife, the Army was in disarray. It was racked by racial antagonism, violence, rampant drug abuse, absenteeism, desertion, crime, and general resistance to authority. One month previously, an official count found that there were sixty-three anti-war newspapers circulating within the forces.

Schwarzkopf's friend and West Point roommate Leroy Suddath was at Fort Bragg, North Carolina, at this time. He, too, had recently come back from Vietnam. As a battalion commander, he was having trouble imposing any sort of discipline. His soldiers were mainly draftees from Vietnam who had returned to Fort Bragg and were impatiently awaiting their discharge.

"Things were in terrible shape," he said. "We were going through a social revolution and we couldn't control it. There were white soldiers being beaten up by blacks and blacks by whites. The black soldiers were showing pride in their ethnicity by growing Afro hairstyles. The place was full of undisciplined druggers. The drug problem was out of control. I saw the worst imaginable things. It was an army in crisis."

The town of Fayetteville, close to Fort Bragg, became known as "Fayettenam." A sleazy strip developed, full of bars and clip joints, and it was frequented mainly by soldiers from the base. Hookers would come down from New York on army payday because business was so good. The local community did not like the soldiers, and the soldiers did not like the locals. Fights and brawls were commonplace. The stockade at the base was always full.

For many professional soldiers of Schwarzkopf's generation, the situation was profoundly disorienting. They had grown into manhood during the 1950s, at a time when America's ability to grow richer, do good, and influence the world had never seemed stronger. They had an almost naïve belief in American power: first General Eisenhower had freed Europe from Hitler, and then, between 1952 and 1960, President Eisenhower had made the country richer than ever. Their view that America should serve as the model for the free world was largely unquestioning. Their decision to go to Vietnam stemmed from the same absolute conviction: the South Vietnamese people should live in freedom and democracy and be rid of the menace of Communism.

Yet here before their eyes was the abject result of what they saw as an essentially noble effort: a discredited military—undisciplined, divided, hesitant, derided. "There was a sense when you came back of being unable to do anything worthwhile," said Adrian Cronauer, who was a military broadcaster in Vietnam. "Many of us had grown up with the feeling that we were the leaders of the world, or at least the free world. Afterward, we had the sense we did not live up to that leadership in Vietnam, and we felt bad about it."

Lieutenant Colonel Schwarzkopf felt very bad, torn by agonizing internal conflicts. On the one hand, he was furious at what he saw as the fickle, traitorous American public, which had turned its back on soldiers who were trying, against a thousand obstacles, to do their job in Vietnam. As he would later say of his return, "Nobody was going to spit at me. *Nobody!*" On the other hand, he was profoundly disillusioned with the Army, disgusted by officers who put their own cares before those of their soldiers, by busy bureaucrats who thought the Army was all about office jobs, and by the lack of the quality that had most attracted him to the Armed Forces in the first place: valor. Alienated from both a society he could not understand and an Army that had disappointed him, Schwarzkopf wrestled to find his bearings in an America abruptly stripped of its reassuring certainties.

On August 22, 1970, Schwarzkopf went with Brenda, now nine months pregnant, to his sister Sally's cabin in Bethesda, Maryland, near Washington, D.C. The occasion was his thirty-sixth birthday. It was a small family celebration. They ate, and Norman talked about the war and his ambivalent feelings. Although it was late, he was hard to stop once he got going on these themes: they were an obsession. Finally, feeling exhausted, Brenda said, "Norm, I think we really have to go now." Three hours later she was in the delivery room.

That evening Norman had said jokingly, "If it's a girl, I want to call her Brunhilda, Brunhilda Schwarzkopf. What a great German name!" But he was hoping for a boy. Not because he wanted to pass on his name—he did not wish to punish another generation of Schwarzkopfs with the dreaded "Herbert" or the burden of explaining the "H." It was straightforward male pride.

Like his father before him, however, Schwarzkopf would have to wait for a son. On August 23, 1970, Cynthia was born, the first of the fifth generation of Schwarzkopfs since Christian's arrival in the United States 118 years earlier.

At the time, Schwarzkopf was back in a desk job, working at the Pentagon in the Officer Personnel Directorate of the Infantry Branch, which was responsible for the careers of about 40,000 army officers. He had always disliked this kind of work, which he tended to dismiss as paper shuffling. Certainly it was not challenging enough to take his mind off the war. At home, in the Schwarzkopfs' unpretentious two-bedroom apartment in Annandale, Virginia, Cindy did provide a great deal of happiness. But his wounds festered.

Even hunting, once a great pleasure, had palled. Norman's father-in-law, Jesse, repeatedly invited him to Virginia, but he was not interested. He had seen enough killing. The idea of hearing shots disturbed him. Because his feelings were hard to explain, he fobbed his father-in-law off with lame excuses rather than get involved in a difficult discussion about the war.

He was not sure that Jesse—or anybody—could understand. "The toughest thing for me to handle was the reaction of the American public to the U.S. military as a result of the Vietnam War," he said later. He saw people spitting at the uniforms; he heard people calling soldiers "baby burners"; he watched television shows depicting officers as "Neanderthal men who with blind, unquestioning obedience burned villages and killed babies." In Schwarzkopf's eyes, it was as if all of Vietnam had been transformed by the media into one extended My Lai massacre.

After work, or during lunch breaks, Schwarzkopf spoke at length with some of his friends and former classmates who had also been assigned to the Pentagon. "We talked about what our expectations were and what had really happened on the front line. We talked about going into combat and the fear that came with it—how much we had all been afraid," said Colonel James L. Anderson, who was at West Point with Schwarzkopf. "Norm told us about his experience in the minefield, not the heroic side of it, but the shaking-of-the-legs part."

They also talked about the country's reaction to the war. "We saw Vietnam veterans laying their medals down on the ground, throwing them away, and trying to blockade the Pentagon," recalled Charles Prather, another classmate. "We didn't like the war, but we felt sorry for those people. We didn't understand their reaction and we didn't agree with it."

Schwarzkopf and his colleagues also saw younger officers refusing to serve their country. This attitude, with its implicit contempt for the "Duty, Honor, Country" motto of West Point, infuriated them. "I resented them for having garnered all of the privileges of being an officer in the United States Army—but all of a sudden, when they were asked to do what they were really paid to do, they said, 'I am sorry, but morally I can't assume that,' " Schwarzkopf later explained.

His resentment toward peace demonstrators was even more virulent. In his eyes, these people were simplistic and callous, unable to understand the war and indifferent to the fate of the South Vietnamese. Indeed, he was so angry that he virtually severed all contact with his sister Ruth, who was still active in the anti-war movement. After seeing her between his two tours of duty, Schwarzkopf never went back to visit her. In a split country, the Schwarzkopfs thus remained a divided family.

Nobody angered Schwarzkopf more at this time than Jane Fonda, who had become a symbol of the anti-war movement. Later dubbed "Hanoi Jane," she had been expelled by the military police from Fort Hood, Texas; Fort Meade, Maryland; and Fort Bragg after distributing leaflets opposing U.S. military involvement in Indochina. She had even financed a trial of U.S. "war crimes" in Southeast Asia. Norman considered her a traitor. He would get upset just hearing her name and for years refused to go to her movies. "Our attitude was crystal clear: the bitch was a traitor," said another of Norman's former classmates, Ward Le Hardy.

The vehemence of Schwarzkopf's reaction no doubt stemmed from the fact that everything he had been raised to believe in was being questioned, abused, tossed in the gutter. Despite all he had seen, he still firmly believed that there were things for which it was worth putting up a fight. Democracy was one of them, wherever in the world it was under threat. To think otherwise, in his view, was simply to leave the road open to a Soviet machine that had already gobbled up half of Europe.

But was the Army, which was supposed to embody his view of the world and to stand up and fight in the name of both freedom and honor, really worthy of this lofty task? After Vietnam, Schwarzkopf had insistent doubts. So, at this midpoint in his life, as he became a father and weighed his future, it seemed at times that he had nowhere to turn.

"I came to understand that carelessness, negligence, lousy leadership, and self-serving officers and generals cost human lives," he said later of Vietnam. "And you just can't forgive that. You cannot forgive that sort of crassness. People who are more concerned with their ambitions than they are with their troops are unforgivable to me. There was a terrible erosion in integrity in the Armed Forces during Vietnam. I don't think that many of us came out of Vietnam and could hold our heads up and say, 'My sense of integrity is still lily-white and pure,' because we all know that we had to lie about body count. We all knew that there had been a lot of other lies, and it did bad things to the officer corps."

Body count—the daily reporting of the number of enemy dead—was particularly galling to Schwarzkopf. He considered it meaningless and dishonest. "I was forced to participate in that lie," he told *Life* magazine. "Many times people would call me up on the radio after a battle and say, 'What was your body count?' I'd say I didn't know what the body count was. They'd say, 'Well, make it up, we have to report a body count.' So eventually, just to get them off your back, you'd say, 'O.K. the body count was 250.' "

For Schwarzkopf, body count, more than anything else, undermined trust, compromised integrity, and contributed to the American public's loss of faith in the Army. "After all, we're only an arm of policy of the United States government. We're public servants. If the public no longer has confidence in us, then what good are we?" he asked.

His dismay was so great that Schwarzkopf often considered resigning from the Army. At times he almost believed he would make the break. But that, in some way, was to become part of the malaise. Would he not be shirking his duty, compromising his own honor, making himself useless to his country, if he chose that course? He remembered the advice he had received in the 1950s from an older officer at a time when he was appalled by the drunkenness and carelessness of his superiors: when everything is broken is not the time to quit. He stayed on, to fix things.

Before doing that, he decided to fix his back. Years of football and parachuting had taken a toll. In Vietnam it bothered him persistently and in Washington the pain kept coming back. But it was not until he was selected for the U.S. Army War College at Carlisle Barracks, Pennsylvania, that he decided he could take some time off to do something about it. His selection—an important step on the ladder to becoming a brigadier general—was communicated to him in November 1970, and he promptly asked for a one-year deferral. Then he checked into the Walter Reed Army Medical Center in Washington, D.C.

At Walter Reed, Schwarzkopf was told he had a hairline fracture which, if aggravated, could paralyze him. He opted for difficult surgery in which parts of both hipbones were cut and grafted to his spinal column. Fortunately, the operation was successful, because it, too, could have left him paralyzed. He remained in the hospital for months with a bulky full-body cast, unable to do much except reflect, read, and receive visits from his family and army friends. These friends would come to the hospital and talk about the same old subjects—war, America, and Vietnam.

These themes were particularly vivid at Walter Reed. He was in the orthopedic ward and so relived the painful experience of seeing soldiers with amputated arms and legs. "I often found him in his bed, teary-eyed," recalled Le Hardy. "He heard so many stories of soldiers stepping on mines or being hit by shrapnel and losing their limbs. It made him even more furious. He was astonished that the rest of the country was not acknowledging the fact that these soldiers were giving their limbs for America. 'Those bastards, not supporting us!' he would say when he saw protesters burning the American flag."

In the end, this fury probably made it easier for him to overcome his ambivalence and stay in the Army. Even beleaguered, it was the institution that stood closest to his own essentially conservative view of the world.

Trust is an intangible and elusive thing, but no army, and probably no organization of any kind, can function without it. In Vietnam, trust evaporated. With it went any possibility of effective leadership. To Schwarzkopf, this was a central dilemma of the Army which he grappled with in his hospital bed: Why did the leaders fall so far short of the great generals of World War II and so far short of their responsibilities?

He had seen for himself that officers in Vietnam were often so insecure they were unable to trust their subordinates. As a reaction to their fears, they threatened and mindlessly punished soldiers, thus passing their insecurity on down the ranks. Lieutenant Colonel Faris R. Kirkland, an expert in military psychiatry at the University City Science Center of Philadelphia, called this phenomenon the "culture of fear."

"In Vietnam," he said, "many battalion commanders were appointed without prior combat experience. I was there, and I saw that many of them were not interested in waging war well. They didn't worry about conducting the campaign with precision, knowledge, and violence, which is what you do when you want to wage war well. They were more interested in not getting in trouble. They had short command tours, and they knew that if there were no embarrassing incidents, they would get a good rating and move up and away from Vietnam. I personally met an artillery battalion commander from the 101st Airborne Division who did not mind spelling it out. 'I never fire more than one gun at a time,' he told me. 'If I fire the entire battery at once, I risk hitting a village or some other wrong target and then I would be relieved.' I had a fit. Instead of worrying about improving the precision of the firing procedures, he thought it was better not to fire at all. Because shooting a single god-damn gun at a time is basically like not firing at all."

By the time Schwarzkopf returned to the United States, an internal reaction to this sort of thing was beginning. In April 1970, Lieutenant General William R. Peers had sent a memorandum to the Army Chief of Staff, General William C. Westmoreland, in which he described cases of officers who were lying, commanding from safe distances, ignoring their men's needs, and failing to enforce safety measures. The report was so compelling that Westmoreland was forced to order an immediate investigation. The result was the War College *Study on Military Professionalism*, in which 415 officers were questioned on the existing climate in the Army. The conclusions were even more shocking than Lieutenant General Peers's assertions and amounted to a perfect reflection of Schwarzkopf's feelings:

Officers of all grades perceive a significant difference between the ideal values and the actual or operative values of the Officer Corps. Their perception is strong, clear, pervasive, and statistically and qualitatively independent of grade, branch, educational level, or source of commission. There is also concern among officers that the Army is not taking action to ensure that high ideals are practiced as well as preached. In fact, there is extensive preoccupation among the younger officers with this condition. There is a widespread feeling that the Army has generated an environment that rewards relatively insignificant, short-term indicators of success, and disregards or discourages the growth of the long-term qualities of moral and ethical strength on which the future of the Army depends. They are frustrated by the pressures of the system, disheartened by those seniors who sacrificed integrity on the altar of personal success. There is a general feeling among junior officers that seniors are untouchable, unapproachable, unreasonable, and constantly looking for mistakes.

The study found evidence of distorted or dishonest reporting of statistics and officer efficiency; technical or managerial incompetence; and disregard for principles. Side by side with this, there was a mindless respect for accomplishing even the most trivial mission with "zero defects."

Schwarzkopf could have written the report. He hated the presence of hordes of senior officers from the Army, Navy, Air Force, and Marine Corps, all trying to protect their parochial interests during the war. He was appalled by the bureaucratic labyrinth in the various headquarters at divisional, brigade, and battalion level. He was disturbed by the fact that after days in the field, troops returned to bases where they found well-fed, well-rested, and well-dressed officers. He knew how all this bred resentment. Indeed, between 1969 and 1972, the Army counted 788 cases of "friendly assaults with explosive devices," a practice mostly directed at officers. Otherwise known as "fragging," this involved tossing a hand grenade from a short distance at another soldier.

There were other conspicuous problems. Schwarzkopf knew that the shortness of commanding tours in Vietnam meant officers were relieved just as they were beginning to know what they were about. He did not agree with the generosity with which medals were handed out: 522,905, a record, in 1970 alone. He despised the self-indulgent attitude of top officers who encouraged the production of weapons "for generals only," such as a 9 mm pistol—known as the "general officers pistol"—which required different ammunition from the regular .45 caliber issue.

The problems were so rampant it was hard to know where to begin. But a first significant step toward change came with the decision made by President Nixon on April 23, 1970, to move to an all-volunteer force and complete this transformation by June 1973. In theory, this switch could address many of the problems haunting Schwarzkopf by bringing professional motivation—and with that, discipline—back to the Army.

The trouble was that to attract and retain educated volunteers, army life had to be rewarding. The reality was different, and the funds to encourage high-class recruitment were lacking. Under pressure from a public more and more exasperated by the war, the Nixon Administration in 1972 presented the first budget since World War II that allocated less money for military than for social spending.

"We found that a wide gap had developed between life in the service and in the civilian community," General Westmoreland concluded in a 1972 report. "In general, life in America had become more affluent and a great deal more liberal. The Army had not kept pace. Some time-honored practices and customs had outlived their usefulness and were irritating to the young. Living conditions were often poor. The Army would have to compete in the open job market for its manpower, and success would depend on substantial improvements in service life, facilities, services and remuneration."

In the early seventies, Schwarzkopf himself felt the Army was offering him little motivation—that is, except for the U.S. Army War College, which he attended from August '72 to June '73. The War College was an opportunity to shift gears and develop a strategic vision, projected toward the international arena. It was also an important step in his career as an officer. Eisenhower, Patton, Bradley, and Haig had gone there, and only the top 6 percent of lieutenant colonels and colonels in any given year were selected. Schwarzkopf studied international defense and strategies and national security issues, with a particular focus on the implications for U.S. foreign policy of Soviet and Chinese power in the international arena. His major writing while he was there was a Special Project Report entitled *Military Merit: How to Measure Who Measures Up*. In June '73, he graduated with the other 233 officers of his class, among them General Carl E. Vuono, the Army Chief of Staff during the Gulf War, and General John R. Galvin, who later became Supreme Allied Commander in Europe.

But apart from the War College, this was the least professionally stimulating period of his life. As a result, Norman became more domestic, especially after his second child, Jessica, was born on March 12, 1972.

Following her birth, the Schwarzkopfs bought a house near Annandale where Norman spent many hours with his two girls and planted his own vineyard. He had a wine-making laboratory, which consisted of mail-order equipment and a bathtub. "We used to call it bathtub wine!" said Le Hardy. "But he was really proud of it and he gave it away as presents. He gave me a jar once and it tasted awful. I gracefully told him that, and he suggested that I let it sit for a while. I let it sit and then tried it again. It tasted worse!"

Schwarzkopf also developed a passion for magic during this period. Back in a job at the Pentagon as military assistant to the assistant secretary of the Army for Financial Management, he found distraction at Al's Magic Shop in Washington. There he bought all sorts of tricks, from fake ropes to special cards. He quickly learned the tricks and started performing at parties at his children's school and at Pentagon social events. Le Hardy remembers that his specialty was pulling flags or long multicolored napkins out of his mouth.

It was also at this time that he took up the game of bocce—a form of lawn bowling—and played with Le Hardy most weekends. But none of these hobbies eased the rancor that Vietnam had left festering inside the fun-loving cadet Le Hardy had known at West Point.

In the spring of 1972 the presidential campaign exacerbated things. George S. McGovern, the Democratic candidate, was an outspoken opponent of the war in Vietnam. His speeches irritated Schwarzkopf, who had never forgotten McGovern's address to the Senate in 1963 calling for an end to the Cold War and denouncing the Armed Forces for fostering the myth of Soviet military superiority. And now he was denouncing the military again on a passionate platform of "End the war now"!

One evening the Schwarzkopfs invited Sally for dinner, and the conversation turned to the forthcoming elections. Sally had voted Democrat since the days of Kennedy and had supported Lyndon B. Johnson's civil rights efforts so strongly that she wrote him a personal letter expressing her support. In the 1972 election she was strongly opposed to Nixon because of his role during the McCarthy era and his conservative domestic policy. She was therefore ready to vote for McGovern. She asked her brother to try to be objective in his feelings about the peace marchers and consider the war from their perspective. "They have their good reasons, too, and they might be right," she said.

Sally was working at the Defense Department at the time. She had entered after college in 1953 and had risen to the senior executive level. She was not in favor of the U.S. presence in Vietnam, but was not opposed to it in the way her sister Ruth was. She could see both sides, and on this particular evening was simply trying to suggest that her brother consider the other side's point of view.

But the wounds were too raw. Sally vividly remembers her brother abruptly bursting into tears and accusing her of betraying her own flesh and blood.

"How can you take the other side?" he asked her. "Goddamn it!" he yelled, not waiting for an answer. He wanted her to leave the house immediately. Sally, who was also crying by then, could not understand his reaction and kept asking what she had done to make him want to throw her out.

Why couldn't people understand? Why couldn't they get it? H. Norman Schwarzkopf was angry. He did not want to spell out why and perhaps he could not, because the hurt was so deeply embedded in his gut. For the same reason that he could not tell his father-in-law why he did not want to go hunting, he could not tell Sally why he was so angry. There were things that were beyond words and beyond analysis. Why couldn't Sally, of all people, the sister he held so dear, just understand?

Brenda was speechless. She had never seen Norm and Sally cry and scream in that way. They had always been very close. Vietnam, which had already been so destructive to the relationship between Norm and his older sister, was now coming between him and Sally. Brenda, raised in a close family, was appalled. Sally left in tears and Norm went to bed without saying a word.

The next morning, he called his sister and apologized. She did, too; and then they both started to cry again, but this time in a cathartic way. Still, they were both traumatized by what had happened, and Sally never again brought up the subject of Vietnam or any politically sensitive issue. She kept politics out of their relationship in order to hold the family together.

As this incident suggests, frustration was building inside Lieutenant Colonel Schwarzkopf. He was very angry and was having great difficulty in coming to terms with his feelings. Having decided to stick with the Army, he needed to get out and rebuild his faith in it. His desk job just accentuated his other preoccupations. Desperate for something new, he decided to volunteer for an assignment—in Alaska—that no one else wanted. And in the fall of

1974, four years after his return from Vietnam, he became deputy commander of the 172nd Infantry Brigade at Fort Richardson in Alaska.

Here, on an assignment where he was sufficiently isolated to apply his own ideas, Schwarzkopf tried to reinvent the army leadership that he felt to be so eroded. Although very few people have a genius for it, effective military leadership is no mystery. Over two thousand years ago, the Chinese warrior-philosopher Sun Tzu laid out the attributes of a great military leader. His ideas have stood the test of time. Since then countless military theorists have modulated and expanded upon the notions he expounded, but nothing has undermined the core of truth they hold.

"Leadership," the Chinese philosopher wrote, "is a matter of intelligence, trustworthiness, humaneness, courage, and sternness. Trustworthiness means to make people sure of punishment or reward. Humaneness means love and compassion for people, being aware of their toils. Courage means to seize opportunities and make certain of victory without vacillation. Sternness means to establish discipline in the ranks by strict punishment."

In Alaska, Schwarzkopf applied a severe discipline that surprised his troops, but at the same time showed great trust in the amount of responsibility he delegated. He became known, for the first time, as "the Bear"—part teddy, part grizzly, as he later described it. The grizzly roared at subordinates who did not listen or care, particularly junior officers who were not looking after their soldiers. But his attacks were not personal or vindictive. The teddy was the humane leader, supportive of his men and demanding nothing he would not also expect of himself.

In the harsh climate of Alaska, he marched his soldiers to the point of exhaustion, instilling a sense of purpose. It was painful, but with the pain came pride. Every mock battle was taken as seriously as if it were a real one. He told them that training made them good soldiers, which in turn made them winners in life as well as war.

Schwarzkopf loved the wilderness. It purged. From his very first days in Alaska, he never missed an opportunity to sleep outdoors with his troops. Normally brigade commanders went back to the base to spend the night, but he never did. Moreover, when the troops were not on bivouac, he spent time outdoors on his own. Brenda would drop him off at the edge of a mountain trail and come back for him three days later. He would thus spend long periods by himself—away from people and problems—alone except for the salmon, the trout, and a few real bears. It was a spiritual and physical exercise, one that even managed to rekindle his love for hunting. Up there, alone in the wilderness of Alaska, he was finally at peace.

The towering landscape, it seems, brought out something that had always been in him. Alone in the mountains, Schwarzkopf may have come to terms with the romantic side of his nature. Although war is about precision, it can also be a heroic thing; and a passionate striving, rather than a cool detachment, always lay at the heart of Schwarzkopf's involvement in the military. It would have been in character for him to find in the stark grandeur of the Alaskan landscape an encouragement to persevere in his longing for fulfillment.

Certainly this natural beauty helped to heal the wounds of Vietnam. He felt a sense of joy and relief and wanted to share this with Sally. In the spring of 1975 he invited her to come fishing with him. Sally wanted very much to spend time with her brother, but did not feel she could leave her mother.

Ruth Schwarzkopf's health had deteriorated sharply. She had been operated on for breast cancer and had moved to Washington, D.C., to be close to Walter Reed Hospital, where she could have weekly chemotherapy. Being a military wife, she was entitled to free treatment there. She did not want to interfere in her daughter's life, so, with great resolve, she found an apartment near Sally's cabin in Bethesda and continued to live independently. But by

1975 she had developed bone cancer and was confined to a wheelchair. Sally had to take her for chemotherapy every two weeks: Alaska would have to wait.

In the summer of 1975 Norm tried again. He invited Sally to come on a camping trip with the family. Ruth wanted her daughter to go. She said that Sally was "turning into a turtle" and needed to get out; and she assured her daughter that she would be fine. With some misgivings, Sally traveled to Fort Richardson, where Norm, Brenda, and the kids were waiting for her with a rented camper. They drove to Mount McKinley National Park. It was a wonderful vacation.

But when Sally returned home, she found her mother in low spirits. The visits to the hospital without help had been difficult and depressing.

From then on, Ruth's health steadily worsened. She died at Walter Reed Hospital at the beginning of October 1976, after undergoing gallbladder surgery. As with his father, Norman was unable to be with his mother before her death. He arrived, with his sister Ruth, the day after their mother died. The children arranged for the funeral, and Ruth was buried the next day beside her husband in West Point Cemetery.

It had been a very long time since the three Schwarzkopf children were together. It was an emotional time—sad, nostalgic, and yet also happy in some way. Norman took the opportunity to scold Sally for smoking so much. In his usual humorous way, he said, "It's easy to quit. I did it three times!" He had stopped smoking once before his first Vietnam tour, but started again while he was there. He stopped the second time while he was teaching at West Point, but began again during his second tour. He finally quit after his return to the States from Vietnam. Sally, on the other hand, had never stopped smoking since she was thirteen.

One evening, reminiscing about the past on Sally's porch, Norman for the first time acknowledged the positive side of their being so different. More at peace with himself after Alaska, he was also more tolerant. The taut strings inside him loosened. "We are such an interesting and diverse family," he said. "We all had the same education and the same upbringing, and yet we're so different." It was true: Ruth, the idealist about peace; Norman, the idealist about war; and Sally, the more pragmatic mediator. Yet they also shared a spiritual sense of some higher value in life worth striving toward. Purged by Alaska, Norman could see such nuances again and was more accepting of diversity.

But if Schwarzkopf healed relatively quickly, his Army did not. The switch to an all-volunteer force had been pursued with slogans like "Today's Army Wants to Join You," and hundreds of recruiting stations were opened around the country. A lot of people signed up. But the recruits were mostly undistinguished, and confusion reigned.

Attempts to liberalize the Army, making it more democratic and less authoritarian, only increased the level of chaos. An army, by definition, cannot be a democratic institution. To be effective, it depends on the exercise of command. But, urged to be more understanding, some officers merely became lax. The result was a softer Army which lacked, and craved, both discipline and leadership. The same Army that had produced leaders such as Robert E. Lee, Ulysses S. Grant, George S. Patton, Douglas MacArthur, and Dwight D. Eisenhower now worried about being nice. It did not work.

Soldiers, naturally, ended up disliking the softness that was supposed to attract them, because it took away any sense of leadership and purpose. "Soldiers felt nobody cared about what they were doing, no one was holding them to any standards, and no one worried whether they were successful as soldiers," said Lieutenant Colonel Kirkland. "For many of them the answer was drugs. So the drug epidemic got even worse. The Army was so worried that it decided to allocate considerable amounts of money to research and detoxification centers. It was later discovered that the problem was made more acute by the higher proportion of 'cat-4s' (those belonging to the fourth category—below-average intelligence) whose number had dramatically increased due to the fact that, being socially out of favor, the Army had attracted the most desperate, those who couldn't get other jobs. Up to 50 percent of the new recruits were cat-4s. Naturally, this was hard to take for many of the good officers. And I remember in the first half of the seventies being personally told by many officers how much they hated it, how difficult it was for them to go to work every day. They felt angry."

Lieutenant Colonel Ned V. J. Longsworth of the XVIII Airborne Corps recalled feeling certain in the mid-seventies that the Army would have to abandon its attempt at an all-volunteer force. The quality of the soldiers was abject, and none of the problems that led to the switch to a professional Army had been solved. In Korea with the 2nd Infantry Division in 1975, he recalls being stationed near the town of Dong Du Cheo. A river ran through the town. On one bank there were clubs for white soldiers; on the other, clubs for blacks. Racial tension led to regular fights.

In Germany, the situation was no better. Major General Barry McCaffrey, now the commander of the 24th Infantry Division (Mechanized), went there in 1976 after a spell teaching at West Point and was appalled. "One-third of our soldiers were the dregs of U.S. society," he said. "Drugs and indiscipline were rampant. There was no joy in the Army, none. We had to throw people out, literally toss them out on the street, because we were that close to being unable to defend the United States."

Changes in tactical doctrine also reflected the disorientation of the Army. For the first time since World War II, the United States began stressing the limits of its power. The neo-isolationist sentiment brought about by the failure in

Vietnam pushed the Pentagon to retrench to the European theater, a smaller and more vital area of influence whose defense was not contested. The Soviet buildup, which had begun in the late sixties and continued through the seventies, and its increasingly aggressive European posture made it even more important for the United States to focus on Europe. Experts at TRADOC, the Training and Doctrine Command, conveniently rediscovered the classic maxim of the Prussian military theorist Karl von Clausewitz that defense is the strongest form of combat. The 1970s—a time of constraints—produced tactics of constraints.

A study of the 1973 Yom Kippur War emphasized the vulnerability of the attacker. The war provided an opportunity to see the results of a modern armored confrontation of proportions not seen since World War II. It showed a new level of destructive capability and confirmed the merits of a strong defense. What happened to the Israelis was particularly significant to TRADOC experts. After absorbing the initial Arab attack, the Israelis counterattacked with little attention to their own safety, thereby exposing themselves to the enemy. The Egyptians, in particular, had carefully planned defenses and managed to inflict high casualties on the Israelis. Depending on the battle, as many as half of the Israeli tanks and armored vehicles were destroyed.

In July 1976 a new Army Field Manual formally introduced the new doctrine of "active defense." It argued that if war was now as lethal as the Mideast conflict suggested, defense should become the Army's major concern. The new manual instructed that "the commander should attack only if he expects the outcome to result in decisively greater enemy losses than his own, or result in the capture of objectives crucial to the outcome of the larger battle." It was a doctrine of retrenchment and of defensive orientation reflecting the overall mood of the Armed Forces. In an Army historically projected toward an offensive war of movement, such a change at the expense of mobility was bound to raise objections and frustrations.

• • •

Against this negative backdrop, at the end of October 1976, shortly after the death of his mother, Norman became commander of the 1st Brigade of the 9th Infantry Division at Fort Lewis in Washington State. It was there that he found out, to his great joy, that Brenda was pregnant again. He was just like his father. He had two girls and loved them, indulging their every whim. But as his father had, he desperately wanted a boy.

Brenda, on the other hand, was quite happy with one child. Then, after their second, she really planned to stop. But Norman kept up the pressure, both at home and in public with close friends. "Brenda, since you don't want to give me another chance of having a boy, I will get a German shepherd," he would say.

By 1977 he had both. He got the dog first, and then on June 20, 1977, Brenda gave birth to a boy. They named him Christian, after Norman's pioneering great-grandfather.

Having a son made Norm think about his own father and how alike they were. His fondness for music, whether opera, folk music, or Handel's "Hallelujah Chorus" (which he would sing at the drop of a hat), came from his father, as did his love for books and the ability to quote from them extensively. Even his competitive nature went back to H. Norman Sr. "Whenever Norm plays games with adults—whether board games or sports—he always plays to win. He is *extremely* competitive, but not a sore loser," said Sally. This assessment is confirmed by Brenda, who has publicly acknowledged the family's refusal to play Trivial Pursuit with him because of his aggressiveness.

At Fort Lewis, Schwarzkopf worked under Major General Richard E. Cavazos, a rugged Texan with a love for hunting and a strong sense of leadership. Cavazos took to his brigade commander immediately.

"Schwarzkopf stood out among my brigade commanders as an outstanding leader," said the now-retired General Cavazos. "He was able to identify weaknesses in his units and correct them without running over his subordinates. He never overreacted, never pounced on them. That, to me, was a clear sign of his leadership skills: he was able to transmit confidence, trust, competence, and at the same time act on the various problems he was encountering. Only a good commander can do that." Cavazos also noticed what he described as "Schwarzkopf's verve for soldiering," which he passed along to his junior officers and troops.

"He was the type of leader that would make men laugh at a bayonet charge," said General Cavazos.

One of his first encounters with Schwarzkopf made a particular impact on Cavazos. In an exercise, one of Schwarzkopf's battalions was taken by helicopter to a predetermined landing spot, and Cavazos told them to set up defensive positions quickly because the enemy would arrive in seventy-two hours. "I wanted them to dig in and show the best defensive posture they could in three days," recalled Cavazos. "The battalion dug a million holes, positioning all its artillery in the wrong direction. Not a single weapon was set up in the right position."

That was the general's first impression of Schwarzkopf's men: disastrous. At "critique time," when the exercise was reviewed, Schwarzkopf was the first to talk. Addressing the general, he said, "Sir, we've just been taught a lesson. We've got to go back to the fundamentals. The battalion commander knows that and I know that. And I recommend that this be the end of the critique. But before you go, sir, one more thing. We screwed up and we'll fix it. Come back and see us in six weeks."

Cavazos was impressed. Schwarzkopf had said "we." Here was a brigade commander whose troops had completely failed an important test, and he was not blaming them or accusing the battalion commander.

"I was used to getting all kinds of excuses from commanders. And there were many other approaches he could have chosen," said Cavazos. "He could have tried to justify the mistakes, or he could have said that the troops didn't do what he had told them to do. But he was not afraid of assuming responsibility or standing up and being counted. He also committed himself to changing things, which he eventually did. That to me was and still is what leadership is all about."

To Cavazos, even the "Stormin' Norman" act was indicative of a style of leadership that worked.

Cavazos saw it as something very calculated and controlled. The anger was precisely modulated. "When Schwarzkopf heard or witnessed something he didn't like, he would have this intense look and make clear how strongly he felt about it. He didn't necessarily raise his voice. I saw him whispering, and I'll tell you, it wasn't any less effective than screaming. But I don't think it's so unique. I saw something similar in a lot of other good army officers. What counts is that he could get mad, but never be disrespectful. People have to know, when they screw up, you cannot let a mistake pass because sooner or later you'll pay for it. You just have to know how to do it. Norman would tell a subordinate that he had done something dumb, but never that *he* was dumb."

While Schwarzkopf was stationed at Fort Lewis, he and Major General Cavazos hunted pheasant near the base. The general admired Norman's hunting skills but not his dogs:

"Norman is a superb wing shot. He is great at bird hunting with a shotgun. Unfortunately, his dogs have always been terrible. He has a soft spot for dogs, and the Labrador he has now, Bear, is no better than the one he had then. Labradors are kind of hardheaded, and you have to be very strict to train them. Unfortunately, Norm loves his dog too much. It's one of his weaknesses. I remember receiving negative reports about Bear and calling Norman up to find out if they were true. He denied the reports. Only after the Gulf War did he finally admit the truth. On March 3, 1991, he wrote me a letter saying (and I quote): 'Be advised, next fall I may show up with a good hunting dog. If I show up with poor old Bear, who definitely needs a lot of work, he'll never live down his mediocre reputation!' "

After two years in Washington State, Norman Schwarzkopf went back to a desk job. In July 1978 he became Deputy Director for Plans at the United States Pacific Command in Hawaii. It was a joint command, meaning that all services were represented there: the kind of post that any senior officer needs to advance. It was not a position that required any soldiering, but it did call for sophisticated political and diplomatic skills. He not only had to learn how to deal with the Navy, the Air Force, and the Marines, but also to serve as liaison between the Pentagon and various countries in the Pacific.

Schwarzkopf traveled often to Asian countries, mainly Korea. Since he had acquired a deftness in adapting to other cultures from his father, diplomacy came naturally to him. "My brother knows how to adapt to the background and interests of his hosts," said Sally. "He can be a willing listener, even though he is usually certain of his views and sometimes can be stubborn."

Eight years after his return from Vietnam, Norman Schwarzkopf could listen again. His angst had abated. Less than a month after his transfer to Hawaii, on August 1, 1978, he received his first star. It was just before his forty-fourth birthday that Schwarzkopf became a brigadier general. After a time of trial, he had come through, while the Army he served continued to search for a new and convincing identity. It was still, in the telling words of General Edward C. Meyer, Chief of Staff in 1979–83, "a hollow army," rich in equipment but poor in spirit.

5

Urgent Fury

War is as much a conflict of passion as it
is of force.
    —General of the Army Omar N. Bradley

"In six months," the new assistant division commander proclaimed in his clipped tone, "I am going to bring down your world and rebuild it."

It was the early morning of August 19, 1980, in Mainz, West Germany. The entire community affairs staff for the 8th Infantry Division (Mechanized) of the U.S. Army, Europe, had gathered in a conference room to meet Brigadier General H. Norman Schwarzkopf, the man just named to take charge of all facilities in the fourteen housing areas used by the 11,000-member military community. They had received advance warning that Schwarzkopf was a formidable character. But his speech still came as something of a shock.

"No stone will be left unturned," Schwarzkopf continued. "And it will be good. You're all going to like it. But to do this in six months, I'm going to be a bear—sometimes even a grizzly bear. At the end of the six months you, too, will be bears and, when necessary, able to turn into grizzlies as easily as I do. At that point I am going to change into a teddy and remain that way for the rest of my tour here—just a nice, cuddly teddy bear."

Lieutenant Colonel David Crotty, who was to become Schwarzkopf's executive officer and right-hand man, was so struck by the speech that he wrote "YOU WILL BE THE BEARS" in capital letters in his notebook. In twenty-four years in the Army, he had never heard a commander say anything remotely like it.

Schwarzkopf immediately told his staff that he was going to do nothing less than mold them in his own image. He added that they should remember they were *serving* the community and should never deny a request without consulting him. "If there is something you think you cannot provide, don't say no—bring it to my attention," he ordered. He told them that he wanted to be kept informed of everything and that they would always have access to him.

A move from Hawaii to Germany such as the general had just made amounts to a considerable culture shock. But Schwarzkopf was used to moving, and wasted no time in listing his priorities in order of importance: serve the soldiers better, serve their families better, and improve relations with the German community.

This initial meeting left its mark on everyone. Most of the staff members had settled into a comfortable routine with the previous commander. But like soldiers from Vietnam to Alaska who had worked under Schwarzkopf before, they would have to get used to a new and extremely vigorous way of doing things.

Schwarzkopf spent the next several weeks on a nonstop tour of the various communities where the soldiers and their families lived. He visited housing complexes and barracks and learned about the buses and schools. He met all the "mayors"; that is, the spouses of soldiers who were elected to be in charge of each of the military villages where the 8th Infantry Division was housed. He encouraged them to voice their problems.

"He had an insatiable appetite for information and a fantastic memory," recalled Lieutenant Colonel Crotty.

"He was determined to hear it all, the good and the bad." Indeed, one of Schwarzkopf's favorite phrases to his staff was "Don't be afraid to give me the bad news."

The problems in Mainz were different from the ones Schwarzkopf was used to. There were close to 200,000 U.S. troops in Germany, forming the core of NATO's European defenses. Inevitably, strains developed at times between this large force and its German hosts. Schwarzkopf proved skilled in dealing with local German authorities. His excellent German came in useful and earned him favor with the community. In general, he tackled his job with the same energy and candor he brought to military issues. He wanted a well-run community for his troops because he believed, as he would often point out to his staff, that a happy soldier is a better soldier.

"On the issue of army-family support, General Schwarzkopf was a true pioneer," said Lieutenant Colonel Kirkland. "At that time, the tradition in the Army could be summed up by the old saying: If the Army wanted you to have a wife, it would have issued one!"

It was in fact only in 1984, four years after Schwarzkopf took the Mainz army community by storm, that *The Army Family Action Plan* was published. This was the first policy statement ever on how the Army should go about bringing fulfillment for soldiers' families as well as the soldiers it constantly shifts around the globe.

In those first few months in Mainz, the grizzly rarely rested. Lieutenant Colonel Crotty was present at one of the fearsome bear's first appearances. Schwarzkopf and his staff were sitting around a table at a meeting. Crotty was on the commander's right and was the first to speak. He brought up a seemingly insoluble problem with services. But the fact that this aggravation had not been eliminated made the commander livid.

Crotty held his breath and warily looked at the general. He remembers Schwarzkopf's reaction to this day. Almost as if it were in slow motion, he can picture the general's left hand slowly closing into a fist as his arm gradually moved higher and higher. Its downward trajectory was much faster. The fist landed on the table with a crash as the general yelled, "Damn it!" The impact of fist on table sent a cup of hot coffee flying into the lap of a sergeant, who jumped up screaming, gazing at his wet, stained pants in amazement. A sheepish-looking Schwarzkopf accompanied the sergeant out of the room and expressed his regrets. His composure regained, Schwarzkopf continued with the meeting and even managed to make fun of his own temper.

It was clear to the staff that their boss had a red-hot temperament. But they realized, as had his subordinates on other bases, that Schwarzkopf did not bear grudges. Moreover, even when he became a grizzly, he was never vulgar. The worst his staff ever heard was "Goddamn!"

"Those explosions were not too frequent and had different degrees of intensity—usually not as hot as the coffee that was spilled that day," said Crotty.

In November 1980, three months after his arrival, Schwarzkopf faced the entrepreneurial challenge of his life. A visit to Mainz by Pope John Paul II was planned. Because no church in the city was big enough to accommodate the anticipated hordes of pilgrims, the mayor asked the U.S. military if it would host an open Mass at Finthen army airfield on the base.

Schwarzkopf saw the request as a way to raise money for his soldiers' recreational activities. The so-called morale support fund—used to pay for everything from Ping-Pong tables to outings to local castles and wine-tasting tours—might get an exceptional boost from the sale of sandwiches to hungry pilgrims. Accordingly, he had his staff purchase hundreds of pounds of ham and cheese. The operation was set up with military precision. Schwarzkopf and his staff, after a detailed reconnaissance of the airfield, carefully chose sites for the stands that would sell the 480 cases of sandwiches.

But the elements sabotaged this shrewd attempt to mix commerce and religion. The day of the papal visit, November 16, 1980, dawned miserably, and the weather remained awful throughout the day. Mainz, which is on the Rhine, near Frankfurt, does not have a particularly clement climate. But even by the town's poor standards the day was exceptionally nasty. It was cold; it was rainy; it was windy; and only a few hundred of the predicted thousands showed up. The Pope, protected by a specially built canopy, said Mass beneath torrential rain. Afterward, those who had turned up were in too much of a hurry to get home to consider their stomachs.

Schwarzkopf was left with more than two thousand ham-and-cheese sandwiches. Hoping at least to recover the money spent to buy all the food, Schwarzkopf decided to store the leftovers in the freezer of a German food company and peddle them as grilled ham-and-cheese sandwiches at every single American club in Germany. "We had a veterinarian periodically checking the sandwiches' shelf life," recalled Lieutenant Colonel Crotty, noting that vets routinely did this sort of thing in Germany. "And after three or four months of hard marketing and sales at any and every imaginable function—from rodeos to field days—we managed to break even."

General Schwarzkopf's sandwich gained such notoriety it even acquired a name: "the Mainz Sandwich." It was dreaded throughout the U.S. Army in Europe. When the supply was finally depleted—either sold or finally beset by putrefaction—Schwarzkopf's staff presented him with a large ceramic replica at their New Year's Eve celebration.

Many of Schwarzkopf's projects were more of a success. By the beginning of 1981, community life for the 8th Infantry Division had improved. He extended hours for important services. For example, the post exchange, or department store, the commissary, and the post office were all kept open until after soldiers came off duty. An automatic teller was added at the bank. He set up a skeet range where soldiers could fire at clay disks thrown from traps to simulate birds in flight. Soldiers got the impression that their commander really cared—not only about them, but also about their families. He wanted to try to make their lives pleasurable enough to ensure that drug use and alcoholism declined.

Schwarzkopf was true to his word where his temperament was concerned. As the six-month anniversary of his arrival approached, the staff noticed the grizzly going into hibernation. The commander was quieter. On February 19, 1981, the day of the anniversary, Schwarzkopf entered the briefing room to find everybody standing at attention and a large teddy bear dressed in army fatigues sitting in his chair. He burst out laughing, as he would when he received another, smaller bear from his sister in the midst of the Gulf campaign a decade later.

In six months, Schwarzkopf had managed to establish his leadership and gain the respect of his staff. He had shown his temper, but also his compassion. He had given people more responsibility than they were accustomed to having. When people did well, he was lavish in his praise; and when they did badly, he was not vindictive. By now these were methods that he had seen work elsewhere. Germany proved no exception.

In July 1981, Major Paul Cullinane joined the staff in Mainz. Eleven years earlier, he had been a lieutenant under Schwarzkopf in the 1st Battalion of the 198th Infantry Brigade in Vietnam. The major's first encounter with the general in Germany was at a staff meeting. Schwarzkopf seemed to ignore him and then, abruptly, gave him a wink. Later, Cullinane told the general what he had been doing for the last ten years. When he mentioned his marriage, Schwarzkopf immediately suggested that Cullinane's wife, Priscilla, meet Brenda.

"With the Schwarzkopfs, the Army got two for the price of one," said Cullinane, now a colonel. "Brenda took my

Herbert Norman Schwarzkopf

NEWARK, NEW JERSEY

Appointed from Ninth District

NEW JERSEY

"SCHWARZIE"

Sharpshooter, Football (4,3,2,1), Basketball (4,2), Indoor Meet (4,3,2,1), Outdoor Meet (3), Polo, Boxing (4,3,2,1), Swimming (2,1), Handball Championship (1), Y.M.C.A. Committees (2,1), Choir (4,3,2), Manager of Handball Squad (1).

H. Norman Schwarzkopf, Sr.'s 1917 yearbook photograph and list of achievements during his four years at West Point.

H. Norman Schwarzkopf, Sr., in his military school uniform at the age of nine.

Ruth Bowman, General Schwarzkopf's mother, who was Assistant Superintendent of Nurses at Columbia-Presbyterian Hospital in New York when she met H. Norman Schwarzkopf, Sr.

Superintendent Schwarzkopf of the New Jersey State Police personally supervised the design and production of a special "Wanted" poster for the Lindbergh kidnapping case. The poster was based on "Wanted" signs of the Old West. It was printed on March 11, 1932, and distributed to fourteen hundred different law enforcement agencies throughout the United States.

Superintendent of the New Jersey State Police, Colonel H. Norman Schwarzkopf, talking to reporters in the New Jersey State House on March 9, 1932. He appealed to the nation for help in the Lindbergh case.

Mrs. Charles Lindbergh (*right*) with Mrs. H. Norman Schwarz-kopf as they leave the Hunterdon County Courthouse in Flemington, N.J., on January 3, 1935. Mrs. Lindbergh had tes-tified at the trial of Bruno Richard Hauptmann, who was accused of kidnapping and murdering the Lindberghs' twenty-month-old son. In court Mrs. Lindbergh identified the night suit her son was wearing when he was taken from his crib in the Lindbergh residence in Hopewell, N.J.

Colonel Charles A. Lindbergh (*left*) with Colonel H. Norman Schwarzkopf, head of the New Jersey State Police, as they enter the courthouse in Flemington, N.J., on June 28, 1932, to testify in a proceeding related to the kidnapping.

Norman with three-year-old sister Sally in 1935 on the lawn of their house in Lawrenceville, N.J.

COURTESY OF SCHWARZKOPF FAMILY

COURTESY OF SCHWARZKOPF FAMILY

H. Norman Schwarzkopf, Sr., with his three children (*left to right*), Ruth, Norman, and Sally, in front of the Bordentown Military Institute.

COURTESY OF SCHWARZKOPF FAMILY

The Schwarzkopf family in the Bavarian resort town of Garmisch, where they spent Christmas in 1948. H. Norman Schwarzkopf, Sr., was serving as deputy provost marshal of the United States Army in Frankfurt, Germany. *Standing, left to right:* Ruth Ann, Ruth, and Sally. H. Norman Schwarzkopf, Sr., is next to his son.

In his Bordentown Military Institute uniform, cadet Schwarzkopf poses for a photograph to send to his father, who was then stationed in Iran.

Brigadier General Schwarzkopf (*right*) salutes cadets at the graduation of the Imperial Iranian Gendarmerie on January 17, 1947. He trained the gendarmerie from 1942 to 1948, thus contributing to the stability of the Shah's regime.

General Schwarzkopf in 1956 with two ancient Persian weapons presented to him when he was in Iran. The front of the horned weapon was filled with sand and used by a warrior on horseback; the other weapon was used only by the royal family.

H. Norman Schwarzkopf receiving his diploma at his graduation from West Point in 1956.

After an eight-month courtship, H. Norman Schwarzkopf and Brenda Holsinger were married at West Point.

Second Lieutenant H. Norman Schwarzkopf in 1957 at the Airborne School at Fort Benning, Georgia, which he attended to learn parachuting.

In August 1965 Schwarzkopf was immortalized in this photograph taken by young AP reporter Peter Arnett as Schwarzkopf helped a South Vietnamese paratrooper wounded in battle. As an adviser to the South Vietnamese Airborne Division, Schwarzkopf won a Silver Star for his courage in this battle.

Captain Schwarzkopf looks fit in a photo sent home to his mother from his first tour of Vietnam, June 1965 to June 1966.

A soldier on guard in Grenada two weeks after the October 1983 U.S. invasion of the Caribbean island. Schwarzkopf, then a major general, was second-in-command of the operation. Schwarzkopf later said that he had been moved by a sign like the one scrawled on the wall in this photograph.

Schwarzkopf (*right*) greeted by Superintendent David B. Kelly of the N.J. State Police on July 12, 1971, on the inauguration of the N.J. State Police Academy's new dormitory in Sea Girt, N.J. The ceremony was held on the fiftieth anniversary of H. Norman Schwarzkopf, Sr.'s appointment as the first Superintendent of the N.J. State Police; the building was dedicated in his honor. Schwarzkopf was accompanied by his sister Sally (*right*) and his wife, Brenda (*left*).

Schwarzkopf with his daughters Cindy (*right*) and Jessie (*left*) celebrates his promotion to colonel on November 1, 1975.

Defense Secretary Richard B. Cheney confers with King Fahd of Saudi Arabia on February 12, 1991, less than two weeks before the start of the ground war. It was an earlier conversation between the two men on August 6, 1990, that opened the way for the massive U.S. troop deployment in Saudi Arabia, a traditionally closed country. To Cheney's right are General Colin Powell, Schwarzkopf, and the Saudi commander Lieutenant General Khalid.

Schwarzkopf and Lieutenant General Khalid, the Saudi commander, exchange words on December 19, 1990. Their relationship began uneasily five months earlier amid Saudi misgivings over the massive U.S. military deployment. But a genuine friendship gradually emerged.

Lieutenant General Michel Roquejeoffre, the commander of the French forces in Saudi Arabia. Schwarzkopf initially had difficulty winning the full cooperation of the French, but by January 1991 they were active partners in the coalition and played a crucial role. Roquejeoffre particularly appreciated Schwarzkopf's deft diplomacy and surprising tact.

The commander of British forces in Saudi Arabia, Lieutenant General Sir Peter de la Cour de la Billiere. Early on in the troop buildup, he called Schwarzkopf "rude," but he came to have enormous respect for the general, whom he always addressed as "Commander in Chief." A firm friendship developed between the two men; Schwarzkopf later said the general's counsel was invaluable.

Major General Barry R. McCaffrey, commander of the 24th Infantry Division (Mechanized), which Schwarzkopf commanded from 1983 to 1985. McCaffrey, three times wounded in Vietnam, typified the aggressive commanders who vowed there would be no repetition in the Gulf of the protracted Vietnam War.

Schwarzkopf earned the same reverence from his soldiers that General Omar Bradley enjoyed in World War II. An infantryman, the general conveyed a passionate concern for the well-being of his men and liked to mingle with them.

Schwarzkopf gives a pep talk to Marines ten days before the ground war began on February 23, 1991. Many soldiers spoke of perceiving the general as a father-like figure in the affection he displayed and the authority he wielded.

At his many press briefings, Schwarzkopf was sharp, articulate, humorous, and authoritative. His manner was so impressive that a video of his final briefing became an instant best-seller and an impromptu manual for corporate managers. Many saw him as a potential CEO or president. But tough restrictions on the press during the campaign left most media organizations disenchanted.

The bat-like F-117A Stealth bomber successfully evaded Iraqi radar to lead the bombardment of Baghdad. It was one of several high-tech successes in the Gulf that suggested some Pentagon money had been well spent.

U.S. M1A1 tanks race toward the desert sands. The swiftness and mobility of U.S. forces proved decisive. Many commanders said the effect of deception and speed was so overwhelming they did not come across any Iraqi unit looking in their direction at the time of the attacks.

The Army's 101st Airborne Division establishing a forward fuel and supplies base, code-named Cobra, after lifting more than 70 miles into Iraq on the first day of the ground assault, February 23, 1991. The base was essential to Schwarzkopf's wide flanking attack on the Iraqis.

Iraqi soldiers surrendering to U.S. Marines on February 25, 1991. The Marines met scant resistance as they marched across Kuwait toward Kuwait City after reaching Iraqi mine-fields on the Saudi-Kuwait border. In all, 70,000 Iraqi prisoners of war were taken by coalition forces.

An Iraqi walking through the ruins of the Amaria shelter in Baghdad on February 15, after bombing by coalition aircraft killed over 300 civilians. The U.S. said the shelter also housed a command and control center. New technology allowed more accurate bombing than in any previous war.

A dead Iraqi soldier, one of an estimated 100,000 Iraqi casualties of the Gulf War. Schwarzkopf's abhorrence of "body count," developed in Vietnam, was such that he went along with a policy which ensured that no information was officially presented to the U.S. public on the number of people killed in the war.

As Iraqis fled north out of Kuwait City to escape the advancing coalition troops, U.S. aircraft and helicopters bombarded and strafed them, leaving a scene of bloody mayhem. This was one of the few striking images of the savagery of battle to emerge from the war.

ALLEN TANNENBAUM/SYGMA

Retreating Iraqi troops started close to 600 oil fires in Kuwait shortly before coalition troops retook the country. Schwarzkopf was appalled by this wanton destruction. When he first saw it from the air on March 3, 1991, he described it as a vision of hell. Months after, the war smoke still shrouded much of the country.

On a blustery April day, Schwarzkopf came home to MacDill Air Base in Tampa, Florida. The reception reflected the Schwarzkopf fever sweeping the country, which confronted the general with a barrage of offers, from book contracts to political invitations. He is flanked by a security guard and his wife, Brenda, who successfully urged Schwarzkopf to open the homecoming to the public after he had initially disappointed the Tampa community by requesting a discreet return.

Schwarzkopf reunited with his family after eight months in Saudi Arabia. Between August 26, 1990, and his return on April 28, 1991, he did not come back to the United States, because he thought it would be bad for his troops' morale. *From left to right:* Christian, Cynthia, the general, Jessica, and Brenda.

wife under her protective wing, coached her, helped her, and became her friend. She cared about community affairs just as much as he did, and was very active in helping wives cope with life on an American military base in the middle of Germany."

The community motor pool was one of Cullinane's responsibilities. The first issue he had to deal with was the unruliness of U.S. children on school buses. The German drivers, used to more disciplined local *Kinder*, repeatedly complained about their behavior. They were further frustrated because they did not speak English and could not talk to the children.

Schwarzkopf summoned Cullinane and barked, "I want this to be solved once and for all. You get that?"

"Yes, sir," Cullinane promptly answered. Then he smiled.

Schwarzkopf smiled back. He knew that Cullinane knew him too well to see the military sternness on an issue like this as anything other than a façade.

Cullinane devised a monitor program in which a soldier or dependent rode on the bus with the children to see that they behaved. If that did not work, the bus was diverted to the Military Police post—and several times it was—where the children would receive a stern warning. In a matter of weeks, the children started behaving and the adults were no longer needed.

In December of 1981 Schwarzkopf faced a much more serious issue. On Christmas Eve a fire started in the stairwell of a residential building on the base. Two young children died and eight families were left homeless. Although the incident happened at two in the morning, Schwarzkopf rushed to the building.

"He was devastated by the loss of young lives. I saw tears in his eyes," recalled Cullinane.

Schwarzkopf was determined to find a place for every family by the next day so that they would not have to spend Christmas without a home. Working with the "mayors" of the various communities, he found new apartments and arranged for the delivery of food and Christmas trees to each of the families. The relocation was successfully completed by Christmas Day.

This was a tense period for Schwarzkopf. On December 17, 1981, just a few days before the fire, Brigadier General James L. Dozier, the deputy chief of staff for logistics and administration for allied land forces in southern Europe, was kidnapped in Verona, Italy. He was seized by members of an Italian terrorist group, the Red Brigades, who entered Dozier's apartment posing as plumbers and took him away handcuffed and blindfolded. Nothing like this had ever happened before to the U.S. Army in Europe; no American general had ever been kidnapped by terrorists. Security suddenly became a major concern for Schwarzkopf and other senior officers. For Schwarzkopf, moreover, the incident was personal. He knew Dozier, who was a fellow member of the class of 1956 at West Point.

At the beginning of January, with Dozier still in the hands of the Red Brigades, the Pentagon sent a special Green Beret commando team to Italy to mount a possible rescue operation. Security was tightened in Mainz. Schwarzkopf had to switch from his regular army car to civilian vehicles. Every day he had to use a different car of a different color, varying his routes to work.

He followed security rules, altering his routine as much as he could. But he insisted on continuing to pick up his four-year-old son, Christian, from school whenever he could. His driver would take Schwarzkopf to the Martin Luther King, Jr., Village, where he would stand on the corner of the street in front of the school until Christian came out. Then he and his son would walk hand in hand back to the waiting car.

On January 28, 1982, a Special Forces team from the Italian police broke into the apartment in Padua where Dozier was being held captive. They freed Dozier and captured several of the kidnappers. It was a rare breakthrough against the Red Brigades, who had terrorized Italians with considerable impunity during the previous years. Schwarzkopf was relieved, but security at U.S. military installations in Europe remained tight, and Schwarzkopf's movements were still constrained.

Five months later, on July 1, 1982, at the Community Club, Schwarzkopf received his second star. He was promoted to major general by the divisional commander, General Carl E. Vuono, who would later be Army Chief of Staff during the Gulf War. Schwarzkopf gave a speech, and as has often happened to him on these occasions, his emotions got the better of him. His voice started cracking and tears welled in his eyes. It was not just the honor of the second star. He knew that he was about to leave Mainz after two years at command, and he had many good memories to recall.

The Army Major General Schwarzkopf returned to in the United States in 1982 was at last beginning to make a comeback. For many, a nadir had been reached on April 24, 1980, when President Jimmy Carter's long-planned attempt to rescue the U.S. hostages held in Tehran ended in humiliating disaster. Eight servicemen were killed in the operation, which fell apart in the Iranian desert before ever reaching the capital.

For military men and women, this was a moment like that of the assassination of President John F. Kennedy in November 1963: they can all remember what they were doing at the moment they heard the news that the mission had been aborted. It was a shameful humiliation. It was suggestive of a U.S. military in which the Army, Navy, Air Force, and Marines had lost the ability to work together and be effective. They had the world's most modern equipment, but they did not know how to put systems together. When it came right down to it, they did not believe in themselves.

The operation reflected America's deep insecurity at the end of the Carter years. But with the election of Ronald W. Reagan in November 1980, the political and psychological climate in the country began to change. The new Administration placed a heavy emphasis on defense, replacing Carter's pleas for human rights with weapons programs for America's might. As a result, the Army became more attractive. It commanded bigger budgets and a bigger share of attention.

Reagan's arrival in power coincided with the presence of a highly effective general at the head of the U.S. Army Recruiting Command, based in Fort Sheridan, Illinois. Major General Maxwell R. Thurman had considerable experience in pushing through change. As a colonel, he had helped in downsizing the Army to 750,000 in 1973 from about 1.5 million in 1968, as part of the switch from a draft to a volunteer force. In 1977, as a major general, he became the director of Program Analysis and Evaluation in the office of the Chief of Staff, responsible for the budgeting, programming, and structuring of the force. In that role, he began shaping long-term policies for the Army of the 1980s. And in November 1979, he took over at Fort Sheridan, where he began work on a publicity campaign that would lay the basis for the new, highly professional Army that most Americans discovered only when it went to war in the Gulf.

When Thurman took over, the recruiting program was in a shambles. The Army was short of soldiers, and the soldiers it did have were often not up to standard. Thurman set to work to attract better-educated young Americans and get rid of the myriad so-called cat-4s—those below the average national intelligence level. Indeed, he set quotas for all recruitment centers, stating just how many cat-4s would be allowed.

Advertising, in Thurman's view, held the key to a breakthrough. In the late 1960s, the Army had started using the oldest advertising agency in America, N. W. Ayer, which had been responsible for the slogan "Today's Army Wants to Join You." That campaign, with its friendly suggestion that the Armed Forces were amenable to the ideas of the general population, did attract enough young people for the change to a volunteer Army. But Thurman was no longer just concerned about numbers. He wanted quality.

In late 1979, Thurman met with Ted Regan, the creative force at N. W. Ayer. The general told him that he wanted to shift from the traditional patriotic approach to an educational, high-tech pitch. To help the agency develop the right approach, Thurman gave N. W. Ayer access to any data it requested and assisted it in all marketing studies.

"We found out that education and personal challenge were very important to young people, but that the idea of making it as a human being transcended the others," said David Means, formerly in charge of the army account for N. W. Ayer. "With that in mind, we developed four different approaches, based on four different advertising strategies. The third one, which we recommended as the most appropriate, was summed up by the phrase 'Be All You Can Be.' We produced a three-minute montage on that theme for a meeting with the Secretary of the Army. Fifteen minutes before the meeting, we showed it to General Thurman for the first time. We were in a small, dark room in the Pentagon; the lights went down, the music went up, and when it was all over and the lights were turned on again, General Thurman took off his glasses, took out his handkerchief, and excused himself from the room. When he came back a minute later, he said, 'You really got me.' "

The ads started airing in 1980. They were among the most successful in American advertising history. When the campaign started, fewer than 50 percent of army personnel had a high school diploma. Thanks to the "Be All You Can Be" campaign, that percentage jumped to over 90 percent within three years. This dramatic transformation was in full swing at the time Major General Schwarzkopf returned from Germany in the summer of 1982.

On his return, Schwarzkopf was transferred to the Pentagon and appointed director of Military Personnel Management in the office of the deputy chief of staff for Personnel. His boss was General Thurman, who, one year earlier, had become deputy chief of staff for Personnel.

"As a great supporter of Thurman's effort to improve the quality and the professional standards of the U.S. Army, Norman was very interested in our recruiting approach," recalled Ted Regan. "He participated in all the big meetings concerning the 'Be All You Can Be' campaign and was always very positive toward the tone and goals of Thurman's marketing strategies."

The campaign was further boosted by the recession that started in the summer of 1981. Layoffs in the civilian sector helped bring a new class of volunteers to the Army. This, in turn, allowed the Pentagon to accelerate the phasing out of many cat-4s.

The soldiers who joined the Army in the early 1980s were generally what the Army calls cat-2s; that is to say, they were above-average intelligence, which is defined as cat-3. According to army analysts, these new recruits tended to learn in a few months what the cat-4s had taken years to master.

At the same time, the Pentagon made promotion procedures more aggressive. The new recruits forged ahead at the expense of the generally slower soldiers recruited in the 1970s. Many of these longer-serving soldiers became angry and left.

Army doctrine was also changing. The restoration of American confidence in the 1980s and increasing Soviet expansionism in the Third World—such as in Angola and in Afghanistan—provoked a reassessment of the defensive posture of the previous decade. This process would lead to the AirLand Battle doctrine so successfully applied in the Gulf.

General Donn A. Starry, who had assumed command of TRADOC (Training and Doctrine Command) in August 1977, was the first to come up with the Battlefield Development Plan, a battlefield analysis that integrated all the elements of air and land battle. Under Starry, the designers of U.S. army doctrine rediscovered the importance of speed and maneuverability; at the same time, they downplayed firepower, which had been the obsession of the previous years. Instead of massive head-on confrontations of armored forces, they started talking about attacking the flanks and rear of the enemy.

In February 1980, the Chief of Staff of the Army, General Edward C. Meyer, contributed to these changes by introducing new strategic and tactical requirements in his White Paper. Meyer wanted his Army to be prepared for what he called "three days of war." What he meant was that he wanted the U. S. Army to develop a threefold strategy. Day One was the "day before," that is, being equipped to deter war. Day Two was the "day of the war," that is, being ready to fight. Day Three was the "day after," that is, guaranteeing the right kind of peace and security. It was a broader strategy than had been previously postulated, and it demanded a new kind of flexibility.

Meanwhile, General Starry moved toward a reformulation of the Army's operations manual. In mid-1980, he came up with a tentative title for the new doctrine initially called the air-land battle: the "extended battlefield." This envisaged an early offensive initiative in the air as well as on land—a first deep attack into enemy positions, followed by a second, even deeper attack with air, artillery, Special Forces, and electronic warfare, all aimed at disrupting the enemy's forward movement and centers of gravity. The basic aim was to exploit high mobility and technology to destroy the enemy's ability to fight as a cohesive unit. Against a highly centralized army such as that of the Soviet Union, this was now perceived as the most effective strategy in a conflict in the European theater. Although its application in the deserts of the Gulf was not foreseen, it *was* a strategy ideally suited to flat, open terrain.

The main elements of what was ultimately known as AirLand Battle were initiative, an offensive outlook, depth, agility, and integration. Returning to Clausewitz, TRADOC emphasized another of his concepts: the offensive-oriented defense—a "shield of blows," as Clausewitz called it. Commanders had to move and strike quickly, demolishing the enemy before it could find its bearings or secure reinforcements. They could not do this unless they were able to "see" deep into enemy lines and assess the enemy's positions and strengths. General Starry therefore called for a major surveillance effort. He also stressed the importance of a rapid forward resupply capability because, as the old military adage says, "what cannot be supported logistically cannot be accomplished tactically." The Gulf War was to provide eloquent proof of the truth of this adage and testimony to General Starry's foresight in emphasizing the improvement of logistical support procedures.

The first articles in military journals presenting the new concept appeared in 1981 and early 1982. Nobody outside the Armed Forces paid much attention. The new manual was sent to General Meyer, the Army Chief of Staff, in August 1981, but changes delayed its final publication. The revised Field Manual 100-5 (Operations) finally came out a year later, in August 1982. A significant change was the formal inclusion of the name AirLand Battle, suggested by General Glenn K. Otis, who had become the new head of TRADOC in 1981.

In line with the more buoyant national mood, the publication showed a major doctrinal shift toward a more aggressive posture. In his essay "From Active Defense to AirLand Battle: The Development of Army Doctrine 1973–1982," John L. Romjue, a historian and staff member at TRADOC, said, "AirLand Battle was an offensively oriented doctrine that the Army found intellectually and analytically convincing."

The offensive orientation of the manual is explicit:

> AirLand Battle doctrine is based on securing or retaining the initiative and exercising it aggressively to defeat the enemy. Destruction of the opposing force is achieved by throwing the enemy off balance with powerful initial blows from unexpected directions and then following up rapidly to prevent his recovery. Army units will attack the enemy in depth with fire and maneuver and synchronize all efforts to attain the objective. They will maintain the agility necessary to shift forces and fire to the points of enemy weakness. Our operations must be rapid, unpredictable, violent and disorienting to the enemy.

There could scarcely be a better summary of the attack General H. Norman Schwarzkopf would direct upon the Iraqis nine years later.

The new doctrine also addressed an issue that had been of deep concern to General Schwarzkopf since Vietnam. This was the question of army leadership, so lacking in Vietnam, so limp in its aftermath. The AirLand Battle field manual declared that "improvisation, initiative, and aggressiveness must be particularly strong in our leaders." In March 1983, TRADOC published a follow-up to the manual, called Pamphlet 525-28, *U.S. Army Operational Concept for Leadership*. This amounted to a clear-cut call for more inspiring leadership and for extreme attention within the Army to finding those officers with true leadership qualities.

After World War II, General Omar N. Bradley, one of the most revered leaders of the U.S. Army, said: "Because war is as much a conflict of passion as it is of force, no commander can become a strategist until first he knows his men." One of the people who did much to turn the Army's attention back to those words was General Richard E. Cavazos, who, as commander of the 9th Infantry Division at Fort Lewis, had profoundly influenced H. Norman Schwarzkopf. According to the TRADOC historian Romjue, "Cavazos was an exponent of the importance of the moral aspect of combat. Cavazos's approach was to view it foremost as a clash of wills, whose outcome was dependent on psychological faculties." By 1983 the Army believed again that leaders really mattered.

Schwarzkopf's opportunity to test his leadership abilities again came after ten months of working under General Thurman in the Pentagon. In June of 1983, he was given command of the 24th Infantry Division (Mechanized) at Fort Stewart, Georgia. It was a plum assignment. The 24th, with its motto of "First to Fight," earned by being the first to attack and shoot down a couple of Japanese planes at Pearl Harbor in 1941, had become one of the best divisions in the Army. Schwarzkopf's predecessor, General Jack Galvin, had trained it aggressively, taking advantage of the high-technology combat simulation program introduced in 1981 at the National Training Center in Fort Irwin, California.

Because of its size and its open terrain, the Mojave Desert near Fort Irwin had been the training area for maneuvers of big tank divisions for years. But the introduction of the new MILES—the Multiple Integrated Laser Engagement System—made everything more realistic and demanding.

Beginning in 1981, soldiers who trained in the Mojave had devices mounted on their weapons which emitted laser beams that simulated the effect of weapons—their range, direction, and firepower. Troops also wore receptors that would emit a continuous buzz when hit by an "enemy" beam. At that point, their own firing devices were paralyzed. Even a near miss could be detected, and was signaled by three consecutive buzzes. Like rifles and machine guns in war, each device was loaded with a limited supply of "ammunition," so that resupply operations were necessary under fire. Other devices were mounted on armored vehicles, so the central command could track all losses of equipment and men during the exercise, as well as evaluate firing precision. It was as close as the Army had ever come to simulating the real conditions of battle, and it did soldiers a great deal of good. Indeed, after the Gulf War, many would comment that their training was tougher than what they actually encountered on the battlefield.

General Galvin was the first 24th Infantry Division commander to train with MILES. He was badly shaken by the results. His troops were repeatedly beaten by the so-called OPFOR, or opposing force—a group of soldiers made up of the 177th Armored Brigade, which is permanently stationed at Fort Irwin and is familiar with the terrain. This OPFOR, comprising about fifteen hundred soldiers, wears chocolate-brown uniforms with red insignias, exactly like those of Warsaw Pact forces, and is equipped with tanks and armored personnel carriers modified to resemble those of the Soviet Union. Their tactics are similar to those of the Red Army; that is, they try to punch through opposing forces at the least defended point with maximum strength. But Soviet tactics are usually predictable and relatively rigid, while OPFOR combines a keen understanding of Soviet principles with a flexibility found more often in U.S. forces. Visiting units such as the 24th were outnumbered about three to one in all engagements in order to simulate troop ratios likely to be found in Central Europe.

After the depressing experience of repeated defeats, General Galvin went back to Fort Stewart and announced a total overhaul of his training program. "I just came back from the Mojave, where our battalions lost every single battle," he said. "What we're going to do now is throw out our training practice and start from scratch. The next time we go out there, I want a win." "Victory at the National Training Center" became a slogan for the

24th. When Major General Schwarzkopf took over, he was determined to keep up the training pressure so that they could get just that.

But Schwarzkopf hardly had time to test his plans for the 24th Division. In the fall of 1983, he was abruptly called away from his new job to wage a real war. In the place of the Mojave Desert, he was sent to the Caribbean island of Grenada, a little-known place less than one-third the size of his own 285,000-acre base at Fort Stewart.

Grenada gained independence from Great Britain in 1974. From that time, its Prime Minister, Sir Eric M. Gairy, assisted by a gang of like-minded hatchet men, known as the Mongoose, ruled the country with a mixture of harsh repression, rampant corruption, and a flagrant misuse of the island's extremely moderate resources. He indulged, for example, in a fruitless but energetic search for UFOs. Despite this, in typical banana-republic style, the country maintained friendly relations with the United States.

On March 13, 1979, Gairy was overthrown in a bloodless coup by a socialist movement known as New Jewel (Joint Endeavor for Welfare, Education, and Liberation). Founded in 1973, New Jewel's main purpose had become the ousting of Gairy. Following the coup, New Jewel's charismatic leader, the thirty-four-year-old Maurice Bishop, became Prime Minister.

Bishop acted prudently after seizing power. He kept Grenada in the British Commonwealth and did not challenge the largely symbolic authority of its governor-general, Sir Paul Scoon, a Grenadian who had been knighted by Queen Elizabeth II. However, his foreign policy assumed a more left-leaning tone and was often indistinguishable from that of Cuba's Fidel Castro.

On November 28, 1979, after Nicaragua fell to the Sandinistas in July, President Jimmy Carter warned Bishop of possible economic reprisals if Grenada pursued its foreign-policy alignment with Cuba. At a conference on

Caribbean trade and development in Miami, Carter said: "The answers for the future are in the Caribbean's own talents and traditions, not in the false promises of foreign models."

In that same month, Bishop had announced plans to build a new international airport near Point Salines on the southern tip of the island. He said that he wanted to encourage mass tourism from the United States and Europe. But the U.S. intelligence community was concerned because the 9,500-foot runway could also be used for long-range military aircraft. Its concern mounted when a Cuban construction group, made up partly of soldiers, arrived to do the work. Castro's financial aid in the airport's construction made the project all the more suspicious.

Relations with Washington continued to worsen with the election of Ronald Reagan, whose Republican Administration was determined to counter more aggressively what it viewed as Soviet expansionism. When, in July 1982, Bishop visited Moscow and obtained a long-term credit line for the construction of a communications installation linked to a Soviet communications satellite, the U.S. government grew more alarmed.

In March 1983, President Reagan went on national television to show the public a classified photo of a Cuban barracks alongside the still-unfinished airfield.

"Grenada doesn't even have an Air Force," the President said. "Who is this [the airfield] intended for? The Soviet-Cuban militarization of Grenada can only be seen as power projection into the region." The possibility that the airfield was intended for jumbo jets filled with tourists was dismissed as laughable in Washington.

But Bishop was not a typical Communist ideologue, and he knew that, in the long run, a break in relations with the United States could only spell trouble for a small Caribbean island. Therefore, in June, he decided to try personal diplomacy. He flew to the United States for a surprise visit. After hanging around for a week in Washington, he managed to secure a meeting with National Security Adviser William P. Clark and Deputy Secretary of State Kenneth W. Dam. He was given a stern warning: Loosen your ties to Cuba and hold free elections. Bishop returned to Grenada with the intention of testing American goodwill. He told his Jewel colleagues he wanted to improve relations with Washington and started toning down his anti-American, pro-Third World rhetoric. This shift in policy was not appreciated, however, by the pro-Soviet faction in his party, led by Bishop's deputy, Bernard Coard.

On October 13, Coard made his move to gain control of the country. He placed Bishop and Jacqueline Creft, Bishop's longtime friend and Minister of Education, under house arrest. Washington interpreted this as a sign of a Cuban attempt to take direct control of Grenadian affairs. The White House was also concerned about the welfare of approximately four hundred young Americans who were studying medicine in a private university on the island.

On the same day as the arrests, October 13, the Pentagon alerted General Richard E. Cavazos that armed intervention in Grenada might be called for. Cavazos, Schwarzkopf's former commanding general at Fort Lewis, was now a four-star general, heading the U.S. Army Forces Command at Fort McPherson, Georgia. As such, he was responsible for providing ground troops to reinforce other commands when necessary. "I was notified that they wanted an army division and two Ranger battalions ready to join a Marine battalion," General Cavazos said.

The bureaucracy was complicated. Since Grenada was a Caribbean island, planning for any intervention there came under the Atlantic Command, based in Norfolk, Virginia. This is a unified command, which means all four forces—Army, Navy, Marines, and Air Force—are represented there. But the overall command was the responsibility of a naval officer, Admiral Wesley L. McDonald. Other services had only token representation. The army officers were of a fairly low rank.

Thus, a situation was created in which a land battle in Grenada—no sea warfare was anticipated, since Grenada has no navy—would be coordinated entirely by the Navy. It was a typical case of inter-force confusion of the kind that had plagued the Armed Forces for a long time.

Six days after the Pentagon's call to Cavazos, on October 19, the situation in Grenada worsened. Several thousand of Bishop's supporters stormed into his residence, freed him and Jacqueline Creft, and then marched to Market Square in the country's capital of St. George's. There Bishop gave a fiery speech and the crowd moved on to Fort Rupert, the Grenadian Army headquarters, which was under the command of General Hudson Austin, a former prison guard close to the Soviet hardliner Coard. At Austin's command, the troops opened fire on the crowd, recaptured Bishop and Creft, and executed them on the spot. General Austin then announced that he was the new leader of a sixteen-man junta. He also ordered a twenty-four-hour curfew. Anyone violating it, he said, would be shot on sight.

Late the next day, October 20, Vice President George Bush convened a meeting in the White House to discuss the implications of Austin's takeover, particularly its impact on the security of the American medical students. At the meeting, it was decided to divert a MEU, or Marine Expeditionary Unit—that is, a strike force of 1,800 Marines trained in special operations—from a fleet that was heading for Lebanon. Also detached from the fleet was the helicopter carrier *Guam*, under the command of Vice Admiral Joseph Metcalf III. It was to serve as the flagship for the mission to Grenada. All this, however, was still just a "precautionary measure." The White House had not given the official go-ahead for an invasion.

On Friday, October 21, the leaders of the six-nation Organization of Eastern Caribbean States—Antigua, Dominica, St. Lucia, St. Kitts-Nevis, Montserrat, and St. Vincent—met in Barbados, where they were joined by the Prime Ministers of Jamaica and Barbados. John M. G. Adams, the Prime Minister of Barbados, pushed most strongly for the countries to appeal for U.S. intervention.

President Ronald Reagan had, in the meantime, decided not to cancel his scheduled weekend trip to the Augusta National Golf Club. Late on Friday, Reagan left for Georgia with Secretary of State George P. Shultz, Treasury Secretary Donald T. Regan, and the new National Security Adviser, Robert C. "Bud" McFarlane. At 2:45 a.m., on Saturday, Shultz received a call from the State Department communicating the Eastern Caribbean States' request for U.S. intervention. At about 3:30 a.m., McFarlane called Vice President Bush to ask him to evaluate the various options. Bush arranged for a meeting of the National Security Planning Group, a select group of high government officials that includes CIA, Department of Defense, and military representatives.

The meeting was held at 9:00 a.m. on Saturday, October 22, in the Situation Room in the White House. Everyone sat around a large table on which maps of the Caribbean were spread. Among those present were Bush, who acted as the chairman of the meeting, Secretary of Defense Caspar W. Weinberger, White House Chief of Staff James A. Baker 3d, Chairman of the Joint Chiefs of Staff General John W. Vessey, Jr., and CIA Deputy Director John N. McMahon (William J. Casey, the CIA director, was away).

The welfare of the medical students was the main concern of the men in the Situation Room. Officials representing the U.S. university in Grenada where the students were enrolled had repeatedly told the State Department that their students were happy, that they were not in danger, and that there was no need for a rescue operation. The State Department accepted this. However, according to reliable intelligence sources, this information was contradicted at the meeting by McMahon of the CIA. The Agency, he said, had "persuasive information" to the contrary, suggesting that the university officials might merely be seeking to ensure that their money-making operation was not disrupted by an invasion.

The CIA determination that the students wanted out was crucial. It swayed everybody in the room toward intervention. The chairman of the Joint Chiefs of Staff (JCS), General Vessey, was in the end the only one who had some reservations. Vessey was personally ready to go, but was not sure that he could sway the other members of the JCS. At this time, the structure of the office of the Joint Chiefs of Staff was such that the chairman was simply first among equals and not in a position to make a decision on his own.

At the Pentagon there were several concerns. Officials thought the Administration might reverse course at the last minute; they feared a possible Soviet reaction; they were afraid that the country would not support a military intervention in Grenada's internal affairs and were, in principle, opposed to any kind of hastily arranged, small-scale surgical operation. The last such effort, Operation Desert One on April 24, 1980, failed when U.S. helicopters crashed in the Iranian desert during an attempt to free the American hostages held in Tehran. The Pentagon did not want to be involved in one more little intervention, full of political constraints and military boundaries.

From the Situation Room, Vice President Bush contacted the President on the golf course in Augusta and told him that the general consensus was to go ahead. The President said that he agreed, and so did Shultz and McFarlane.

At that point, the operation was officially on. It was decided that the President would stay in Augusta so as not to create suspicion. But hesitations continued to haunt the operation. The Joint Chiefs of Staff still doubted the wisdom of the decision and continued to believe that the operation might be called off at the last minute. Consequently, the JCS moved slowly in preparing the invasion.

At 2:27 a.m. on Sunday, October 23, President Reagan was awakened in Augusta by the news of the suicide bombing of the Marine barracks in Beirut, Lebanon. A Mercedes truck filled with explosives had crashed through the security barriers at the Marine headquarters, blowing up and killing 241 Marines. Now there was no question that the President's sojourn in Georgia had to end.

At 7:17 a.m., Air Force One took off from Augusta, and later that day, in Washington, the President called for a new round of meetings. Shaken by the tragedy in Beirut, the military pressed for another consultation on Grenada. That afternoon, a second National Security Planning Group meeting was called, which lasted several hours. There Vessey expressed the continuing reservations of others in the JCS. But the President confirmed his earlier decision; he wanted the invasion and wanted it fast. The Beirut disaster, in his view, had made it even more urgent for the United States to show determination on the international scene.

A bitter debate then ensued at the meeting over whether the operation should take the form of a surgical strike or a full-scale invasion.

On the one hand, the CIA pushed for a Special Forces operation, conducted primarily by the Marine Expeditionary Unit already diverted to Grenada. On the other, the military pressed for a much bigger show of force. The CIA was convinced that only air support was needed for the MEU. There was no real need, in its view, for any Rangers or airborne division from the Army to be brought in. By patching together a mixed force, including Army and Marine units, the Pentagon would only create confusion, CIA officials argued.

The military countered by arguing that a surgical strike with a small force was too risky and would end up causing many more American casualties. The Army was especially determined to go ahead with a big array of force in order to overwhelm the enemy. "The Navy backed us on that," recalled General Cavazos, who, even now, dismisses the idea of a surgical strike: "People who want to have little wars, and have it nice and neat, are of no use to the military." In the end the military view prevailed, but it had taken two full meetings of the National Security Planning Group—on Saturday morning and Sunday afternoon—for the Pentagon to be convinced that the operation was going ahead regardless of its reservations. Meanwhile, valuable planning time had been lost. So on Sunday evening the operation, which had been named Urgent Fury, still had to be organized.

As soon as the second White House meeting ended on Sunday, the chief of staff called General Cavazos at Fort McPherson and asked him to prepare two Ranger battalions. Cavazos was also told that the chief of staff had decided to provide a liaison officer to act as coordinator and adviser to Vice Admiral Metcalf, who would command the invasion.

Cavazos immediately suggested sending H. Norman Schwarzkopf. "It was a Navy show and the Army had no real voice. Therefore, I felt we needed a strong army personality but also someone capable of dealing with other services," Cavazos said.

But convincing the Army Chief of Staff, General John A. Wickham, Jr., turned out to be difficult. According to Cavazos, "There was a lot of division on whom to send. A lot of people did not want to send Schwarzkopf, and Wickham had someone else in mind. In fact, he thought of two other officers. I had a heated discussion on the phone with Wickham. He liked Schwarzkopf, but did not like the idea of taking an active division commander away from his post. The two guys he had in mind had no post, so they would not have been missed. I told him that if we needed him we could always get Schwarzkopf back."

At the end of the telephone conversation Wickham was persuaded to bring Schwarzkopf into the key liaison role in the invasion.

H. Norman Schwarzkopf had spent that Sunday morning fishing near his base in Georgia. He and Brenda had invited Ward Le Hardy for dinner and were planning to cook fresh bass. While Schwarzkopf was preparing the fish in the kitchen, the telephone rang. It was Cavazos's office.

"What are your plans for the next three weeks?" Cavazos's deputy asked.

There was brief silence. Schwarzkopf immediately thought that there were plans to send him to Beirut because of the suicide bombing. He was not thrilled, but confessed that he had no special plans.

"Since you have nothing too important to do, we're giving you a special mission," the deputy added, refusing to give him the time or place of the mission on the phone. "We will call you later with more details."

Within an hour, Schwarzkopf was ordered to Norfolk, Virginia. When Le Hardy arrived, Brenda let him in and said, "I'm sorry, but Norman is not here. And the strange thing is, he didn't tell me where he went. All I know is that he was called by the Army."

Schwarzkopf was in such a rush that he could not even wait for his personal aide, who was at a reunion at West Point that weekend. That same evening, Schwarzkopf flew from Fort Stewart to Atlanta, where he was briefed at Fulton County Airport before continuing to Norfolk.

At the same time, Vice Admiral Metcalf had left the flagship *Guam* and flown to Atlantic Command, where he was informed of the go-ahead and appointed commander of operations.

On Monday, October 24, at 7 a.m., Metcalf called a meeting with the commanding officers. Here he met Schwarzkopf for the first time and informed him of the details of the mission. Schwarzkopf, then, had no say in the planning of Operation Urgent Fury. He was told that the plan was to use massive force to overwhelm the enemy. A Marine contingent was supposed to arrive by helicopter on the northern part of the island to gain control of Pearls Airport and then move south toward the capital of St. George's. Simultaneously, the Rangers were to be parachuted to the southern tip to seize Point Salines airfield and then immediately move a few miles north to the True Blue campus, where the American students were. From there, they would then march north toward the capital to join the Marines.

But there were so many unanswered questions and unknown factors. Military commanders had not received maps of the island from the Defense Mapping Agency. In addition, the army and the navy units had incompatible radio systems, so extra radio equipment was needed to enable them to communicate with each other. The Marines of the MEU were in no better shape. Their ships had been loaded for an administrative landing; that is, they had been loaded to full capacity and not in the appropriate order for a combat landing. There was little room for maneuvering quickly off the ship, which is essential in an invasion, and the amphibious vehicles were not at the front, ready to disembark. Time was of the essence, so the Marines had to rearrange the equipment at sea. The operation was in some disarray.

The meeting with the commanding officers of the operation went on until about 10:30 a.m., after which Schwarzkopf and Metcalf flew to Barbados. They spent the trip reviewing the plans, and then a Marine helicopter took them from Barbados to the carrier *Guam*. They landed at sunset on Monday, October 24.

Maps were still a problem. "We had maps from the Navy Hydrographical Office and an old British chart, but no operational maps from the Defense Mapping Agency," Metcalf said.

Moreover, up until a few hours before the beginning of Operation Urgent Fury, many still thought that there would be a last-minute cancellation. Schwarzkopf later said, "The prevailing thinking was 'We're going, but it's not going to happen.' I can remember sitting in the dining area on the USS *Guam* and all of a sudden the watch officer or someone came in and said, 'It's a go.' And we all said, 'A go?' 'Yeah, tomorrow morning . . . ' "

At 6 p.m. on Monday, President Reagan signed an order that gave the final go-ahead. Thirteen years after Vietnam, H. Norman Schwarzkopf was going back to war. Memories, fears, and doubts all surged back.

"I remember standing outside the command bridge in the dark of night saying, 'Gee, we're going into Grenada. This is a military operation involving lethal force. Are we getting involved in another Vietnam? Is this something the American people will or will not support?' " Schwarzkopf said.

Any doubts or reluctance he may have had were short-lived. After more than a quarter century in the Army, H. Norman Schwarzkopf knew that his role was to implement policy, not to make it. And his duty was to obey the orders of the President of the United States.

Messily assembled, amid procrastination and doubt, Operation Urgent Fury seemed jinxed from the beginning. While little resistance was expected, reconnaissance efforts were launched to verify the enemy's defenses. But the air reconnaissance flight that Metcalf ordered on Monday failed to detect what would turn out to be strong artillery positions around the Point Salines airfield. On the same day, two four-man SEAL teams, the navy commando units, failed to accomplish their mission. The SEALs were parachuted into the water from a low-flying C-130 aircraft. One team was knocked unconscious by the impact, dragged under by the weight of weapons and equipment, and drowned. The other team managed to clamber into their rubber boat and get the engine started.

However, while proceeding toward the beach, they saw a local fishing boat and decided to switch off the engine, and they could not get it started again. Currents dragged them back out to sea. Eleven hours later, they were picked up by a navy ship.

At exactly 5:36 a.m. on Tuesday, October 25, United States forces attacked an enemy in a foreign country, albeit a tiny one, for the first time since Vietnam. Aboard troop helicopters, four hundred Marines took off from the *Guam*, roaring toward Pearls Airport, in the northern part of the island. Thirty-six minutes later, about five hundred Rangers departed from an airfield in Barbados and parachuted from their C-130s onto the airfield under construction at Point Salines in the south. But while the Marines' landing proceeded relatively smoothly, the Rangers came under heavy fire from artillery positions that had not been detected by surveillance.

Schwarzkopf later described the scene: "You have to visualize literally a cone of tracer fire, green tracer fire, coming up into the air, C-130 aircraft flying in directly underneath this cone of tracer fire, paratroopers dropping in the air and then being shot at, in the air, from all sides on the ground. I can't recall any combat operation that the United States has ever been involved in that could have been more intense than that."

Fortunately for the Americans, the most threatening anti-aircraft machine gun was not correctly positioned at Point Salines. The U.S. planes were able to fly right under its fire. "If it had been at the right angle it could have been a real problem," Vice Admiral Metcalf now admits. "Not detecting it was a significant intelligence failure."

Schwarzkopf confirmed this assessment to PBS: "We really didn't have good intelligence on their ability as anti-aircraft gunners."

Under much stronger enemy fire than anticipated, the U.S. forces kept coming in. After the attack helicopters, the PsyOps (psychological operations) army helicopters flew in, announcing through loudspeakers to the local population that they were coming in to free them.

Metcalf and Schwarzkopf ran Operation Urgent Fury from the flag-plot room, the command post on board the *Guam*. From that small room they could watch helicopters take off from the ship and land on the island about a mile away at Pearls Airport.

Within two hours, the Marines declared that Pearls Airport was secure. But the Rangers at Point Salines, having evaded the artillery fire, were confronted on landing by Grenadian and Cuban construction workers as well as armored personnel carriers. While the Rangers outnumbered these forces, they had not anticipated confronting this level of opposition. Consequently, an operation that was supposed to take a half hour ended up consuming almost two hours.

At 8:30 a.m., the soldiers finally entered the campus and converted an outdoor basketball court into a helicopter lift-off pad to get the students out. But, to their dismay, only some of the students were on that campus. Another 224 had remained on the main campus, Grand Anse, which was two miles away, in an area still held by Cubans and Grenadians.

"I was shocked. Stunned," Schwarzkopf said later. "There's no other word for it ... If it had been a Hollywood movie, it would have kind of gone like this: the Rangers would have broken through the door and said, 'Ta da, we're here, you're rescued,' and the students would say, 'Yeah, but what about the rest of us?' And the Rangers would say, 'What do you mean, what about the rest of us?' and they'd say, 'Oh, we're the small campus. They're all located someplace else.' I mean, you can imagine the shock!"

The rescue of the medical students was the major objective of Operation Urgent Fury, but neither Metcalf nor Schwarzkopf had been informed that there was more than one campus.

Since the American troops at both ends of the island were meeting more resistance as they forged toward the capital, the Pentagon decided to send reinforcements. On Tuesday afternoon, it dispatched two battalions of the 82nd Airborne Division from Fort Bragg. "We got a lot more resistance than we expected," admitted the chairman of the Joint Chiefs of Staff, General Vessey.

The SEALs seemed particularly unlucky. Twenty-two of them had landed on the island in small boats, five miles north of Point Salines, and moved up the hill toward the capital to rescue the governor-general and his family, at his residence. But as soon as they entered Sir Paul Scoon's building, Grenadian soldiers and three Cuban-manned BTR60 armored amphibious vehicles arrived. Equipped with only small arms, the SEALs were forced to retreat; they barricaded themselves in the residence and radioed for reinforcements.

To help them, Schwarzkopf improvised a plan to stage an amphibious Marine landing near the capital and then mount a flanking attack on the town, with Marines on one side and the Army, now marching north, on the other. At 8 p.m. on Tuesday, October 25, special amphibious landing craft carried 250 Marines and five M60 tanks to the beach at Grand Mal, just north of St. George's.

This landing on an unsurveyed beach went against military doctrine. There had been no reconnaissance or preparation. The Marine commander was opposed to the idea and pointed out all the risks. But Schwarzkopf insisted on the need for improvisation, and after a half hour of discussion, Metcalf approved the plan. Schwarzkopf had seen enough of war to know that sometimes improvisation has to take the place of doctrine in battle.

At the end of Tuesday, the first day of fighting, the vice admiral ordered all commanders to the flagship to work on the plans for the second day. At the meeting he announced the on-the-spot appointment of Schwarzkopf as deputy commander of operations. "He was sharp. He was great. He knew what to do and was clearly superior to the others involved in that operation. He also showed he was balanced and even-handed in dealing with the Marines and the Navy," Metcalf said. All this was just what General Cavazos had anticipated when he pushed for Schwarzkopf's involvement in the mission.

A much tougher decision at that meeting involved the press. Metcalf was asked to bring hundreds of journalists into the area of operations. "We were still fighting, we couldn't handle four hundred journalists. Therefore, I made a rule: no press on the island until things are squared away," Metcalf said. The Pentagon took the same position, but the reasons were political rather than practical.

It was a highly controversial decision, one without precedent in U.S. military history. Giving access to the media to cover military conflicts had been an established practice since the days of the Civil War. (Even then, however, General William T. Sherman had accused war correspondents of "inciting jealousy and discontent and doing infinite mischief.") But Vietnam had led General Schwarzkopf and his generation of military leaders not to trust the media. They came out of that long war believing that all their failings had been magnified, their achievements belittled. The hostility of the country in the 1970s, they believed, stemmed largely from the hostility of newspapers and television. Now, as generals and admirals, they were determined not to expose their troops to what they considered inimical media organizations. It was a primitive fortress mentality. But it was tenacious; and the vestiges of it would still be apparent eight years later in the Gulf War, when the movement of the press was strictly confined.

At 3 a.m. on the second day of the Grenada War—Wednesday, October 26—a second Marine company landed at the Grand Mal beach and started moving toward the governor-general's residence. Four hours later, at 7 a.m., Scoon and his family were freed and flown out.

They had breakfast with Schwarzkopf and Metcalf aboard the *Guam*, and Schwarzkopf quickly put the governor at ease. After breakfast, as the fighting was easing, the vice admiral decided to go ashore and visit the airfield at Point Salines.

Schwarzkopf stayed on the *Guam*. By the second day, he was taking care of all operational and military matters. Metcalf was dealing with Atlantic Command in Norfolk and the political aspects of the mission. There was still a major problem: the students at the second campus in Grand Anse had not seen any Marines.

Schwarzkopf later reconstructed the situation: "The progress on the ground was extremely slow. That terrain is terrible. The heat was terrible. The enemy was there. The *Guam* was sitting right off the coast, and you could look off the side of the aircraft carrier and there was Grand Anse. I mean it was there. You could see it. And one of the things that you saw was a wide open spread of white beach that would make an ideal helicopter landing zone. The other thing you saw, sitting right there on the deck of this aircraft carrier, were all these helicopters! So it didn't take any great military genius to load some forces on board, fly right in from the sea, land right there, run an air assault operation, and rescue the students."

Perhaps not a military genius, but it did, in this case again, take H. Norman Schwarzkopf to bring some improvised and faster movement to the operation. Indeed, throughout Urgent Fury, all the improvised military solutions came from him.

In response to his orders, Marines and Rangers with blackened faces and weapons ready rushed into six helicopters and landed on Grand Anse in a matter of minutes. "In twenty-six minutes, we evacuated 224 students without a single casualty to the students and only one light wound on the part of the Rangers. It was absolutely a classic operation and it came off without a hitch and was a great success," the general told public television.

On Thursday afternoon, as the fighting was subsiding, the U.S. forces captured the two leaders of the Grenadian government, Bernard Coard and General Hudson Austin. A Marine unit found Coard hiding in a residential area near the capital and arrested him. Ushering him into custody, they had to protect him from the rage of the local population. Soon after, Austin surrendered to American forces. The two men were brought aboard one of the U.S. ships, interrogated, and then turned over to the authorities of the new Grenadian government.

By late Thursday, with over five thousand paratroopers, nine hundred Marines, and five hundred Rangers in Grenada, Admiral McDonald, the head of Atlantic Command, reported that all major objectives on the island had been secured, although on the next day he did admit that there were "scattered pockets of resistance and fighting still in progress."

The operation was over, the mission successfully completed. Schwarzkopf flew into the island on a helicopter. From a distance he saw a sign scrawled on a wall. It reminded him of signs he had seen throughout the world—in Berlin, in Vietnam, in Tokyo, even on the walls of the Pentagon. They usually said something like "Long Live Marxism" or "Down with the United States." But in this case Schwarzkopf was surprised as he drew closer. The sign said "God Bless America."

Schwarzkopf is an ardent patriot. "The Star-Spangled Banner" can bring him close to tears. He believes with a military man's intensity in America's commitment to the freedom of nations. This belief is not unquestioning—Schwarzkopf is too intelligent for that—but it is strong enough to outweigh all doubts. That small sign, with its clear message that sometimes people around the world could appreciate America's efforts, moved him.

His return home surprised him. It was triumphal. "I had expected to come home just the same way I came home from war the last two times: no big deal. It was going to be routine. But the airplane landed, the band was out there, and there were big signs saying, 'WELCOME HOME,' and I walked out of the airplane and everybody started cheering and my wife and kids ran up and hugged me, and I didn't understand what was going on!" he told the writer C. D. B. Bryan.

But Operation Urgent Fury was scarcely a triumph. It was successful largely because it pitted a giant against a pygmy. The giant proved inept and maladroit—but it was still a giant. Seven U.S. battalions, in addition to elements of two other battalions, had fought against 679 Cubans, fewer than fifty of whom were professional soldiers, and a few hundred badly trained Grenadian troops.

Many mistakes were made. The most tragic was the bombing of a mental hospital near the Grenadian army post at Fort Frederick. Corsair jets were sent to bomb the fort. The pilots attacked the hospital instead, leveling a three-story wing and burying many of the occupants under the rubble. In a partial cover-up, the Pentagon did not officially acknowledge that the air strike had taken place until October 31, four days after the end of the invasion. Even then it claimed that enemy troops had been firing from the hospital.

With the Vietnam body count controversy still fresh in their minds, top officials at the Pentagon refused to provide even rough estimates of enemy or civilian casualties. Schwarzkopf stated openly that a deliberate decision had been made not to focus on bodies.

The White House did not react any better. "I am told there is a religious custom that the Grenadians bury their dead very soon after they die," White House spokesman Larry Speakes claimed, rather grotesquely, as he tried to justify the lack of information available to the public. When told that most Grenadians were Catholics or Anglicans, Speakes said, "The custom may not be religious."

Almost three weeks after the invasion, Pentagon officials announced that U.S. Forces had captured 300 shotguns, 24,768 flares, and 5,615,582 rounds of ammunition. But no numbers were given for Grenadian civilian or military casualties. The loss of nineteen Americans was, however, conceded.

Over the following months, behind closed doors, the Pentagon rigorously examined its failures in Grenada. According to subsequent reports, the Defense Department in a closed congressional hearing presented a written assessment which admitted that the mission was fraught with confusion brought on mainly by hasty planning. Two naval officers were also reported as having said, "We went into combat the first day with absolutely no knowledge of, or coordination with, the Ranger operation." The Defense Department, in its assessment, tried to shift some of the blame to the intelligence community, stating that there was "an almost total lack of intelligence data about the situation on the island." In other words, the aftermath brought on a deluge of typical interservice quarreling, of the kind that had also plagued the 1980 mission to rescue the hostages in Tehran—where pilots from several services were used, not on the basis of merit, but on the basis of the need, in the words of one officer familiar with the operation, "to spread the wealth between Army, Navy, Marines, and Air Force."

At one point, according to reliable officials, General Vessey, the Joint Chiefs of Staff chairman, went to William J. Casey of the CIA to complain about the lack of tactical intelligence. But the general was strongly rebuffed by the Agency. Vessey was told that the CIA had informed the military about the heavy machine guns around Point Salines and had said that there was reason to fear the Cubans. Even more important, the Agency had made information available on the *existence of two different campuses* and had offered to put "certain CIA capabilities on the ground" at military disposal. The fact was that the CIA had the ability to provide tactical information, but, in the rush, the Pentagon never asked for it. Vessey had no counterarguments, and the issue of the CIA's failure to provide intelligence was dropped.

In private, Schwarzkopf admitted his unhappiness with the way Operation Urgent Fury had been conducted. "He thought it was badly planned and that the intelligence was badly gathered. He considered the whole thing a sloppy affair," said his sister Sally.

Disturbing questions were raised by military experts at the congressional level. Severe criticism was directed at inter-service competition and lack of coordination. On the Senate floor, Sam Nunn (Democrat of Georgia) declared, "A close look at the Grenada operation can only lead to the conclusion that, despite our victory and success, despite the performance of individual troops who fought bravely, the U.S. Armed Forces have serious problems conducting joint operations."

A later study released by William S. Lind, an aide to Senator Gary Hart (Democrat of Colorado) and founder of the Military Reform Caucus, concluded that the invasion plan developed by Atlantic Command was "overruled by the Joint Chiefs of Staff, who demanded that all four services be involved—just as in the Iran rescue mission." According to Lind, the subsequent "pie-dividing contest" allowed a relatively small Cuban contingent "to form and maintain a fairly effective defense." About the only tactical element that Lind found worthy of praise was the Marines' ability to "adapt swiftly to circumstances as they changed"—an indirect but clear recognition of Schwarzkopf's contribution to Urgent Fury.

Assessments like this opened the way for the Department of Defense Reorganization Act of 1986. This significantly improved the chances of cohesion in a U.S. military operation. Until Grenada, the chairman of the Joint Chiefs of Staff had been constrained by his position as first among equals. His main worry had been to reach a consensus among the various chiefs and to ensure that all views found some reflection in an operation. It was an attempt at war as democracy, and the successful conduct of warfare cannot be achieved through equal representation. It relies on a clear chain of command.

Under the new act, the chairman remained the spokesman for the chiefs. But he also became the main military adviser to the President and the National Security Council, thereby replacing the JCS as a group. He was finally allowed to present opinions and suggestions that were his own and were not necessarily shared by the others.

To make these changes work in practice, the Joint Staff was made responsible to the chairman rather than to the collective body of the Joint Chiefs, and a new position of vice chairman was created to assist the chairman, act on his behalf in his absence, and help him make "jointness" really work. The empowerment of the chairman indirectly reinforced the CINCs (commanders in chief in the field), whose priorities could now be represented by a single voice.

The law also increased the individual authority of the CINCs in the theater of operations, allowing them to organize and command all operational forces with a greater degree of autonomy from Washington and a greater power to integrate different systems and forces into one fighting team. All this would make a big difference to Schwarzkopf when he was the commander in Riyadh.

Back at Fort Stewart, in command of the 24th Infantry Division, Major General H. Norman Schwarzkopf continued his policy of modeling his forces in his image. He had a motto: his soldiers came first. If his ideas did not coincide with those of the U.S. Army, he would always try to change the U.S. Army before renouncing what he thought was best for his soldiers. When the Army's position was an expression of bureaucratic obtuseness, he would ignore it. This is what he did during the Christmas holidays of 1983.

In an attempt to save energy, the Pentagon had forbidden outdoor lights at all military posts that Christmas, and soldiers were told not to decorate trees or houses. The ruling maddened Schwarzkopf. He considered the minor savings derived from the conservation program negligible compared to the loss of morale for the troops. He decided to allow the 24th to ignore the rule. This, however, did not go unnoticed by the conservationists at the Pentagon. Before Christmas, General Cavazos, who was Schwarzkopf's direct superior and rating officer, was informed of the violation.

Cavazos called Schwarzkopf at Fort Stewart. "Oh, you found out about the Christmas lights," Schwarzkopf said. "Yes, I have," replied Cavazos, "and so have the energy conservation freaks."

Cavazos waited. Then Schwarzkopf asked him, "Have you also found out about the personal check for four hundred dollars that I made out to the U.S. government to pay for the electricity?"

Schwarzkopf had calculated the amount saved through the Christmas lights policy and paid the government so as not to deprive his men. Cavazos, a Texan, laughed and admitted that he did not like the energy policy either.

In May 1984, the close professional relationship between Schwarzkopf and Cavazos came to an end. Cavazos retired. Before departing, however, the Texan visited all the posts under his command, including Fort Stewart. He gave explicit instructions that there should be no goodbye ceremony. But when he walked out to the airfield after visiting Schwarzkopf and his officers and soldiers, the division band was there. It played the national anthem and then "Amazing Grace," Cavazos's favorite song. All this was a direct violation of his order, but emotion prevailed. When Cavazos turned to Schwarzkopf, he was crying, and the departing general started to cry, too. He saluted and boarded the plane.

Part of what had drawn Schwarzkopf to Cavazos had been his style of leadership. He was an emotional man involved with his men and determined to lead by an example of true moral courage. When he first met Cavazos in the mid-1970s, this sort of leadership had been a rarity in the Army. But by 1984 Schwarzkopf was convinced that leadership in the forces had never been better. A striking transformation had taken place.

He was therefore incensed when, in September 1984, he read an article in the *Armed Forces Journal* written under a pseudonym by an active-duty U.S. Army general and devoted to a ferocious attack on the Army's promotion policy.

The pseudonym, Colonel Yasotay, was borrowed from the name of the foremost warrior in Genghis Khan's army. The article suggested such warriors were scarce. "Warriors, competent combat leaders," it said, "are an endangered species in our Army. We bend over backwards to kill off our warriors at a young age and give them less consideration in our promotion process . . . We have become an Army of clerks, not killers." It concluded with a nostalgic evocation of pre-Vietnam days: "In those days the warriors were far and above the majority of the people on selection boards. Warriors came first and the needs of the Service after . . . The conclusion is obvious: ours is an Army of clerks, not fighters, and they are running the show!"

"Colonel Yasotay" was none other than Schwarzkopf's classmate at West Point John "Doc" Bahnsen. As was the case with all his other classmates, Doc had gone to Vietnam. He had returned as one of the most decorated officers of the entire class of '56. Some of his old friends at West Point knew that "Yasotay" was his pen name. Ward Le Hardy, who at that time was conducting a study for the Army on the same issues the piece addressed, was one of those who knew. "I found that article very irritating.

In numerous private conversations with Doc, we got quite mad at each other," recalls Le Hardy. "I challenged Doc to come out in the open and say what he had to say—writing his own name at the end of the article."

Schwarzkopf, who was unaware of Yasotay's real identity, was infuriated both by the article and by the author's anonymity. He wrote a response to the editor of the *Armed Forces Journal*. Referring to Yasotay's exaltation of the allegedly lost warrior, he said:

> There is certainly a philosophical appeal to all of us who have dreamed at one time or another of following in the footsteps of John Wayne. But Yasotay's broadside at the entire officers corps really misses the mark when measured against the quality of today's officers. It can best be characterized as an anonymous backshooter's cheap shot. I don't know where Yasotay hangs his helmet, even if he wears one, but I write him to come down to Fort Stewart (Georgia) and I will proudly show him my fine company, battalion, brigade commanders. They are warriors by every measure. They proved it over and over again in the field in the Mojave Desert, far tougher than any that Yasotay and I have fought on. They are not afraid to stand up and be counted. In the 24th Infantry Division we display our names proudly on our uniform. If you print this, make sure you sign my name. SCHWARZKOPF.

Brigadier General Bahnsen was astonished when he received the letter from the editor of the *Armed Forces Journal*. He was especially stunned by the vigor of the attack; he could not believe that his old friend could be so angry. Bahnsen was sure if old Schwarzie had known who Yasotay was, he would not have attacked his integrity and certainly would not have accused him of cowardice. He immediately wrote to Schwarzkopf, revealing his identity. "Norm didn't know it was me, and when he found out he was apologetic," said Bahnsen, adding, "He knows that I have eighteen decorations, five Silver Stars, two Purple Hearts. And *mine* are for killing, not saving lives!"

But finding out who Yasotay really was did not make Schwarzkopf any less angry. He wrote a letter to Bahnsen. It began: "Doc, you crazy S.O.B., you could always get my juices going."

Much of Schwarzkopf's anger stemmed from the fact that he had worked so hard to improve army leadership. This leadership, he believed, was uniquely enhanced by the National Training Center at Fort Irwin, where he regularly worked his forces hard. "He wanted tank crews that could really shoot, and he certainly pushed us," recalled Brigadier General Joe N. Frazar, who was at the time a battalion commander in the 24th. "But he was also generous in his praise, and told us that battalion commanders were a lot better than when he had been one, as a result of the National Training Center. He gave you great latitude as a commander—once you had earned his confidence, you could do what you liked, so long as you met his broad goals."

Defeats were never held against battalion commanders. They were told they would not get relieved even if defeat was humiliating. "I want you to go out there, have fun, learn how to fight, and learn about your equipment," Schwarzkopf said.

In general, Frazar believes that many soldiers were in awe of Schwarzkopf. He could get angry—Frazar particularly recalls his fury at one incompetent sergeant major—but the anger quickly passed. "It's flash anger," he said, "not denigrating anger." And underlying everything, there was a tremendous concern for his men. For example, when Frazar, in 1985, was selected for the Naval War College and mentioned that he would rather go to the Army War College, Schwarzkopf silently went to work. Three weeks after this conversation, Schwarzkopf called and told Frazar he was now going to the Army War College.

After two years with the 24th Division, Major General H. Norman Schwarzkopf once again returned to a desk job at the Pentagon. There were no soldiers, but the job was both prestigious and demanding. He became assistant to the deputy chief of staff for Operations and Plans, his War College classmate Carl Vuono, and was therefore involved in coordinating U.S. military policy worldwide.

The assignment lasted exactly one year. In June 1986 he was again transferred to Fort Lewis, Washington, to serve as the commanding general of the I Corps. On July 1, 1986, he became a lieutenant general, receiving his third star, just in time for his thirtieth reunion at West Point. However, in the anniversary book, where each classmate related events since the last reunion, he did not mention his three stars. He wrote mainly about his family:

> Brenda, my first wife (and only one), is still putting up with me, and the moves, although I often wonder why. Cindy, our oldest, is a junior in high school with ambitions to be a psychologist. (She considers herself qualified after living with her father.) Jessica, our high school freshman, has loftier ambitions. She intends to be a rock star or anything else that will cause her to be filthy rich. The ambitions of Christian, who is now 9, lie somewhere in the nexus of hamster breeder, horny toad trainer, astronaut or Garbage Pail Kid. Finally Bear, the ever-present dog, has just gotten out of jail where I sent him after he attacked the dogs of both the chief of staff and the chairman of the joint chiefs of staff. Hang in there. The next 30 years are gonna be just as much fun as the last 30!

Schwarzkopf spent just fourteen months at Fort Lewis. In August 1987 he was called back to the Pentagon to take over his former boss's position. As deputy chief of staff for Operations and Plans, he was once again taken away from the soldiers he loved. But his new position was considered an important step toward a fourth star. "The DCSOPS is possibly the most demanding job in the U.S. Army in terms of sheer volume of work, and it is the toughest and most challenging three-star job in peacetime," said retired Lieutenant General Sidney "Tom" Weinstein, another former West Point classmate.

The general spent long, tiring, and sometimes frustrating days at the Pentagon, but never turned into a bureaucrat. He managed to add his own personal touch to the position. Every Thursday morning there was a half-hour meeting in the army operations center in the basement of the Pentagon, where the DCSOPS could briefly analyze the most recent events on the international scene with the chief of Army Intelligence and a few other big shots at the Pentagon. Despite the early hour, these 6:30 a.m. meetings were soon to become something special. Schwarzkopf and Weinstein set a humorous, informal tone that filled the room with more staff than had been seen at such meetings before.

Schwarzkopf's impetuous nature made it difficult for him to deal with political issues, but behind the desk in his office, as the operations chief, he showed restraint. Indeed, one day, while discussing budget cuts for the 1989 fiscal year, he told staffers who were complaining about the cuts, "What we get is really a *lot* of money, and if we can't run the Army on seventy-six billion dollars we ought to all go to jail."

However, the Kafkaesque nature of life at the Pentagon bothered him. Periodically he would find something that disgusted him, as in the case of a congressional decision to store tons of ammunition in a state merely to satisfy a congressman who wanted to save jobs. Schwarzkopf knew the ammunition would never be used, and it never was. Sometimes his frustration would be so great he would arrive home short-tempered and tired. Like his father, he had a basic dislike of politics and politicians. But he was about to be thrust into the most political job of his life: a military assignment that would take him to the Middle Eastern countries which he had first discovered as a child under his father's guidance.

6

A Bargain Command

Who do you think gave us oil in the first
place?
—The late Saudi King Faisal, on being
  asked whether it was oil, rather than
  God, that made Islam strong

Saudi Arabia's King Fahd is the eleventh of the forty-
three sons of Abdul Aziz Ibn Saud, the founder of the vast
desert kingdom. Although oil money has transformed the
country since the days of his father—littering the desert
with six-lane highways, Nissan pickups, electricity transmission towers, and spindly communications towers—the
King likes to preserve some of the old Bedouin customs.
At dusk he will go out into the desert to pray; and for a
quick break from the arduous grind of government, he is
likely to go hunting with falcons in the empty expanses
around the capital, Riyadh.

His is a mobile court. Royal caprice shifts it to wherever is deemed most commodious in this thinly populated
country that sits on top of close to one-third of the free
world's proven oil reserves. In summer, King Fahd's whim
generally takes the court 550 miles west to the Red Sea
coast, where the heavy-eyed monarch takes up residence
at his al-Salama Palace in Jidda. The gentle sea breeze
makes it far cooler than the al-Yamama Palace in the
capital. So it was to this ancient port, just fifty miles from
the birthplace of the Prophet Muhammad in Mecca, that

General H. Norman Schwarzkopf came on August 6, 1990, with a secret plan to convince King Fahd to throw open the doors of a kingdom long wary of outsiders and allow the sudden influx of more than 200,000 foreign troops.

The general was accompanied by Defense Secretary Dick Cheney, Deputy National Security Adviser Robert M. Gates, Under Secretary of Defense for Policy Paul Wolfowitz, and Charles W. Freeman, Jr., the U.S. ambassador to Saudi Arabia. Just over a week earlier, Mr. Freeman had been preparing to go on vacation in the United States and had asked intelligence officers whether the abrupt massing of over 100,000 Iraqi troops on the Kuwaiti border was reason enough to cancel his plans. The reply was no: the Iraqi move was probably no more than saber-rattling, and an invasion was unlikely. So, on July 28, Mr. Freeman left for his vacation in America—only to have his summer idyll brusquely interrupted on August 2 by the news that Iraqi troops had swept, almost unopposed, into Kuwait City.

The ambassador's surprise was widely shared. His counterpart in Baghdad, April Glaspie, had also taken off on vacation on July 30. Although the rapid Iraqi buildup had been carefully monitored through U.S. spy satellites since it began in earnest on July 20, the general consensus in Washington had been that Iraqi President Saddam Hussein was merely applying some rather unsubtle pressure on the Emir of Kuwait, Sheik Jabir al-Ahmad al-Jabir al-Sabah. Saddam's aim, officials in Washington believed, was to mount a show of force to convince the Emir that Iraq's economy, reeling from a foreign debt of over $80 billion, needed help. He wanted Kuwait to cut oil production, pump some $10 billion into Iraq's war-ravaged economy, and reach a settlement over exploitation of the disputed Rumaila oil field, which straddles the border between the two countries. Right up until the eve of the invasion—when it was already too late to do anything about it—the possibility of a rapid Iraqi sweep all the way to Kuwait City was dismissed by the State Department and the Pentagon. At worst, a shallow Iraqi incursion to take the whole of the Rumaila oil field was considered possible. Only the Central Intelligence Agency predicted a full-scale invasion—and that was not until the eve of the Iraqi sweep to Kuwait City.

"In retrospect, it's absolutely clear we misread the situation," said Richard W. Murphy, the former Assistant Secretary of State for Near Eastern and South Asian Affairs, who visited Iraq in March 1990 and was struck by the bellicose tone of Iraqi officials. "Even in March, Iraqi officials were screaming that there would be an Israeli attack. They were also ranting about how humiliating and demeaning it was for Iraq to be considered one more economically squeezed Third World country after it had staved off Iran in the war, and how ungrateful the Gulf states like Kuwait were. But we took it all as rhetoric rather than literally."

Part of the cause of this misreading was an enduring U.S. view that some compromise with Iraq was necessary. In April 1990, the influential Strategic Studies Institute of the Army War College had published a report on Iraqi power that urged Washington to adopt a conciliatory approach to Baghdad. Calling Saddam a force to be reckoned with after what it termed the "Iraqi defeat of Iran" in the 1980–88 war, the report said: "It does not seem sensible under such conditions to antagonize what is now the strongest power in so vital an area of the world." Such thinking was widespread in Washington.

The Arab world had also taken the view that Saddam was bluffing; or that if he was serious, he could be coaxed out of his plans. Kuwait never believed that Iraq would invade. When he visited the country between May 4 and 8, 1990, Colonel Ralph Cossa of the Institute for National Strategic Studies in Washington was struck by the way his Kuwaiti hosts scoffed at Saddam's mounting threats: "They kept saying the Iraqis are our brothers, our Arab brothers, and we underwrite them. You don't bite the hand that feeds you." Until Iraqi troops crossed the border, the Kuwaiti government, never a great supporter of a strong U.S. presence in the Gulf, blithely continued to ignore repeated U.S. requests that it spell out its security needs.

Reassuring calls to President Bush in late July from King Fahd, Egyptian President Hosni Mubarak, and King Hussein of Jordan also helped lull the U.S. Administration into a sense that its summer would not be disturbed by a troublesome but distant Arab dictator. Awakened during the night of August 2 with the news that Kuwait had been invaded, King Fahd is said by Western diplomats in Riyadh to have replied, "By whom?" Since the downfall of the Shah of Iran in January 1979, Saudi fears had focused on the fundamentalist Shiite power of that country, just across the Persian Gulf from the immensely valuable Saudi oil fields. The Persians, after all, were historic enemies of the Arabs. But the brutal invasion of an Arab country, Kuwait, by another Arab power, Iraq, was unthinkable.

General Schwarzkopf had been less sanguine in his view of the Iraqi buildup. He himself did not believe that the Iraqis would sweep all the way to Kuwait City. It was more likely, in Schwarzkopf's opinion, that Saddam would stop at a shallow invasion, seizing the Rumaila oil field. Still, in the assessment of former Air Force Chief of Staff General Michael J. Dugan, Schwarzkopf delivered a distinctly sober analysis to the Joint Chiefs of Staff on August 1, the day before the invasion. "Schwarzkopf laid out what was going to happen," said Dugan. "He gave us a briefing on the capabilities of the Iraqi Army and predicted it would take them five to six hours to reach Kuwait City. As it turned out, he was about right. He said they could do it quite easily if they chose. But he also stressed that it could still be mere intimidation by Saddam. In any event, we noted that there was nothing we could do to intervene at that point."

General Schwarzkopf's concerns over a potentially explosive Gulf conflict involving Iraqi aggression had been growing steadily for some time. Since taking over in November 1988 as commander in chief of the Florida-based U.S. Central Command, whose responsibilities include the entire Gulf area, he had made several trips to the Middle East. One such visit took him to Saudi Arabia between October 2 and 7, 1989. In Riyadh, he conferred at length with Ambassador Freeman. Their joint conclusion was that an Iraqi invasion of Kuwait and subsequent threat to Saudi Arabia was now the main potential menace to the region's stability. Over the previous several years, a fundamentalist Shiite eruption in Saudi Arabia's eastern, oil-producing provinces coupled with an Iranian incursion had been regarded as the chief possible threat to the conservative Saudi regime.

The reasoning of Schwarzkopf and the ambassador was straightforward. Since August 1988, Saddam had been freed of the crippling burden of his eight-year war with Iran. Yet, rather than concentrate on reviving his debt-burdened economy, the Iraqi leader was pressing ahead with a frenetic buildup of his military arsenal. The abrupt retrenchment of his main ally, the Soviet Union, had also given him a freer hand to pursue his radical ambitions. He was suddenly beholden to nobody. On his doorstep stood the Gulf states—oil-rich, irritatingly conservative, and largely defenseless before his 1.2-million-man army. Kuwait alone, if conquered, would extend Iraq's coastline from just 37 miles to 225 miles. And it was Kuwait and the other Gulf states, Saddam believed, that were pushing down the price of oil through overproduction, thus suffocating an Iraqi economy that was reeling, in part, from the exorbitant cost of its arms imports.

On February 8, 1990, four months after his trip to Riyadh, General Schwarzkopf made his concerns known to a U.S. Senate Armed Services Committee hearing on "threat assessment, military strategy, and operational requirements" throughout the world. Noting that Iraq was devoting about 35 percent of its GNP to military spending, and that the proportion of Iraqi men in Saddam's armed forces was now equivalent to a 13-million-strong U.S. Army, he told the assembled senators that "Iraq has the capability to militarily coerce its neighboring states should diplomatic efforts fail to produce the desired results." He added that since the Soviet threat had faded, "we in Central Command now consider our most dangerous scenario to be the spillover of some local conflict leading to a regional war which threatens American lives and vital U.S. interests." As to what those U.S. interests in the Gulf are, General Schwarzkopf was blunt, listing the first objective of his command as "to ensure continued access to Arabian Peninsula oil."

But despite the fact that more than one in every four barrels of oil imported by the United States comes from the Middle East and that the area accounts for 77 percent of the non-Communist world's proven oil reserves, General Schwarzkopf's testimony had no discernible impact. He himself was reluctant to forsake entirely a conciliatory approach to Saddam. The general, like other U.S. officials, still saw the Iraqi President as a possible counterweight to Iran and advised that "the U.S. should continue to develop its contacts with Iraq by building selectively on existing political and economic relationships." These "relationships" included an extensive food-aid program.

The main problem, however, was that the Pentagon's attention lay elsewhere. At a time of congressional pressure for a "peace dividend" in the form of a 20 percent cut in military budgets, the Gulf was a seven-thousand-mile-distant problem in an area where the United States had never had a major military presence. According to several officials, the U.S. military establishment remained transfixed by Europe, long the imagined theater of any major conflict, and the ramifications there of the apparent winding down of the cold war. By comparison, the Gulf seemed faraway, murky, and intractable.

Indeed, one State Department official who has worked closely with General Schwarzkopf said that during the early part of 1990 the general even had to lobby against cost-cutting suggestions from the Navy that it terminate the small but symbolic presence in the Persian Gulf that it had maintained since 1949.

"The Joint Chiefs of Staff really discovered the Middle East on August 3, 1990," retired Marine Corps General George B. Crist, the former vice director of the Joint Chiefs and the predecessor of General Schwarzkopf at Central Command, contended.

Nonetheless, General Schwarzkopf had proceeded with careful planning for a potential Iraqi aggression. Throughout the first half of 1990, he worked to shift the focus of Central Command's activities from preparation for a Soviet or Iranian attack in the area—which had been its chief raison d'être since its establishment by President Reagan in 1983—to readying a rapid response to a potential Iraqi invasion of Kuwait. On June 15, 1990, he visited Saudi Arabia again for two days, and his conversations with U.S. and Saudi officials during this trip only confirmed his inclinations. His planning culminated on July 23 as Iraqi troops massed at the Kuwaiti border. It was then that Central Command began a five-day exercise at Hurlburt Field and Eglin Air Force Base in Florida. Called Internal Look '90, the exercise was blandly described in a press release as "testing rapid deployment, mobility, and combat readiness of American forces to protect air and sea lines of communication in the exercise region, and to exercise command, control, and communication activities."

Its real intent is still officially classified. But many of those involved now speak freely of how about 350 members of the command staff, as well as commanders from other army units, worked their way through a scenario that proved uncannily prescient. What General Schwarzkopf did in Florida in late July was to examine how the United States would respond to an Iraqi invasion of Kuwait. "Saddam did for real in August what we had been practicing for in July," said Colonel Tony Gain of Central Command. "We had been focused on Iran for years, but then we totally refocused on Iraq and examined this in our Internal Look exercise. We became very familiar with the geography, the country, and the politics."

Indeed, when he arrived in Saudi Arabia one month after the exercise, Major General Barry R. McCaffrey, the commander of the 24th Infantry Division (Mechanized), found that "the maps from Internal Look had acceptable battle graphics on them for the conduct of this operation." In other words, the war games coordinated in Florida were perfectly applicable to the real situation in Saudi Arabia.

It had thus been no great surprise for General Schwarzkopf when JCS Chairman General Colin L. Powell called him on August 2 to announce that Kuwait had been invaded. The CentCom commander replied, "I really thought they would."

Over the next three days, General Schwarzkopf was able to draw on his Internal Look preparations to provide thorough briefings to the President and the National Security Council in meetings at the White House and Camp David. His role was to present the military options. It was clear that Saddam's move, which had already given him control over 27.3 percent of Middle Eastern oil production, posed a serious threat to the very lifeline of Western economies. As CIA satellite photographs showed Iraqi divisions sweeping on southward toward the Saudi Arabian border, bringing Saddam's army within a few hundred miles of oil fields that earned Saudi Arabia $44.6 billion in 1990 alone, his message assumed a dramatic immediacy. The troop deployment Schwarzkopf talked about—over 200,000 U.S. servicemen and -women to defend Saudi Arabia in a four-month buildup, and considerably more forces if the aim was to drive Saddam out of Kuwait—was alarming to the President and his closest advisers. But if, as President Carter had first insisted in

1979 following the Soviet invasion of Afghanistan, any attempt to gain control of the Persian Gulf amounted to "an assault on U.S. vital interests," then a firm response from Washington was imperative. At the very least, President Bush determined that the Saudis must be defended.

But what would Saudi Arabia say? A country forged by its own rulers, rather than carved out on the whim of retreating imperial powers, it is more pragmatic and less prone to hysterical rhetoric than many of its neighbors. Still, it remains hard to fathom. With more than four thousand descendants of the kingdom's founder, Ibn Saud, making up the royal entourage and liable to put in a word at King Fahd's informal majlis, or court, divining the direction of Saudi policy bears some resemblance to gauging the inclinations of the Vatican or the pre-Perestroika Kremlin. But there is an added twist. The House of Saud is a family, albeit a vast and exceptionally powerful one; and the labyrinthine intricacies of family intrigue, raised to the level of national political policy, can make the ploys of devious cardinals or ardent apparatchiks seem like mere child's play.

Moreover, the Saudi monarchy has for decades been torn between its desire for U.S. support of its rigidly conservative, vehemently anti-Communist system and its anger at U.S. backing of Israel. This has led to ambivalence.

In times of vulnerability, such as the moment when an Egyptian-supported Yemeni invasion seemed imminent in 1963, the Saudis had turned to Washington. On the other hand, stating that "America's complete support of Zionism against the Arabs makes it extremely difficult for us to continue to supply U.S. petroleum needs," it was the Saudi King Faisal who imposed the shattering oil embargo of October 20, 1973, which shook the basic assumptions of Western policymaking and effectively ushered in a new economic era. Saudi uncertainty over the country's relationship with the United States grew in 1979 after Washington allowed its staunchest Middle East ally outside Israel, the Shah of Iran, to be summarily ousted. An insistent question began to be heard in the corridors of power in Riyadh: What sort of ally is the United States for a conservative Arab regime surrounded by radical and fundamentalist movements?

So, when General Schwarzkopf arrived in Jidda on August 6, armed with the plan that would become known as Desert Shield, neither he nor Defense Secretary Cheney had a clear sense of the response they would get from the sixty-eight-year-old King Fahd. Would the King share the U.S. view that Saddam now posed an imminent threat to Saudi Arabia's eastern oil fields? Would he accept the arrival of huge numbers of American troops in his devoutly Islamic, deeply secretive kingdom? Would he believe that, this time, Washington was in earnest? General Schwarzkopf's own view, which he related to his family, was that King Fahd would listen carefully and then request a few days in which to reflect.

The delegation's arrival had been preceded by four days of intense discussion within the Saudi royal family, including what diplomats describe as some sharp exchanges between the King and his younger half brother Crown Prince Abdullah, who was intensely wary of any conspicuous U.S. presence. Perhaps as many as four hundred people were involved in these talks; and King Fahd's views were ultimately shaped by an inner circle of about thirty. While such negotiations can rage within the palaces of the desert kingdom, and reveal a whole gamut of views, once a decision is made, it is final and the whole family abides by it. For a central principle of Saudi Arabia is that, in public, the royal family never disagrees. On his deathbed, the founder of the kingdom, Ibn Saud, had summoned his two oldest sons, Saud and Faisal, and told them, "Join hands across my body and swear that you will work together when I am gone. Also swear you will quarrel only in private." Despite the complexity of governing a country that has become the free world's largest oil producer, King Fahd abides by this basic precept.

Schwarzkopf, Cheney, Gates, Wolfowitz, and Freeman were ushered into the King's luxurious quarters. According to the recollection of one of the officials present, the meeting took place in a large room, immediately outside the King's personal suite, where he meets during the summer with his council of ministers. On the left side of the room, beside the King's desk, is an armchair, and it was from here that King Fahd conducted the talks. The U.S. delegation, with Secretary Cheney in the place of honor immediately to the King's right, was seated on a series of banquettes fanning out around the armchair. Although the King speaks reasonably good English—and his command of the language improved dramatically during the crisis—Prince Bandar Bin Sultan, the Saudi ambassador to the United States, acted as an interpreter. Crown Prince Abdullah was also present.

The King opened the talks by recalling his father's meeting with President Franklin D. Roosevelt at the end of World War II. The meeting took place on board the USS *Quincy* in the Great Bitter Lake in the Suez Canal on February 14, 1945. It was on this occasion, in the view of the Saudi royal family, that the special relationship between Washington and Riyadh was formally established. Roosevelt, just two months before his death, promised the Saudis that the United States would be a true ally to them—and a photograph of the meeting still hangs in the U.S. ambassador's office in Riyadh as a reminder of the occasion.

After this formal opening, Secretary Cheney did most of the talking for the U.S. delegation, explaining the President's deep concern over Saddam's invasion and his determination to protect Saudi Arabia. But when the King asked what specific military plans the United States had to confront Saddam, it was Schwarzkopf who, in his firm, clipped tone, outlined the strategy.

Kneeling at one point beside the King with a map, he explained how more than 200,000 troops could be rapidly deployed in northeastern Saudi Arabia, close to the Kuwaiti border, to head off the threat of an Iraqi invasion. Because of the months of preparation that had gone into the plan, he was able to outline in considerable detail the proposed desert deployment of the XVIII Airborne Corps, America's contingency force trained for swift deployment. The general spoke with a genuine conviction born of his own long reflection. Illustrating his points with satellite photographs, he gave the King the latest U.S. intelligence on Iraqi positions. The photographs made the Iraqi advance toward the Saudi border abundantly clear. At that point there is little doubt that, as Schwarzkopf would say later, the Iraqis could have "just driven down the highway and taken" Saudi Arabia's oil fields, the richest in the world.

When Schwarzkopf had finished, the Saudi monarch reflected for a moment and then spoke with an enthusiasm that surprised the U.S. officials. He said that the proposed deployment made sense and expressed his distrust of Saddam. He also underlined that Saudi Arabia was not interested in "some purely symbolic gesture from the United States."

The King's words were carefully measured. In 1979— a watershed year in the Middle East—it was not only the U.S. reaction to the fall of the Shah that had disturbed the Saudis. When conflict in Yemen, on Saudi Arabia's southwestern border, threatened to spill over into the kingdom, King Khalid, Fahd's predecessor, asked President Jimmy Carter for help. The response was the dispatch of two AWAC (airborne warning and control) planes and a squadron of unarmed F-15s: this, in Saudi eyes, was risible. "The last thing the Saudis wanted," said one Western diplomat in Riyadh, "was that the United States arrive with a single aircraft carrier and try to look busy."

The other major Saudi concerns were twofold: that the U.S. deployment should not turn into a permanent presence, and that sensitivity be shown toward the unusual mores of the country. On the first point, Secretary Cheney offered repeated reassurances, while intimating that it would not be a bad thing to leave some equipment behind on the ground at the end of the mission. The second concern was a complex one to address. Saudi Arabia is a nation where everything stops five times a day for prayer, slavery was abolished only in 1962, cinemas are banned, the constitution is the Koran, and women are so concealed by their long black robes, or abayas, that American soldiers would come to refer to them as "BMOs"—black moving objects. But assurances were given to King Fahd that the United States would try to keep its presence discreet. General Schwarzkopf—who had been obliged as a twelve-year-old boy in Iran to learn respect for Islam—was emphatic in his view that Saudi customs and beliefs would not be profaned.

Following the two-and-a-half-hour meeting, Secretary Cheney and General Schwarzkopf returned to the al-Hamra, a Japanese-designed guest palace in Jidda. From here, Secretary Cheney called the President with the news that the Saudis had given the go-ahead for Desert Shield. The President convoked the National Security Council. The next day, August 7, the first American F-15 fighters started to arrive in Dhahran on Saudi Arabia's east coast. The day after that, August 8, the President was ready to tell the nation that "a line has been drawn in the sand" and 50,000 U.S. troops would be deployed in Saudi Arabia as part of a multinational force on a purely defensive mission to be known as Operation Desert Shield. The figure of 50,000 was a deliberate understatement, designed to attenuate political alarm. Meanwhile, General Schwarzkopf returned home to MacDill Air Force Base in Florida knowing that— just as his thirty-four-year army career had appeared to be easing toward a quiet conclusion—he suddenly faced the most complex challenge of his life at the head of the largest U.S. military effort in the two decades since Vietnam.

• • •

But it could easily have been somebody other than H. Norman Schwarzkopf, four-star general, leading this massive deployment in the Middle East. For some time before his appointment to Central Command in November 1988, he had been toying with the idea of retirement, convinced that his best days in the Army were probably behind him.

A passionate outdoorsman and a soldier's soldier, he had never enjoyed life at army headquarters in the capital. There was too much paper-shuffling and political maneuvering for General Schwarzkopf's taste. The Army had attracted him for old-fashioned reasons: its grandeur and its capacity to bring out the heroic in individuals suddenly caught up in something much greater than themselves. The bureaucracy of the Pentagon is the diametric opposite of this.

So his appointment as the Army's deputy chief of staff for Operations and Plans in August 1987 did not thrill him. And as the Washington job palled in the first few months of 1988, while prospects of further promotion appeared somewhat remote, he considered leaving the service. Apart from anything else, he had three children to put through college and he was worried about finding himself financially squeezed.

Schwarzkopf, as usual, shared his concerns with his older sister Sally. In mid-1988, he told her that promotion from three-star rank at the Pentagon to four-star rank was a presidential decision; and that although his job often led to a fourth star, he was not sure he could win out among a plethora of officers nearing the end of their careers and jostling for a few choice appointments. He was tired of the Washington job. It offered him little opportunity to get things done, let alone go fishing, shoot skeet, or spend time with his children. He confided that one four-star job he had hoped for had recently been given to somebody else. And he suggested that he might be better off in a civilian job, perhaps a business involving exchange of students from different parts of the world.

Sally discouraged him from anything precipitate. Over many years, she had developed a profound sense of her brother's visceral attachment to the Army. Through times of disillusionment, she had seen this emotional tie to military life and tradition win out over moods of disgust and impatience. So she told him, "You will be sorry if you leave. It's very different as a civilian. Stick with it, at least for now."

Shortly after this conversation, General Schwarzkopf learned that he was being considered for the four-star post of commander in chief at Central Command. This Florida-based command had been established in 1983 by President Reagan to give a permanent structure to the Rapid Deployment Force set up by President Carter to focus on the Middle East following the Soviet invasion of Afghanistan and the fall of the Shah. But, although involved in a highly sensitive and strategic area, it had never been considered a particularly prestigious place by the Pentagon. Unlike the much-longer-established European, Pacific, Atlantic, and Southern Commands, CentCom has no headquarters in its sprawling area of responsibility, which stretches from Sudan to Pakistan through what many in the military saw as nineteen troubled, distant, and generally mysterious countries. The lack of a base in the countries it monitored reflected many things: uneasiness in many Middle Eastern countries over a conspicuous U.S. presence, U.S. apprehension after the killing of 241 Marines in Beirut in 1983, and the fact that the U.S. alliance with Israel is so strong it has traditionally made other Middle Eastern alliances sensitive. Israel does not fall within CentCom's area of responsibility.

Housed in a two-story prefabricated headquarters at MacDill Air Force Base near Tampa, several thousand miles from the countries it monitors, CentCom was widely seen as a bit of a sleepy hollow. With a permanent staff of just eight hundred, it tended to live up to its reputation. For the Pentagon, the Middle East was a place where the French and British had traditionally been more active than the United States. It was intractable; it was 6,500 miles away by air, as much as 10,000 miles away by sea; and it was treacherous.

"The Joint Chiefs of Staff never took Central Command quite seriously," said General Crist, who was commander there for three years before General Schwarzkopf's arrival. "We'd never fought in the Middle East. Europe and Asia were where we'd been. And it was not a place we wanted to be involved in—certainly not if it took away from Europe."

The command did, however, earn a new prestige in 1987. The Iran–Iraq War threatened shipping in the Gulf, and thirty-seven U.S. soldiers were killed after an Iraqi Exocet missile hit the Navy frigate USS *Stark* on May 17, 1987. Operation Earnest Will, involving about 18,000 U.S. servicemen and -women, was then mounted to defend shipping in the Gulf. Several Kuwaiti tankers were reflagged—placed under U.S. flags—and protected with U.S. navy escorts and army and navy helicopters. The operation suffered from one conspicuous blot: on July 3, 1988, the USS *Vincennes* accidentally shot down an Iranian airliner in the Gulf, killing the 290 people on board. In other respects, the operation was generally a success.

However, General Crist said he still felt some foot-dragging from the Pentagon. When, for example, he wanted minesweepers sent to the area after the Kuwaiti supertanker *Bridgeton* hit a mine on July 24, 1987, he found he had to fend for himself. The Navy declined at that time to commit the ships to the area: it was costly and a distraction from Europe. Moreover, the Navy still believed the Gulf operation would be, as the general put it, "a walk in the sun." So Crist was obliged to hire a couple of Kuwaiti oil equipment service vessels and fit them with World

War II minesweeping equipment unearthed in Norfolk, Virginia. The service-vessels-turned-minesweepers were then renamed *Hunter* and *Striker*. It was only several months later that the Navy did commit its thirty-year-old minesweepers to the area.

The Earnest Will operation would prove important to the future success of the Gulf War operations. The Saudis were extremely touchy about being seen to be helping the U.S. effort in the Gulf. For example, U.S. army helicopters flying out from Saudi Arabia to platforms in the Gulf had to do so after dark and complete the operation before dawn. But the Saudis, while wishing to present an image of independence from the U.S. Earnest Will mission, were in fact extremely concerned about a potential Iranian attack combined with a Shiite uprising. They therefore did a lot of work in 1987 and 1988 with the U.S. military on a communications and command infrastructure, complete with secure telephone lines. The work included the equipping of a special command bunker beneath the Ministry of Defense, which would be used by Schwarzkopf and his staff. An Air Command and Control Center was also constructed in Dhahran on the Gulf coast. Without all this, it would have been far more difficult for Schwarzkopf to install himself and his staff in Riyadh and Dhahran as quickly and effectively as he did.

The Saudi insistence during Earnest Will that the presence of U.S. helicopters in the country not be made public was typical of the general uneasiness in the Middle East over revealing American ties. When CentCom's biannual Bright Star joint military exercises with Egyptian troops were held in Egypt, the fact that some joint military exercises were also taking place in Oman and Jordan was glossed over. When U.S. Ranger and Special Forces troops trained with the Saudis, this, too, was not publicized. The Pentagon, more taken up with events in Europe, was content with this low profile for CentCom. When Crist wanted to pre-position materials for an air base in Oman,

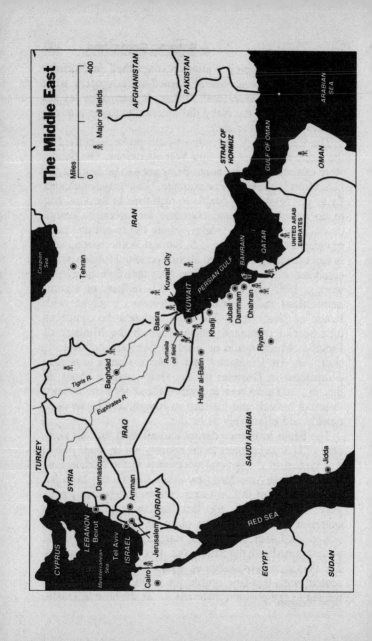

"it all had to be done under the table, with a nod from Secretary of Defense Weinberger, against the foot-dragging of the Joint Chiefs of Staff." In a clear indication of Central Command's standing, Arab military leaders who came to the United States were ushered discreetly to Tampa, far away from the Washington limelight. Concerns over Israeli sensitivity contributed to this practice.

Despite its mixed reputation, General Schwarzkopf was attracted to the Central Command job. It would take him back to more active duty and away from the gloomy corridors of the Pentagon; it would earn him that elusive fourth star; and it would allow him to visit again an area whose mystery and exoticism had seduced him in his childhood years with his family in Tehran. He had been surprised to learn that he was in the running for the post; but once he knew, he was eager to get it.

"He liked the idea of being involved with issues beyond purely military considerations," said retired Lieutenant General Sidney "Tom" Weinstein, a classmate and former deputy chief of staff for Intelligence. "He felt Central Command would be intellectually challenging. And there was also the nostalgic connection."

But there was serious competition for the job. It grew out of a typical inter-service spat. The Navy, impressed by its performance escorting shipping through the Gulf, had decided that Central Command should become a naval job. It recommended Admiral Henry C. Mustin, the Navy's director of plans. The Joint Chiefs of Staff, under chairman Admiral William J. Crowe, Jr., was split. But General Crist wrote a strong recommendation for General Schwarzkopf, noting that the heads of service in the Arab world were all army men—and these were the people that CentCom's commander would be dealing with. In the end, the Secretary of Defense, Frank C. Carlucci, nominated Schwarzkopf and his appointment was approved by President Reagan.

Moving had become a way of life for the Schwarzkopf family. After twenty years of marriage, the general's wife, Brenda, had become a model of the army spouse: supportive, but independently strong, and deeply concerned with the well-being of military families wherever she happened to find herself. So uprooting after less than eighteen months in Washington was not especially difficult.

Florida had much to offer the Schwarzkopfs. The CentCom headquarters building, with its windowless ground floor and narrow tinted windows on the second floor, is not particularly attractive. But it is surrounded by palm trees and azaleas and is in a singularly lush base that abuts the sea. There is a golf course on the premises; and soldiers are often seen jogging along the seafront. The base is an ideal place for long walks and for living the sort of outdoors life that General Schwarzkopf and his family prefer. Washington immediately seemed no more than a gray memory.

A two-story, four-bedroom Spanish-colonial-style house, with a red-tile roof and white stucco walls, awaited them. It was comfortable, although not as luxurious as some of their former homes, such as the mansion they had in Fort Lewis, Washington. Only the dining room, in deference to the tastes of the Arab generals who would be entertained there, was huge. The family settled in quickly. Taking up his duties on November 23, 1988, Schwarzkopf plunged with relish into his new responsibilities, traveling widely in the Middle East as he gradually developed the ideas that he would be called upon to demonstrate in August 1990.

His family immediately saw a change in him. He was delighted to return to the Islamic world that had intrigued him as a child, and he bubbled over with enthusiasm. Always, like his father, an avid collector, the general came back from his visits with assorted souvenirs: Arab coffeepots, tea sets, beautiful ivory rhinoceroses and elephants, brass objects, and rugs. His wife despaired of the clutter filling their home. There was scarcely an empty space left on the walls, despite the fact that, unlike many military men, General Schwarzkopf does not hang up his medals, badges, awards, and accolades for all to see.

On one Middle Eastern trip, to North Yemen in early 1989, General Schwarzkopf was accompanied by Lieutenant General Weinstein. There Schwarzkopf made such an impression on President Ali Abdullah Saleh that he insisted on seeing the general alone, much to the chagrin of the U.S. ambassador, who was asked to leave the presidential suite. From North Yemen, Weinstein and Schwarzkopf went on to the small state of Djibouti, across the Gulf of Aden, where they stayed in a hotel with a casino. For years, the two men had been talking about going to Atlantic City: Schwarzkopf has a taste for blackjack. So, having failed to reach the New Jersey resort, they agreed to make up for it by meeting at 9:00 p.m. at the entrance to the Djibouti casino.

Weinstein waited, but Schwarzkopf never appeared. After a grueling day, he had fallen asleep. "He didn't miss much. It was a terrible casino and I lost," Weinstein recalled.

On a subsequent trip, to Kuwait in 1989, the general was asked by his hosts to don a traditional long dishdasha robe. This deferential gesture came naturally to him— and it was also appealing to the romantic side of General Schwarzkopf. He could not resist performing a quick twirl in front of his hotel mirror. The vision that came to him was of T. E. Lawrence, the legendary Lawrence of Arabia, who had scoffed at his British commanding officers' poker-faced disapproval of "going native." Like Lawrence, Schwarzkopf was drawn to the Middle East by more than official duty; and he was prepared to adapt to an environment where rules are replaced by infinite nuance and where form can be as important as substance.

The other vision that came to the general was that of his father, who, forty-six years earlier, had first depicted the robes of the Arabs to him. In a long letter to the family dated April 23, 1943, Schwarzkopf Sr. had described a visit to the Iranian town of Khorramshahr near the Iraqi border, where he noted that there were many Arabs. He went on to describe the habitual dress of most men as being very much like an old-fashioned nightgown, adding that the men all wore some kind of rag around their heads. It was Schwarzkopf's father who first taught him the art of pliancy amid the languor and varied customs of the Middle East.

But his new command had frustrations. As he traveled, the general noted how Middle Eastern countries, especially Saudi Arabia, were turning increasingly to other countries, such as Britain, France, and Brazil, for their military hardware. Everywhere, U.S. commitment was questioned. Convinced that U.S. security assistance was the cornerstone of safeguarding vital U.S. interests in the area, the general could not always hide his irritation at the way the changes sweeping the Soviet Union and Eastern Europe became the obsession of the top brass in Washington. As he would comment acidly to senators early in 1990, "With no permanently assigned ground forces, CentCom must be considered a bargain command." It was, however, about to prove its worth.

Between August 7 and 13, 1990, there was a chaotic scene at the steamy port of Savannah, Georgia, that typified General Schwarzkopf's problems as he sought to make the plan he had shown to President Bush and King Fahd a reality. Transporting over 200,000 men and women and all their equipment to a distant country was a colossal undertaking.

The 24th Infantry Division (Mechanized)—the so-called Victory Division, for which Schwarzkopf had conceived a particular affection when he commanded it in 1983–85—was hustling to load its tanks, Bradley fighting vehicles, supplies, water, ammunition, air defense equipment, and

POL—petroleum, oil, and lubricants—onto the first of a series of ships that would travel the eight thousand miles to the port of Dhahran on Saudi Arabia's eastern seaboard in the Persian Gulf. Dhahran, in the heart of the desert kingdom's oil-producing area, was the best base from which to move north into defensive positions closer to the Kuwaiti border.

But the loading operation at Savannah did not go smoothly. "We had to assemble the ammunition from nine different plants around the United States, and we had hundreds and hundreds of truckloads of ammunition coming in," said Major General McCaffrey, the division's forty-eight-year-old commander, a veteran of Vietnam with the heavy scars of a machine-gun wound on his left forearm. "We had to waive hundreds of regulations of the Coast Guard, the port of Savannah, and the interstate highway system, because we shipped fully uploaded for combat, and I was not going to have it any other way. At one point, there were three hundred people in a giant bureaucratic battle in Savannah, and we were being told: *You can't do it this way.* You must go to Saudi Arabia and meet your ammunition and your fuel there. And my answer was no. We're going to upload this ship so we're ready to fight. And when we're finished, you tell the Chief of Naval Operations why the ship won't sail!"

Without knowing it, McCaffrey was setting the tone for the conduct of the entire seven-month campaign. General Schwarzkopf had long ago learned to be a leader who gives considerable leeway to the commanders he trusts and respects. That trust has to be earned, but, once earned, it is generous. While keeping a careful scrutiny of the overall operation under his command, Schwarzkopf never meddled in details—or asked questions about how things got done so long as they were done. Given this freedom, which they tended in turn to entrust to their own subordinates, commanders improvised unceasingly in an effort to solve the problems of an operation of staggering complexity. Their attitude was eloquent testimony to the reforms in military leadership pushed through since Vietnam, as mindless severity was gradually replaced by a discipline based on the intelligence and responsibility of a professional group of men and women. As Lieutenant General William G. "Gus" Pagonis, the chief of logistics in Saudi Arabia, later commented, "Everything goes wrong every minute. What you do is fix it!"

McCaffrey's own fix-it attitude was rooted in a sober pragmatism. As the first ship was loaded, in six days six hours and fifteen minutes, he could only guess what might await the 24th on arrival. "We had no idea what we'd face when we got there. What if Dhahran had been taken by Saddam and we'd had to unload in the Red Sea or go into Cairo? There was no way I was going to agree to meeting my ammunition over there. Then I had a fight with the Navy over how many soldiers could ride on the ship to take care of the equipment. Normally, it's no more than eight; they don't like too many army soldiers hanging around the ship. I wanted one hundred soldiers, and I got them. I also got a doctor on board, and a minister and a major and our chemical warfare equipment. We were going to fight to defend our ship no matter what we faced."

Back in Tampa, as he prepared to depart for the Gulf, General Schwarzkopf was also desperately worried about what the first troops on the ground in the area would find. Everything was moving with astonishing speed and it was hard to keep pace with events. But the general was proud to have just completed the Internal Look exercise, which gave him a very useful head start. He was also pleased by a development that was to play a crucial role in the campaign. Chairman Powell was not a very familiar figure to Schwarzkopf before the crisis broke. He had been appointed chairman of the Joint Chiefs of Staff after Schwarzkopf's departure for Florida from Washington. But as Schwarzkopf got to know him in the days after the Iraqi invasion of August 2, 1990, he was enormously impressed by Powell's candor and clarity. Before leaving for the Gulf, Schwarzkopf had, in the words of his sister Sally, decided that "Powell's terrific. He's very straight. Norm's kind of guy."

A strong partnership was needed to confront Saddam. He had shown his determination by annexing Kuwait on August 8; and he had revealed, yet again, his ghoulish taste by declaring a week later that "thousands of Americans will return home in body bags." As the first battalions of the 101st Airborne Division (Air Assault), the 82nd Airborne Division, and the 24th Infantry Division arrived in the Saudi Gulf coast towns of Dhahran, Dammam, and Jubail in August, they were indeed acutely vulnerable. The Iraqis were only 250 miles away in Kuwait, with a huge array of tanks.

In the view of retired army Colonel David C. Hackworth, "The U.S. forces initially amounted to no more than speed bumps in the desert for Saddam's tank army. A huge risk was taken in the early days." Although they had some air protection, particularly from the aircraft massing on U.S. carriers in the Gulf, the U.S. forces were at first little match for the Iraqi tank divisions gathered at the Kuwaiti-Saudi border.

Major Richard Rowe of the XVIII Airborne Corps was among the first soldiers into Saudi Arabia. He arrived on a C-141 transporter that left Pope Air Force Base adjoining Fort Bragg on August 8—the day President Bush announced he was drawing a line in the sand— and arrived in Dhahran on August 9. There were seventy-seven people on board, the vulnerable fore- runners of a force that would, by the following Feb- ruary, exceed 500,000. They did not have much more than their personal weapons, some shoulder-fired Sting- er surface-to-air missiles, and a few so-called Humvees, the latter-day jeeps whose initials—HMMWV—stand for "high-mobility, multi-purpose wheeled vehicle."

"We got off that plane with our helmets on," Major

Rowe recalled, "because we thought the Iraqis might attack at any moment."

In fact, it is now clear that the first of Saddam's many mistakes was not to pursue his blitzkrieg in August on down the Saudi coast to Dhahran—a 250-mile swoop that would have given him control of vital ports and airfields, as well as Saudi Arabia's oil. As General Powell was to comment later, "It would have taken us a lot longer, and it would have been a much more difficult proposition, to have to kick the Iraqi Army out of Saudi Arabia as well as Kuwait." Put bluntly, the U.S. Armed Forces would no longer have had the ports they used to get into Saudi Arabia at a point close to Kuwait. The alternative site for a Saudi landing, the Red Sea coast, is almost a thousand miles away.

But General Schwarzkopf trusted his instinct that a man who had thought he could invade Kuwait with impunity would not take the great additional risk of invading Saudi Arabia, because that would inevitably bring an eventual armed response of massive proportions. He also knew that if Saddam pushed down the coast, the move would extend his fragile lines of communication and logistics to a point never tested in the largely static Iran-Iraq War. Schwarzkopf used every means to intimidate Saddam. One was to ensure that the press had good access to film the equipment and soldiers that were arriving in Saudi Arabia, so fostering the illusion that the United States was already present in force. It was not the first time that Schwarzkopf—a man who can charm the press but also harbors a basic mistrust of newspapermen that was inherited from his father—would manipulate media coverage of the war to his advantage.

In the midst of his anxious preparations, on August 22, General Schwarzkopf celebrated his fifty-sixth birthday. It was a bittersweet occasion. The day before, in a phrase he would not be allowed to forget, Saddam promised "the mother of all battles" if an attempt was made to free Kuwait by force. With such invective hanging over them, it was impossible for the Schwarzkopfs to feel carefree on an occasion marked in past years by the general's self-deprecating buffoonery, magic tricks, and good humor. The family celebrated alone. Sally gave her brother a lithograph of two polar bears by the artist Martin Solberg. Schwarzkopf is a lover of works depicting nature. Although tense, Brenda was able to joke about having to buy a mansion to accommodate this alongside the family's growing art collection.

By this time, Schwarzkopf had brought together his three children, Cynthia, Jessica, and Christian, and explained to them that he would soon be leaving on an important mission that should be a source of pride to them.

But there was a pained moment when they asked, "Dad, what do you want for Christmas?"

After some reflection, General Schwarzkopf replied, "Well, I might not be home for Christmas."

In a family for whom Christmas is a sacred and elaborate occasion, this was hard to swallow. But the general did not want Brenda or his children to harbor any illusion that his Middle East mission might not take many months. Accordingly, Brenda worked on preparing for a long haul: she did not want to be disappointed.

She did this, in part, because she knew from the outset that it would be a point of honor with the general that, once gone, he would not return to the United States even for a briefing. He simply did not want his troops to feel that he had privileges they were denied. This was quintessential Schwarzkopf: an understated gesture that, over the course of many months, did much for the morale of his soldiers, particularly on holidays such as Thanksgiving and Christmas when thoughts turned to home with particular poignancy.

Four days after his birthday, on Sunday, August 26, General Schwarzkopf departed for Riyadh, an ugly city crisscrossed by new six-lane highways and dotted with bright new buildings combining oil-funded monumentality and traditional Islamic motifs in a seldom felicitous blend. On arrival in this sprawling capital in the middle of the desert, he set up his secret headquarters in the heavily guarded basement, two floors beneath the Saudi Ministry of Defense and Aviation, that had been equipped during Operation Earnest Will. The modern ministry, with its tapestries, ficus trees, and ground-floor mosque, is a bright building, a far cry from the gloom of the Pentagon. But for security reasons, General Schwarzkopf made his base in an airless place reached through nine-inch-thick doors that give the impression of entering a safe.

To get there, the general had to walk every day past a faintly ominous sign reading: "All weapons must be cleared (unloaded) prior to entering the command center." Then he went down one floor in an elevator, and continued downward on a long flight of stairs, leaving the bustle of King Abdul Aziz Street far behind. This bunker, with its harsh lighting, its white floors, its countless clocks, maps, TV screens, and portable computers, was to be the place where the general spent most of the next seven months. At times, he felt starved for the sounds of nature to the point that he would listen to a tape of birdsong and other sounds of the outside world. It was one way to overcome the sometimes suffocating sense of being cocooned from the living and breathing world.

In his bedroom, initially a comfortable place in the ministry and later a rather Spartan cell in the bunker itself, he arrayed photographs of his wife and children. He also placed a photograph of his father and found his thoughts turning to him with an insistence he had never known before. Where the Lindbergh case had been the moment of truth for his father—the instant in which the slow passage of life built suddenly to a crisis—this was Schwarzkopf's hour. He knew that his father would be proud of him; and he looked to him as never before for inspiration. Old precepts—the West Point motto of "Duty,

Honor, Country," respect for the ways of other cultures, care and fairness toward those in one's command—which had been drummed into him as a young man guided him. But more than that, so, too, did his father's emotional way of expressing his love for his children.

Several years earlier, the general's sister Sally had given him a special gift for Father's Day. It consisted of a series of photographs in which she illustrated the uncannily parallel courses of the two men's lives. There was a picture of General Schwarzkopf as a young boy in uniform beside a like one of his father. There was another of the general as a West Point cadet, next to his father during his unruly West Point days. On later pages there were photographs of the two men with their children, who were born in the same order: each had a daughter, then a second daughter, and then a son. General Schwarzkopf had looked at the album in silence for some time. Then he had risen from the sofa where he was sitting. When he reached Sally and hugged her, he was crying.

As he thought of his family, such overwhelming emotion often affected the general during the months in Riyadh, but he never let it show. For example, when his eyes watered during an interview with *U.S. News & World Report*, he urged the magazine not to use that photograph. He was determined that Saddam should see nothing he might interpret as weakness. He also had to set an example to the gathering allied military force in Saudi Arabia.

Schwarzkopf's arrival at the ministry had been preceded a couple of days earlier by that of many of the Central Command staff who would work most closely with him. Colonel Tony Gain, who oversaw the Joint Operations Center, arrived on August 24. The center acted as the Operations and Intelligence headquarters for the campaign. It was just down the corridor from the War Room itself, where General Schwarzkopf ensconced himself in a large leather executive-style chair facing a wall of maps. Here he received the information sifted and passed on to him twenty-four hours a day by the Joint Operations Center. A staff of about seventy people, mainly plucked from CentCom in Florida, worked twelve-hour shifts seven days a week for seven months. "An eight-hour shift was insufficient to really master the battlefield," said Colonel Gain. "And our fighting people were going twenty-four hours a day, so we had to keep pace with them."

The staff included navy, air, army, marine, air defense, intelligence, and civic affairs officers. There were lawyers to provide expertise on the rules of military engagement, experts on chemical warfare, and communications specialists who rapidly set up satellite communications. On his table in the War Room, General Schwarzkopf had a bank of sixteen secure phones, including a red one that was the hot line to Chairman Powell and another hot line to the President.

The Command Center, using several cameras, regularly beamed information to the general on three television screens in the War Room. The fourth screen was often tuned to CNN—a useful source of information, and an occasional source of extreme irritation, throughout the war. Maps were constantly updated with the latest Iraqi troop movements, and, according to his staff, Schwarzkopf would spend hours poring over these as he worked to pinpoint the most effective strategy for confronting Saddam.

The general's overwhelming initial concern was that there might be an Iraqi attack. In late August, intelligence reports still suggested Saddam might be ready to move down the Saudi Arabian coast. A priority was to organize effective air defense for the still-flimsy forces on the ground. In a key move, General Schwarzkopf placed Air Force Lieutenant General Charles A. Horner, another hardened Vietnam veteran, in charge of the coalition's air operations, declaring in effect that "if you don't want Horner to be the boss, take your air force home." After his long experience of interservice squabbles, Schwarzkopf was clear on one thing: he was going to make the goals clear and then get everybody to work together toward them.

Diplomatic efforts by President George Bush and Secretary of State James Baker had already brought several European and Arab countries into a rapidly expanding coalition to confront Iraq. In time, this coalition would come to embrace thirty-three countries. Working together in a clear chain of command was more essential than ever.

A few days after he arrived, Schwarzkopf flew by helicopter to Dhahran, where many of the first U.S. troops into Saudi Arabia were still huddled. On the tarmac at Dhahran airport, a forlorn-looking blue-and-white Kuwaiti Airlines Boeing 747 would stand throughout the coming months: the airline's slogan became "To Kuwait Any Day Now."

From the scattered plants of the Arabian American Oil Company (Aramco), smoke billowed into the clear blue sky. It was not far from Dhahran airport, on March 20, 1938, that an American engineer, Karl S. Twitchell, first struck oil in what was to become the biggest and richest field in the world. Originally owned by Standard Oil of California, the fields came under a hundred percent Saudi ownership only a decade ago. But as the Aramco name suggests, Saudi oil remains at the root of the special U.S.-Saudi relationship; and several thousand Americans still work at the company's plant. Indeed, a big sign just outside the headquarters, written in English, reads: "Drive Carefully. Your Family Awaits You."

As early as 1942, a U.S. government memorandum stated that "it is our strong belief that the development of Saudi Arabian petroleum resources should be viewed in the light of the broad national interest." And a year later, on February 18, 1943, President Frankin D. Roosevelt called Saudi Arabia "vital to the defense of the United States" when he approved a large aid package.

Schwarzkopf had studied the region's history. And as his statement to the Senate Armed Services Committee earlier in the year suggested, he knew that the precious liquid beneath the sands around Dhahran was central to his mission. The Persian Gulf is the world's oil headquarters, and the world's only remaining superpower was not about to abandon it to the whims of an Iraqi from Tikrit who had made good through a combination of ambition, guile, and terror.

Schwarzkopf was returning to an area familiar to his father, who had visited the Gulf, from the Iranian side, in April 1943. There he had noted a rather daunting scene for the gendarmerie he was establishing. Iranian smugglers were ferrying wheat, opium, and dates across the Gulf to Arab traders, who gave them cloth, rifles, and ammunition in return. The gendarmerie was supposed to break up this activity, but with no communications, transportation, or coastal patrol, their task was rather hopeless.

Thirty-seven years later, the task before the general also seemed daunting. Around Dhahran, Schwarzkopf found the U.S. mission in a state of rather dismal confusion. Thousands of soldiers were holed up in several warehouses at the nearby port of Dammam, where they were sleeping on makeshift cots. The temperature was close to 120 degrees and the humidity 100 percent. The MREs, or army-issue "meals ready to eat," that would later earn considerable popularity among the Bedouins for such dishes as chicken à la king, had not yet arrived. So soldiers from the 24th Division, many of whom arrived on August 23, were eating whatever the Saudis could provide. There was very little transportation available, so commanders were renting civilian vehicles.

The 101st Airborne had arrived. So, too, had the 82nd Airborne with nine parachute infantry battalions and the Marines with five infantry battalions. But there was still alarmingly little on the ground with which to confront any Iraqi assault. There were some M551 Sheridan light tanks in the area around Dhahran, but most soldiers had little more than their personal weapons, hand grenades, and some anti-tank rockets. Certainly, any Iraqi attack would have faced a pounding from navy and air force aircraft. But the U.S. commanders knew they would have been hard pressed to withstand Saddam even in the last ten days of August.

"The thought I had was that he might come, he sure might," said Lieutenant General Gary E. Luck, the commander of the XVIII Airborne Corps, whose divisions include the 1st Cavalry, the 82nd Airborne, the 101st Airborne (Air Assault), and the 24th Infantry (Mechanized). "And if Saddam did, we would do what we could to make it painful for him. With our Apache helicopters and aviation, we could do that. I'm not saying we could have defended against him or defeated him. But we could make it painful. And the Iraqis knew that, too."

Nervousness was running high. A mechanized division like the 24th is trained to exploit speed and mobility in wide-open spaces. As it was, when Schwarzkopf visited, they were still trying to get out of the city into the desert. On the weekend before he came (August 25 and 26), speculation over an Iraqi attack reached fever pitch. The division hurriedly developed a plan to fight as light infantry in the city of Dhahran. Air attacks, Scud missile attacks, or chemical attacks were expected at any moment. Every night, generals would put together impromptu plans called Desert Dragon (the dragon is the symbol of the XVIII Corps) to outline what they would do in the event of an immediate Iraqi attack. Later, Schwarzkopf would insist that they maintain this policy, ensuring every night, before they went to bed, that they were ready, if necessary, to go to war the next morning. "God, it was nasty," said Major Tom O'Brien of the 24th Division, recalling those early days in Saudi Arabia.

When Schwarzkopf arrived, soldiers crowded around him. His very presence—the knowledge that the commander in chief, or CINC (pronounced "sink"), was in the country—was a tremendous morale boost. Several years earlier, when he was the commander of the 24th Division—

known as the Victory Division—the general had become famous for the rousing speech he made every year on Victory Day. It became known as the "Carve-a-V-in-the-Forehead" speech. Schwarzkopf, then a two-star general, would stand in front of 16,000 soldiers at Fort Stewart, Georgia, and bring them to a frenzy as he declared that "we're gonna carve a V in the forehead of every enemy soldier."

Now, in a more sober mood, he still exuded a conviction that all would be well: that out of this rather unseemly morass at the port a victorious force would be forged. He shook hands with soldiers, mingled, conveyed that he was one of them; such scenes were to become familiar in Saudi Arabia as the general sought to make each soldier his own.

Corporal Stephanie Hikia recalled that at one point General Schwarzkopf gave her and her husband a big bear hug: "He brings you in real nice and tight, like he's your dad." On a separate occasion, Major Tom Nickerson, of the Army Public Affairs staff, had the same reaction. A six-foot man with bulging muscles, he felt small when the six-foot three-inch CINC approached him. "I don't consider myself a small guy," he said, "but when the general put his arm around me, I felt like a little kid." It was Schwarzkopf's unusual achievement to retain authority over his troops while conveying this intimate sense of caring that made soldiers feel they had a father-like figure ordering them into battle.

More than two thousand years earlier, the Chinese warrior-philosopher Sun Tzu had written: "Look upon your soldiers as you do infants, and they willingly go into deep valleys with you; look upon your soldiers as beloved children, and they willingly die with you." Schwarzkopf, as he would throughout the campaign, embodied this ancient military wisdom even as he waged war with the most elaborate instruments of destruction created by modern technology.

While he became a father figure to his troops, Schwarzkopf never stopped worrying about his own children. As a child, he had suffered the prolonged absence of his own father during World War II. He knew the enormous—and enormously treacherous—task confronting him. Returning to Riyadh, he called home, as he would about twice a week through most of his stay. At the end of the conversation, he told his family, "Pray for peace."

Over the coming months, he would end every conversation with them with those three simple words.

7

Strength Against Weakness

To me an unnecessary action, or shot, or
casualty, was not only waste but sin.
—T. E. Lawrence

General H. Norman Schwarzkopf came to Saudi
Arabia with an open mind. In wars in Asia and the
Caribbean, he had seen the unexpected happen far too
often to be a believer in rigid plans or the strict application of military doctrine. Flexibility, he knew, would be
essential; and he suspected that Saddam Hussein, drilled in
his country's mulish eight-year slugging match with Iran,
might lack this ability. But on one thing the general and
his top commanders were utterly inflexible: there would
be no repetition of Vietnam. In place of a war like Vietnam,
fought with vague objectives and limited means, here in the
Gulf—if General Schwarzkopf had anything to do with it—
there would be a war waged with precise objectives and
unlimited firepower.

On his return from Saigon twenty years earlier,
Schwarzkopf had declared roundly, "I hate what Vietnam
has done to our country. I hate what Vietnam has done to
our Army." An enthusiastic young officer when he left for
Asia, he had returned to state publicly that he was unsure
whether he would ever go to war again. In the pursuit of a
mission that increasingly appeared senseless, he had seen

lives lost through the stupidity of self-serving officers—something he is unable to forgive to this day. He had observed officers of integrity reduced to lying over body counts; indeed, he had been obliged to make up some numbers himself.

In 1965, on his first Vietnamese tour, stationed close to the Cambodian border, he had also seen the futility of a limited war: the Viet Cong would repeatedly flee across the border and regroup because they knew that political constraints on the U.S. military left Cambodia a safe haven. And be had watched as soldiers' legs were ripped off by mines in the capture of strategic hills that were then abandoned to the Viet Cong a month or two later.

In the end, Vietnam, the longest war in the history of the United States, had not been measurable in terms of the defeat of enemy forces or the capture of territory—the clear yardsticks that made the struggle in World War II a source of pride to Americans and the other Allied forces. It had been measurable only in terms of the steady accumulation of years and deaths. During the Gulf operation, Schwarzkopf was determined that, in absolute contrast to the Vietnamese debacle, clarity, clout, cohesiveness, and dispatch should prevail.

At the age of fifty-six, Schwarzkopf was a mature man. He had seen death close up and come close to it himself. His fascination with the great battles of history had been tempered by his knowledge of what he calls the "profanity of war." He had raised a family and achieved professional recognition. He knew his two very different weaknesses: his soft heart and the coiled spring of energy inside him that could snap suddenly into rage; and he had learned to control them both. Surrounded by people who saluted him, he had not smothered his emotions in order to play the role of the martinet.

Thus he embarked on the biggest mission of his life with these conflicting qualities: the equanimity born of long experience and self-knowledge; and the peculiar, bristling restlessness born of his unquenchable emotional nature. As a battalion commander in Vietnam, he had felt the extraordinary weight of his responsibility: the responsibility of ordering young men into situations where they risked their lives. As the commander in chief in Riyadh, hundreds of miles from the front on the Kuwaiti border, that sense of personal accountability for the half-million men and women under his command continued to grip and haunt him as if he were still under fire in the lush environs of My Lai.

He was not alone in this attitude. The Gulf operation was led by men who were lieutenants, captains, majors, and lieutenant colonels in Vietnam.

From up close they had all seen jaws shot off, limbs amputated, young lives extinguished. This experience changed them. They had understood, with a mixture of rage and disgust, what political meddling and procrastination can do on a battlefield. Theirs was the shame of defeat in a war they felt they were never allowed to fight; theirs the humiliation of public hostility. They became, many of them, soldiers' soldiers, and they worked quietly over many years to refashion the Armed Forces. Wherever Schwarzkopf turned—to Chairman Powell, deputy commander Army Lieutenant General Calvin A. H. Waller, Marine commander Lieutenant General Walter E. Boomer, Air Force commander Lieutenant General Charles A. Horner, deputy air commander Brigadier General Buster C. Glosson, Army commander Lieutenant General John J. Yeosock, Navy commander Vice Admiral Stanley R. Arthur, chief logistician Lieutenant General William G. "Gus" Pagonis, XVIII Airborne Corps commander Lieutenant General Gary E. Luck, or VII Corps commander Lieutenant General Frederick M. Franks, Jr.—he found men for whom Vietnam had been a pivotal experience. General Franks lost his right leg there, and everyone lost something of himself. As General Boomer said, "We made a lot of stupid mistakes in Vietnam, mistakes we were not going to repeat here."

Even beneath this top level of command, there were many who had been shaped by the Vietnamese trauma. Brigadier General Joe N. Frazar, for example, was the assistant commander for Support in the 24th Division (Mechanized) in Saudi Arabia. He had done two tours in Vietnam, in the 11th Armored Cavalry Regiment in 1966–67, and then in the 3rd Squadron of the 5th Cavalry Regiment in 1969–70. His views were virulent:

"I personally despised the experience of Vietnam. For ten years afterward, I never talked about it, never read a book about it. I did not believe in the war at all. I did not know if it was relevant or irrelevant. I don't think we were trained for the fight. I don't think our leadership was good. In fact, it let us down. There was too much political meddling. As a lieutenant, I had no idea what our real objective was over there. My own military objective was one thing. But when was this thing going to end? How were we going to fight it? So I think that when we committed ourselves to this war in the Gulf, we all made a personal commitment that, for our part, we were not going to let our soldiers, airmen, navy go through the same experience, or have the same outcome as Vietnam. I felt that personally from General Schwarzkopf. For one thing, if possible, we were not going to rotate soldiers, because the annual replacement system in Vietnam just destroyed coherent units and their will to fight. For another, we were not going to talk body count. For another, we had the personal assurance of General Schwarzkopf that President Bush was going to allow the military to fight this war."

Major General Barry McCaffrey, the commander of the 24th Division in Saudi Arabia, was another member of General Schwarzkopf's generation who was deeply marked by Vietnam. He spent two and a half years there, was wounded three times, lost his brother-in-law and his best friend. He said, "Vietnam was a great tragedy, a tremendous tragedy. We fought a war for idealistic purposes, and we tried to do it on the cheap. We forgot that armies don't fight wars, countries fight wars. There were tremendous political and military constraints that prevented any serious possibility of resolving the conflict. I never lost a fight in Vietnam, *ever*, as a company commander, or as a battalion adviser to the Vietnamese airborne. I did okay. The country lost the war. And coming out of it, my generation—the people now leading the operation here in the Gulf—felt abused by the generals, by the politicians, by the country. So what did we do differently here? Oh, God bless them, everything! Powell and Schwarzkopf would never allow us to be put in that situation. They would have taken off their uniforms before they allowed that."

As he settled into his defensive mission, Schwarzkopf worked continually to ensure that the lessons of Vietnam were applied. From the time of his arrival on August 26, he worked seven days a week, often putting in fifteen-hour days, beginning with staff meetings at 7 a.m. and continuing well into the evening. He ate in the War Room and slept no more than four to five hours a night. Every day, he talked to Powell, usually in the midafternoon. There was unity of purpose between them: they were running the show. In Defense Secretary Cheney and the President they found two civilians equally committed to avoiding political micromanagement of the battlefield. As Cheney said on September 12, 1990, "The President belongs to what I call the 'Don't-screw-around school of military strategy.' "

Unlike President Johnson in the Vietnam years, Bush, a former pilot during World War II, would never try his hand at selecting bombing targets. The President was emphatic: "This will not be another Vietnam. This will not be a protracted, drawn-out war." He added, "If there must be a war, we will not permit our troops to have their hands tied behind their backs. If one American soldier has to go into battle, that soldier will have enough force behind him to win and then get out as soon as possible."

That force arrived faster than initially believed possible. Troops and cargo poured into Saudi Arabia in September. They arrived on ships and the big C-5A/B Galaxy, C-141B StarLifter, and C-130 Hercules transports, gradually easing the acute problem of vulnerability that the general faced in August. By the end of September, when the M1A1 tanks of the 24th Division started arriving, the allied positions, on Saudi Arabia's east coast between Dhahran and the Kuwaiti border, were reasonably secure. Every day the window was closed a little.

But if more troops and armor brought security, they also sharply compounded the problems of organization. One of the Vietnamese lessons Schwarzkopf kept in mind was the importance of avoiding inter-force rivalry. This was a problem that had also plagued the Armed Forces in their abortive 1980 mission to rescue the U.S. hostages held in Tehran and again in the 1983 Grenada invasion. Nowhere was integration more essential than in the air, where divvying up between forces had often caused chaos during the Vietnamese air war.

Early on, it was evident to Schwarzkopf that one area where his coalition had clear superiority over Iraq was in the air. His ground forces, although growing stronger daily, would depend heavily on the support of aviation to withstand any Iraqi attack. So he pressed Lieutenant General Horner to develop a cohesive air option as quickly as possible. When Air Force Chief of Staff General Michael J. Dugan visited Riyadh on September 12 and 13, this preparation was in full swing; and it continued after Dugan's dismissal a few days later for revealing to the press that Baghdad would be targeted in any air campaign. Dugan's letter to Schwarzkopf thanking him for the hospitality in Riyadh was never answered.

After the initial arrival of Air Force F-15 Eagle fighters on August 8, a mass of other air power was becoming available in the form of U.S. Air Force F-4G Wild Weasel air-defense-missile-hunting fighters, the F-111 Aardvark fighter-bomber, the F-16 Falcon attack fighter, veteran B-52 bombers, the bat-like F-117 Stealth fighter, AWAC planes, the ungainly A-10 Thunderbolt anti-tank aircraft known as the "Warthog," EF-111 Ravens for electronic jamming, French Mirage fighters, British Tornado F3 interceptors, U.S. Navy F-14 Tomcat interceptors and A-6 Intruder attack bombers, U.S. Marine F/A-18 Hornet fighters, and Saudi Tornado GR1 bombers. It was an awesome array of destructive force. Horner and Glosson, based in another bunker at the headquarters of the Royal Saudi Air Force, not far from Schwarzkopf's War Room in the bowels of the Ministry of Defense, worked furiously to mold these and numerous other aircraft into a single force capable of unleashing the most lethal air assault in the history of warfare. Their preparations, in offices that became known as the "Black Hole," would eventually allow an armada of over 2,500 warplanes to work from the same computerized common tasking order: Horner called it "a sheet of music that everybody sings the same song off."

Singing the same song was even more difficult on the ground. From shortly after Iraq's August 2 invasion, President Bush and Secretary of State James Baker had worked adroitly to put together what would become a thirty-three-nation military coalition.[1] Forging such a coalition was a tremendous political achievement. But it created a military dilemma. Schwarzkopf was presented with the strategic and diplomatic challenge of fashioning a unified force from this disparate bunch, a task that was, in its way,

---

[1]*The members of the coalition were Afghanistan, Argentina, Australia, Bahrain, Bangladesh, Belgium, Britain, Canada, Czechoslovakia, Denmark, Egypt, France, Germany, Greece, Italy, Kuwait, Morocco, the Netherlands, New Zealand, Niger, Norway, Oman, Pakistan, Poland, Qatar, Saudi Arabia, Senegal, South Korea, Spain, Syria, Turkey, United Arab Emirates, and the United States.

perhaps more complex than that of General Eisenhower during World War II. At the same time, Schwarzkopf had to ensure that the old rivalries between the four U.S. forces—Army, Navy, Marines, and Air Force—did not resurface.

He proved remarkably adept. Initially perceived by the British and some others as a caricature of the U.S. military man—the loud, guffawing commander made notorious around the world in shows such as "M*A*S*H"—he went on to surprise them with his sensitivity and tact. The British were struck by the way Schwarzkopf would sometimes talk about his boyhood in Iran, his respect for Islam, and the importance of sensitivity to Saudi feelings.

More often than not, in meetings, the public bluster of "Stormin' Norman" was replaced by a thoughtfulness that impressed his partners. At one point, Lieutenant General Sir Peter Edgar de la Cour de la Billiere, the commander of the British forces, called him rude. But Air Vice Marshal Ian Macfadyen, the chief of staff of the British forces, said people quickly discovered that "his rudeness was not aimed at people, it was aimed at things. He was a considerable diplomat, even as one sensed that he could overpower people if he wanted. Like all great commanders, he could see the big picture. We quickly got a sense that we were at the top table, and the old Anglo-U.S. special relationship was working."

Indeed, over the months, General de la Billiere and Schwarzkopf became very close friends. Schwarzkopf told his family that the British general's expertise on the Middle East was invaluable, and that he had come to depend on him a great deal. De la Billiere, in turn, formed an enormous respect for Schwarzkopf, whom, in their daily meetings, he always addressed as "Commander in Chief."

In his dealings with the French, General Schwarzkopf was also able to establish a good understanding. His achievement was considerable and took time. He managed to fashion an effective partnership with a nation known for its prickly assertion of national sovereignty as well as its Cartesian ways of reasoning, which tend to leave the Anglo-Saxon mind cold.

This was not easy. From the time the first French helicopter regiment arrived in August, it was not clear for many months whether the French were really ready to cooperate. They declined to come under coalition command. Instead, they insisted that they report only to President François Mitterrand. Then they said that in the event of an Iraqi attack, they would go under Saudi command. Only on January 17, 1991 (January 16 in the United States), when the air war began, did the 14,000-strong reinforced French 6th Light Armored Division, known as "Daguet," formally come under what was called "the operational command" of the U.S. XVIII Airborne Corps.

Despite these travails, General Schwarzkopf was patient. He never forced the issue. British officials had the distinct impression that he was maddened by the French ambivalence. But he never let it show. Rather, he slowly established an entente with the French commander, Lieutenant General Michel Roquejeoffre, who arrived in Riyadh on September 19, 1990. This was not based on Schwarzkopf's command of French—his knowledge of the language is in fact slight and the stories of his fluency untrue—but on his sensitivity to French self-importance. Roquejeoffre was won over. "I understood quite quickly that I would get on well with General Schwarzkopf," he said. "I sensed that he had an unusual intelligence and capacity to synthesize information and make the right decision. In addition, he seemed *good*, a man with a big heart. We often talked about the need to avoid casualties. That was a priority for him. He would never have engaged the troops until he knew every precaution had been taken to avoid losses."

In the end, the French played an important role. When the air war began, they initiated the vast westward shift of troops that was the basis for Schwarzkopf's flanking attack. By so doing, they covered the movement west of the XVIII Airborne Corps behind them. It was this secret maneuver that set up the devastating left hook that caught the Iraqis by surprise. And when the ground war began, the French fought in highly effective partnership with the 2nd Brigade of the 82nd Airborne Division, taking the Iraqi air base of As-Salman and subsequently protecting the allies' western flank. Schwarzkopf's patience paid off.

"After the war," recalled Roquejeoffre, "he called me by my first name, Michel. Before that, he had always called me General. I was very moved. I went on calling him General because I did not feel I could call him Norman. But his gesture was a sign of friendship I will always remember." This was one small instance of the ways in which Schwarzkopf conjured away mistrust within the coalition.

He was equally adroit in his dealings with the Saudis and the various Arab members of the force. Lieutenant General Khalid Bin Sultan Bin Abdul Aziz, the Saudi commander and nephew of King Fahd, is a loud, blustery character used to getting his own way. Prior to the war, he had a mixed reputation. Some saw him as one of the more corrupt members of the Saudi royal family; others, as one of the more intelligent. Initially, he was extremely prickly about the American presence, suggesting in early September that no U.S. unit could engage in any offensive operation without prior consultation with the Saudis.

From the beginning, Schwarzkopf had to reassure the Saudi commander that he was not in Saudi Arabia to usurp any of his power, and that the Arab role in the gathering coalition force would be one of substance. In the end, he succeeded in allaying Khalid's insecurity—which stemmed in part from the fact that the last time that Saudi Arabia had gone to war was on camel- and horseback in the 1930s—while conceding to him a role of real importance.

Khalid, who speaks excellent English, came to be a good friend to Schwarzkopf. He acted as a highly effective mediator between Schwarzkopf and the Arab forces. These included an Egyptian corps, which proved to be the best Arab fighting force in the Kuwaiti campaign, a Syrian division, a Moroccan battalion, a Kuwaiti and an Omani brigade, a Bahraini motorized infantry company, and mechanized battalions from Qatar and the United Arab Emirates. Senegalese, Bangladeshi, and Pakistani forces were also placed under General Khalid. By delegating authority to Khalid over what would become known as the Joint Arab Task Force, Schwarzkopf at once lightened his own overburdened work load and smoothed relations with the Saudis. Khalid, in the end, proved skilled in overcoming Egyptian and Syrian hesitancy about whether they were prepared to attack Kuwait or be part of a force also sweeping over Iraqi territory. While he left Khalid much leeway, Schwarzkopf knew that, in a crunch, the Saudi commander would always defer to his own vastly superior military experience.

This gradual harnessing of soldiers from all over the world proved to be a source of fascination to Washington. Almost half the Senate and a third of the House came over to see what was happening. So, too, of course, did all the service chiefs. Schwarzkopf used to joke to the U.S. ambassador, Charles Freeman, that "we have become the chief park rangers in the world's largest military theme park!"

Not everything worked smoothly, however. Before Schwarzkopf's arrival, tensions with the Saudis had built up over a series of minor incidents. In so closed a society, these were probably inevitable. But Schwarzkopf immediately set to work to ensure that matters did not get worse. Several things annoyed the Saudis: armed U.S. soldiers in local souks, or markets; female military personnel driving trucks in a society where women are forbidden by law to drive; soldiers setting up camp on empty tracts of desert that were in fact owned by somebody. The list was endless, and potentially very irritating. Schwarzkopf opted for tact.

On August 30, 1990, he issued General Order No. 1 for Operation Desert Shield. This pointed out that "Islamic law and Arabic customs prohibit or restrict certain activities which are generally permissible in Western societies." It went on to say that any sexually explicit material was banned—adding that, in the eyes of Saudi Arabia, this included "body-building magazines, swimsuit editions of periodicals, lingerie or underwear advertisements and catalogues, as well as visual mediums which infer but do not directly show human genitalia, women's breasts or human sexual acts." Women were encouraged to wear abayas, the all-concealing robes of Saudi women, and instructed to dress modestly at all times. Shorts were banned, as were short sleeves and certain bright colors. In some companies, women were at first told not to drive. This, according to Staff Sergeant James L. Washington of the 598th Maintenance Company, "enraged a lot of people."

Schwarzkopf worked closely with the U.S. embassy and the consulate in Dhahran on the Gulf coast to set up liaison procedures with the Saudis that would nip problems in the bud. It did not always work: a demonstration by defiant Saudi women driving their cars around Riyadh was an embarrassment. The demonstration declared, in effect, that what U.S. women in the Army could do, Saudi women should be allowed to do, too. But, in general, Schwarzkopf was helped by the fact that 95 percent of his troops were in the Eastern Province, which is used to the presence of foreigners working for Aramco and is therefore more liberal than the heart of the country is.

His measures in Riyadh, the capital and so the most politically sensitive place, were draconian. Many of the troops there spent much of their time in Saudi Arabia shuttling between the dormitory villages on the outskirts of town to bases near the airport, about twenty miles out of the center. For long periods, they were not allowed to come into the city. As a result, most Saudis had very little sense of the massive American presence.

Religion was a particularly sensitive area. Here the general was determined to find a compromise between U.S. principle, which establishes freedom of religion, and Saudi law, which countenances nothing but Islam. In the end, Jewish and Christian services were regularly celebrated on Saudi soil, but the press was banned from covering them. Rosh Hashanah in the land of Mecca would have made a great story, but no journalist was allowed to witness the Jewish services. As in other areas, Schwarzkopf placed political and military interests above the freedom of the press. Indeed, the press and the question of body count proved to be the two areas where the general could be most prickly and ruthless.

To assuage Saudi concerns still further, Schwarzkopf allowed the Mutawa'iin, or government-funded Society for the Promotion of Virtue and Suppression of Vice, to visit the troops out in the desert. The Mutawa'iin can be a fearsome group. With their long beards and short thobes (the shirt-like garment worn by Arabian men), its members represent the fierce asceticism of the Wahhabi interpretation of Islam on which the royal house of Saud is founded.

Muhammad ibn Abdal-Wahhab, who lived in the eighteenth century, was the Martin Luther of Islam in Arabia; and his railings against idols, opulence, and any loose interpretation of the Sharia, or law of God, are the modern-day battle cry of the Mutawa'iin. T. E. Lawrence, the British officer who became known as Lawrence of Arabia, had observed the Wahhabi as he orchestrated the Arab Revolt of 1917 that put an end to the Ottoman Empire in Arabia and Mesopotamia and opened the way for the creation of the modern Arab states. Among the Wahhabi, he wrote, there was "little coffee-hospitality, much prayer and fasting, no tobacco, no artistic dalliance with women, no silk clothes, no gold and silver headropes or ornaments.

Everything was forcibly pious or forcibly puritanical." He put their ascetic creed down to "sun, moon, wind, acting in the emptiness of open spaces" and weighing on the unhurried minds of the desert dwellers.

The creed has not changed. In 1989, the Mutawa'iin became very angry when a Cajun band played at the U.S. embassy during the holy period of Ramadan, and as a result, the whole diplomatic quarter was temporarily sealed. But if they expected to find rampant vice among the U.S. troops, they were disappointed. Schwarzkopf commanded, on the whole, an army of God-fearing people from the heartland of America.

The forces were highly trained and highly motivated. Their values revolved around family life, religion, and patriotism. They were, in the end, very conservative. Their discipline was reinforced because alcohol is banned in Saudi Arabia. As the British chief of staff, Macfadyen, commented, "The fact there was no booze was an absolute godsend. No problems with alcohol mean no problems at all. It's a great lesson in war. If we do not have any alcohol, we will be all right."

The professionalism and earnestness of Schwarzkopf's troops represented a crucial difference from Vietnam. The ultimate success of the decade-long struggle of the 1970s to establish a professional and motivated Army was evidenced in the absence of drugs or major morale problems. In the place of drafted nineteen-year-old grunts on a one-year tour, Schwarzkopf had committed troops with an average age of twenty-six and extensive preparation. The CINC was aware of this. The knowledge was reassuring. But he would awaken as many as fifteen times a night wondering how to resolve the crisis quickly so as not to lose his troops' enthusiasm. There was a lot to be said for speed. At the same time, however, he did not want to lose one life more than was necessary. There was a lot to be said for caution, too. Somewhere between dispatch and prudence, the answer lay.

• • •

General Schwarzkopf came to Riyadh to defend Saudi Arabia. He had no political mandate to oust the invading Iraqis from Kuwait. During the five months before the air war began, he continued to hope for peace. In conversations with his family, he would express his frustration at what he saw as the lack of diplomatic activity. "I wish the diplomats would get going," he said repeatedly. "They don't seem to be doing a damn thing."

Although he seldom let it show, he was often anxious. He would sit in the War Room for long hours, studying maps, seldom appearing in the Joint Operations Center down the corridor where intelligence was gathered daily on the huge Iraqi Army. The Operations Center became known as "the Bullpen." The staff thought of themselves as spotters studying the adversary's plays in order to prepare their bear-like coach. In the War Room, targets were indicated on the maps in various colors: Iraqi ballistic missiles in pink, chemical weapons in yellow, the Republican Guard in purple. On Schwarzkopf's right sat the deputy CINC, Lieutenant General Calvin Waller, and his chief of operations, Major General Burton Moore; and on his left the chief of staff, Major General Robert B. Johnston. They were colleagues and they were friends. Still, he missed his family; and, at times, he ached for the opportunity to be alone, walking on the beach at Tampa Bay or out skeet shooting.

Occasionally the tension showed. Lieutenant General Roquejeoffre once saw Schwarzkopf explode and swear when something he had asked for had not been done. Most of the time, however, he showed great self-control. He never paced the room. He stuck to a healthy diet, avoiding what one staff member called "the temptation to reward himself with packs of M&M's."

His sense of humor never left him. When his sister Sally made a batch of the family's beloved sand tart cookies and sent them to him, he called her and said, "You Iraqi subversive! You made me gain a thousand calories!"

On the whole, however, his mood was somber. He had seen too much of war to seek it. His favorite passage from the Bible he kept beside his bed was "Dear Lord, make us the instruments of your peace." As he said while in Riyadh, "If anyone thinks this is an enjoyable experience, they are dead wrong. I've known a lot of generals who were war lovers. They scare the living hell out of me, and they're also not very good generals, not by my measure."

But if it seems clear that General Schwarzkopf genuinely hoped for peace, it is also clear that it did not take him long to start preparing for an aggressive, rather than a purely defensive, campaign. He was always skeptical that the trade embargo imposed by the UN on August 6, 1990, would prove effective in persuading Saddam to withdraw from the country he renamed Iraq's nineteenth province on August 28. Even if 90 percent of Iraq's imports and exports were cut off, Iraq was not a land where public misery made much difference. There were no channels for protest. The country was clamped under the forbidding control of Saddam and his Baath Party cronies from his hometown of Tikrit.

Studying the Iraqi dictator's psychology, Schwarzkopf saw a stubborn, cunning, but extremely limited man, used to getting his way by force and ill equipped to gauge the resolve of a world in which he had scarcely traveled. Like any megalomaniac—and Schwarzkopf concluded that Saddam had a megalomaniacal desire to lead the Arab world—he was deluded. He was, in short, a parochial thug with dangerous fantasies. One official close to the general said that Schwarzkopf tried to put himself in Saddam's shoes and concluded that the Iraqi dictator was likely to be misled by several things: his eventual success against Iran in a war of atavistic brutality; American failures in Vietnam, in the aborted hostage-rescue mission in Iran in 1980, and in the disastrous foray of the Marines into

Beirut in 1983; the apparent fragility of so wide a coalition, with several Arab members, especially if Israel was attacked; and a conviction that U.S. commitment would prove extremely tenuous as soon as the body bags started piling up.

Accordingly, as early as September, Schwarzkopf quietly began to develop his ideas for evicting Saddam by force. On September 13, just over two weeks after his arrival, he indicated his thinking to Richard Pyle of the Associated Press, declaring that "a war in the desert is a war of mobility and lethality" and adding, "I don't think any military commander will ever tell you that you can win a mobile war with air forces alone." In other words, if it came to war, Schwarzkopf was going to avoid, at all costs, getting into a slugging match like the Iran–Iraq War, and he was going to complement air power with the unique ground-gaining ability of his beloved infantry. He stressed: "I want to use my strength against his weakness."

It was a telling phrase, one that would guide the general. In effect, it was an adaptation of an idea first outlined by Sun Tzu two thousand years earlier. He had written: "For the impact of armed forces to be like stones thrown on eggs is a matter of emptiness and fullness. *Attack complete emptiness with fullness.*"

Sun Tzu also advised generals to "appear where they cannot go, head for where they least expect you. To travel hundreds of miles without fatigue, go over land where there are no people." He emphasized that "a military operation involves *deception.* Without deception you cannot carry out strategy, without strategy you cannot control the opponent. When you are going to attack far away, make it look as if you are going just a short distance." He observed: "I have heard of military operations that were clumsy but swift, but I have *never* seen one that was skillful and lasted a long time. It is never beneficial to a nation to have a military operation continue for a long time." He said that, "on the attack, your movement is swift and your cry shattering, *fast as thunder and lightning,* as though coming from the sky impossible to prepare for." And he noted that "a victorious army *first wins and then seeks battle.* A defeated army first battles and then seeks victory."

As is clear from these passages, General Schwarzkopf, who had read Sun Tzu, did not invent anything in the Gulf. Schooled in military theory, fascinated by the maneuvers of great generals, he brought the knowledge of the ancients to bear on the use of twenty-first-century technology.

Later, Schwarzkopf said the key to victory was superb equipment, and Lieutenant General Horner called it a "technology war." It is true that F-117A Stealth tactical fighters slipped past radar to deliver laser-guided bombs; that the M1A1 Abrams tanks with their lethal 120 mm cannons moved faster than tanks ever did before in warfare; that divisions took CNN dishes and portable TVs to the banks of the Euphrates to keep up their intelligence on Saddam; and that U.S. night-vision equipment reduced the Iraqis to a state of dismay. But the key to success lay in Schwarzkopf's inspired use of the classical military precepts he had long studied. This was no Nintendo game. It was a war in which a general's inspiration and twenty-first-century technology blended. The gadgetry would not have had remotely the same impact without the ideas.

Schwarzkopf knew that he had several important advantages likely to make any war utterly different from Vietnam. The desert terrain, a far cry from the lush hills of the Asian jungle, was ideal for the use of air power. It was also familiar to many of the troops, who had gone through tough training at the National Training Center in the Mojave Desert. Moreover, the area was flat, just like the imagined Central European theater for a war with the Soviet Union, which had been the basis on which the Army's AirLand Battle doctrine of extreme mobility and coordinated air-and-land strike power had evolved. Finally, the geopolitical situation was vastly different from that which had prevailed two decades earlier. The drastic retrenchment in the Soviet Union meant there was no chance of the conflict escalating. China was not a worry either. Saddam was isolated, with no significant friendly flank (such as the Cambodian border in Vietnam) to buttress him. Schwarzkopf could plan his war knowing that his enemy was isolated.

Further, in many ways Saudi Arabia made his planning easy. While utterly foreign in some things, it is in others a comforting place for an American. There are excellent ports, six-lane highways, and an abundance of airfields. The faxes work, and so do the phones. Much of the country's ultra-modern command, control, communications, and intelligence, or C^3I, infrastructure had been installed by the U.S. military. It provided an excellent basis on which to build. Unlike the situation in Vietnam, there was not that much for the Army's engineering units to do. Nor was there a great likelihood of terrorism to worry about. The kingdom is, on the whole, remarkably secluded from the maelstrom of Arab extremism and nationalism that made Beirut such a killing field for the Marines in 1983. Certainly, the U.S. buildup in Saudi Arabia provoked demonstrations in Amman and Cairo, but, for Schwarzkopf, that was a far cry from having suicide bombers or sizable protests on his doorstep. In short, for a place more than 6,500 miles from home, Saudi Arabia was as close to an ideal setting for a U.S. general to plan a war as could be imagined.

Work proceeded at a furious pace. By early October, over 200,000 troops were in place. "We were no longer a deterrent force at the end of September," said Lieutenant General Luck, the XVIII Airborne Corps commander, "we were a genuine defensive force. It was not long before we were sending invitations to Saddam saying 'Come on, we're ready!' " But as Desert Shield was rounded out, differences over planning began to emerge.

According to people who worked closely with him, General Schwarzkopf was aware of acute timing pressures that Washington was initially reluctant to address with much urgency. By October 1, the general had become convinced that sanctions would not budge Saddam. The Iraqi dictator had rapidly built up his force in Kuwait from 100,000 on August 2 to over 430,000 by the end of September. Schwarzkopf saw a very narrow "window" within which an offensive operation should be conducted. This was in January and February, before the dust and rain storms of late February and March, and before the holy period of Ramadan beginning on March 17.

After that it would be too late. The fiercely hot summer weather would return, as severe in its way as a Russian winter, and that would be no time to fight a war. The whole question of how to tackle Saddam would probably have to be put on hold until the fall of 1991. That, in turn, would probably mean reducing the forces during the summer. Would public support continue? Would the troops' morale hold up? Would the desert turn to quicksand for the servicemen and -women who were determined to get the job done and go home?

Schwarzkopf wanted to be ready to move in January. But, for logistical reasons, that meant a political decision had to be made by the end of October. Studying the steady Iraqi buildup in Kuwait—its widening minefields, barbed-wire defenses, thousands of tanks, and increasing strength in depth—he knew he needed at least another corps (that is, about 100,000 troops) to take on Saddam. As he said, if he was going to fight he wanted to be able to "guaran-damn-tee" victory.

But bringing in another corps would take time. Moreover, as Schwarzkopf watched the Iraqi dictator pouring troops into the Kuwaiti sandbox, his attention focused increasingly on the enemy's exposed, empty western flank.

Going in that way might have the twin advantage of reducing casualties and rounding up the crack Republican Guard forces of about 150,000 lurking close to the Kuwaiti border in southern Iraq. But a three-hundred-mile flanking move to the west would also take time. It would necessitate an enormous logistical effort. Put bluntly, if he did not get a green light from Washington by the beginning of November, Schwarzkopf did not see how the various pieces would fit into place and be ready for that optimum January–February period.

Some people in the Pentagon, Congress, and State Department, however, did not see the need to hurry. They wanted time for sanctions to work; or they thought 200,000 troops were enough for an offensive option; or both. "For a while in October, he was exceedingly frustrated," said one State Department official familiar with Schwarzkopf's thinking at that time. "He was not getting political guidance because the political process was taking its time. He would have been content with a clear statement that the defense of Saudi Arabia would be his only mission, or a statement that an order to switch to offensive planning would come. But living in a situation where he knew what he would have to do, but had no order to do it, was frustrating."

Schwarzkopf made his point through military channels; the U.S. embassy in Riyadh lobbied the State Department, where Secretary of State Baker was long reluctant to contemplate any offensive planning. The message, in essence, was: "If you are not prepared to let sanctions go on forever, make some decisions now."

Particularly infuriating for Schwarzkopf was a demand from Washington in early October that he submit a plan for evicting Saddam without any further reinforcement of the roughly 200,000 troops that were already in Saudi Arabia. This request appeared to reflect a twofold concern in Washington: a desire not to pay the political price of a protracted deployment in Saudi Arabia, and at the same time a desire not to pay the political price of sending more troops. Referring to the quest for an offensive plan with the troops he had in October, Schwarzkopf later told the British TV interviewer David Frost:

> I immediately went back and I said, "I don't have the necessary forces to do that." And they [in Washington] said, "Yeah, but if you had to do it right now with the forces you have, what would you do?" So we put together a plan, which, based upon the forces that were available at that time, would be the plan that we would have to use. But when the plan was briefed . . . it was immediately followed by a statement which said:
>
> "That is not what the commander in chief of Central Command is recommending. It is a weak plan and it is not a plan we choose to execute. And here are the things that are wrong with it: A, B, C, D, E, F, G, H, I, J, and a lot more . . . and if, in fact, we are serious about ejecting them from Kuwait what we need is more forces to be able to execute a proper campaign."

A breakthrough in Schwarzkopf's lobbying came when General Powell visited Riyadh on October 21. Powell had been skeptical about moving to an offensive operation. As early as August, he had given Schwarzkopf the impression of being a man bent, if possible, on conciliation. "Powell is not a cowboy," Schwarzkopf confided to his family. By contrast, Defense Secretary Cheney had struck him as a more hawkish character.

As a military man, however, Powell was determined that an offensive operation, if approved, should be conducted with the force necessary to guarantee success. Schwarzkopf's argument found a receptive listener. They talked for several hours, reaching agreement that the VII Corps stationed in Germany and the 1st Infantry Division (Mechanized) from Fort Riley, Kansas, would constitute the ideal reinforcement, offering both punch and the speed necessary to mount a flanking attack. But what

Schwarzkopf wanted—a doubling of troops and the cancellation of the troop rotation that most people in the United States regarded as inevitable—amounted to political dynamite, particularly on the eve of the November 6 congressional elections.

In the long run, however, the alternative could be even more damaging to the Administration and to the military: sitting it out in Saudi Arabia for a very long time without being equipped to make a move. In Cheney, Powell had a Defense Secretary who was not only skeptical of sanctions but also determined to listen to the military's view. On his return to Washington, Powell got down to detailed planning of how a force increase could be speedily accomplished. And on October 30 he and Cheney took the question to the President, who had always been concerned about the political effects of a drawn-out deployment of troops without any visible sign of progress. Also present at the meeting were Secretary of State James Baker and National Security Adviser Brent Scowcroft.

It was at this October 30 meeting that the doubling of the force in Saudi Arabia to over 400,000 was decided, and the diplomatic drive set in motion that would culminate with UN Security Council Resolution 678 of November 29, giving Saddam until January 15 to get out of Iraq or face eviction by force. Bush had been won over both by the argument for a military victory and by the hope that this demonstration of will might lead Saddam to withdraw. But, because of the looming elections, he waited over a week, until November 8, to announce the doubling of forces to the nation.

"I have today directed the Secretary of Defense to increase the size of U.S. forces committed to Desert Shield," the President said, "to ensure that the coalition has an adequate offensive military option should that be necessary to achieve our common goals."

Well before those words were uttered, however, Schwarzkopf had learned that the VII Corps and 1st

Infantry Division, or "Big Red One," were on their way, accompanied by other units. In all, Schwarzkopf's force was to be doubled to over 500,000 U.S. soldiers. Secretary of State Baker had been in Riyadh between November 4 and 7 discussing the situation. Schwarzkopf knew that he could proceed with his planning to humble Saddam in the first months of 1991.

General Schwarzkopf had not been alone in thinking about how to recapture Kuwait. At corps and division level, his generals were inevitably speculating and planning. Lieutenant General Pagonis, the logistics expert, Major General McCaffrey of the 24th Infantry Division, and Major General J. H. Binford Peay III of the 101st Airborne Division had all spent many hours discussing which way to do it. Although their mission remained officially defensive, there was some skepticism from the outset about whether it would remain so. It seemed inconceivable that so much equipment was being shipped more than 6,500 miles just to park it in the sand for an indefinite period. Their planning at get-togethers in the Dhahran area was informal, but it went ahead during the month of October. They called their aggressive plans Desert Sword. From the "Shield" to the "Sword" seemed a logical step.

The generals concentrated on Kuwait itself. They considered an attack aimed initially at capturing the airfield to the west of Kuwait City, then encircling the city, and finally luring the Republican Guard into a major tank battle in northern Kuwait. They were convinced that superior allied firepower and mobility would win the day. But they were concerned that casualties would be high.

Like General Schwarzkopf, these generals were working with intelligence that tended to inflate the Iraqi Army's power. In April 1990, just three months before Saddam's invasion of Kuwait, the respected Strategic Studies Institute of the U.S. Army War College published a ninety-five-page report on Iraq, calling it "a formidable power" and "the most powerful state in the Gulf." The report reflected a general failure of the intelligence community to provide an accurate assessment of the capacity of the Iraqi Army before the war.

The report amounted to a panegyric on Saddam's firepower and growing military prowess, hailing the Iraqi campaign against Iran of April–August 1988—during which Saddam won five decisive battles and recaptured the Al Faw Peninsula—as an illustration of Iraqi mastery of "complicated large-scale military operations."

It emphasized that any army facing Saddam would confront an opponent who was "armor heavy, including a large number of T72 tanks," "rich in long-range field artillery," equipped with a "large number of a variety of types of attack helicopters," and "in possession of a very large, mostly modern air force which has shown itself capable of conducting deep interdiction and battlefield interdiction missions."

The report added that Saddam was "capable of, and doctrinally attuned to, employment of chemical weapons by all available means, to include mortars, helicopter fire, aerial delivered bombs, and rockets and artillery." It speculated that he might fire "large quantities of Scud variants with conventional and possibly chemical warheads with moderate accuracy." It suggested that the Iraqi Army was "routinely practiced in the art of strategic deception" and "capable of raising the banner of pan-Arabism against an outside force by identifying it with Israel."

Saddam's army, moreover, was "capable of tenacious defense of their homeland and well practiced at the tactical level with intricate defense systems"; and it was "doctrinally inclined toward fighting set-piece battles seeking to lure their enemy into prearranged killing zones where, once Iraqi artillery had broken the momentum of an attack, an armor-heavy counterattack would be launched." To cap it all, the Iraqis were "equipped with some of the Middle East's best educated troops" and "capable of considerable adaptation to changing circumstances as evidenced by the tremendous speed-up of the Al Faw operation."

Quite apart from this report, the overall numbers were scarcely reassuring: the over-one-million-man army (of whom about half would make their way into the Kuwaiti theater), the eight divisions of highly trained, elite Republican Guard, the 5,500 main battle tanks, the 350 long-range SAMs (surface-to-air missiles), the 800 aircraft and 160 armed attack helicopters. All this in a fighting force hardened by eight years of slugging it out with Iran and expert in the waging of war in a desert terrain.

On Saturday, November 10, two and a half months after his arrival in Saudi Arabia and two days after the President's announcement that the U.S. force would be doubled, General Schwarzkopf summoned his army, navy, air force, and marine commanders to the officers' club at the Dhahran air base. In all, there were about forty people in the room. The general's purpose in calling the meeting was to tell the commanders what he intended to do to the reputedly formidable Iraqi forces. The CINC told the commanders that he did not yet have political directions to retake Kuwait, but "if I get them, here's the plan I'm working on." At that point, covers were removed from maps behind Schwarzkopf, revealing what, in very broad outline, would be the strategy followed in the recapture of Kuwait. In the month since he had presented the President with a plan for an attack with just 250,000 troops, Schwarzkopf and his staff had been working on this new plan relentlessly; and in the coming months it would be relentlessly adjusted in its finer points.

The reaction was one of general astonishment. There, behind Schwarzkopf's burly frame, was what one general described as "an extraordinary giant sweeping arc."

All the basic elements of the campaign were there. Way out to the west—farther than they ultimately went—was the XVIII Airborne Corps, sweeping around behind the Iraqi lines and cutting off the Euphrates River valley. To the east of the XVIII Corps was the VII Corps, surging into Iraq closer to Kuwait's western border—the so-called Wadi al-Batin corridor—and then wheeling eastward into Kuwait itself and attacking the Republican Guard in the north of the country. Closer to the Persian Gulf, moving directly over the Iraqi minefields and on toward Kuwait City, were the 1st and 2nd Marine Expeditionary Forces and the Arab forces. In the Gulf itself was the coalition's massive naval power, preparing a possible amphibious assault, although, in General Schwarzkopf's mind, there was already the growing thought that this would probably end up as no more than a feint. The much-publicized Imminent Thunder rehearsal for an amphibious landing, which began five days later on November 15, would set the Iraqis up for this deception.

The General called the plan Desert Storm, which he preferred to Desert Sword. The lunge of a sword comes from a single place; a storm is ubiquitous. Schwarzkopf, schooled in the Army's AirLand doctrine of "deep battle"—that is, destroying the enemy's ability to fight as a coherent force through deep strikes behind its lines—wanted to come at the relatively static Iraqis from all sides. As he would later say in describing his attack, "We're going to go around, over, through, on top, underneath, and any other way!"

Even in its broad outline, it was a plan of astonishing audacity. The logistics alone were absolutely daunting. Schwarzkopf's idea was that none of the troops shifting out to the west should move into their pre-attack positions before D Day—the name chosen by CentCom for the start of the planned air campaign. This campaign, already elaborated in some detail, was to be directed at Iraq's main Scud missile-launching sites; its airfields and air defense systems; petrochemical factories and electrical power plants; communications systems and crucial roads and bridges; chemical and biological weapons facilities; and, lastly, Republican Guard divisions near Basra and the troops in Kuwait.

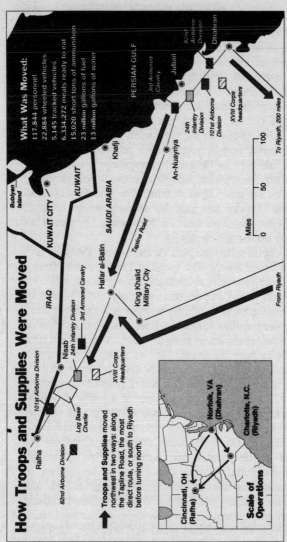

How Troops and Supplies Were Moved

What Was Moved:
117,844 personnel
22,884 wheeled vehicles
5,145 tracked vehicles
6,334,272 meals ready to eat
15,020 short tons of ammunition
23 million gallons of fuel
13 million gallons of water

PERSIAN GULF

82nd Airborne Division

3rd Armored Cavalry

Jubail

24th Infantry Division

101st Airborne Division

XVIII Corps headquarters

Dhahran

Bublyan Island

KUWAIT CITY

KUWAIT

IRAQ

Nisab

101st Airborne Division

24th Infantry Division

3rd Armored Cavalry

Khafji

An-Nuayriya

SAUDI ARABIA

Tapline Road

Hafar al-Batin

King Khalid Military City

XVIII Corps Headquarters

Log Base Charlie

Rafha

82nd Airborne Division

To Riyadh, 200 miles

From Riyadh

Miles
0   50   100

➤ Troops and Supplies moved northwest in two ways: along the Tapline Road, the most direct route, or south to Riyadh before turning north.

Norfolk, OH
(Rafha)

Norfolk, VA
(Dhahran)

Charlotte, N.C.
(Riyadh)

Scale of Operations

In the 21 days after January 16, 1991, when the air campaign began, the XVIII Corps moved as far as 530 miles from its defensive to its pre-attack positions, setting up Schwarzkopf's surprise flanking attack. Never before in the history of warfare has an army moved so much so far so fast. The distance covered was the same as that between Norfolk, Virginia, and Cincinnati, Ohio. The whole maneuver was conducted in complete secrecy. The move involved 1,252 flights by C-130 transporters, and 5,476 trips by trucks.

Only after D Day, when this campaign began, would Schwarzkopf be sure that Saddam's eyes had been taken out, and thus have some reasonable hope that the massive flanking movement would remain secret. Moreover, although the VII Corps was preparing to move into positions southeast of the Saudi town of Hafar al-Batin, about two hundred miles inland from the Gulf, and would therefore be placed much farther west than the defensive positions of the XVIII Corps about thirty miles inland, between Dhahran and An-Nuayriya, it was the XVIII Corps that Schwarzkopf wanted to move to pre-attack positions some 370 miles inland from the Gulf.

"Schwarzkopf could have just said 'Everyone take four steps to the left.' It would have been easier, and that's what somebody less imaginative would have done," said Major Richard Rowe of the XVIII Corps. "But he wanted our corps, and not the VII Corps, out wide on the flank."

The commander in chief had good reason for this. The XVIII Airborne is America's contingency corps, trained to move at speed to wherever conflict happens to break out. The VII Corps is at the heart of NATO's European defense, prepared to take on the Russians in a massive tank battle. With almost one thousand helicopters and only one heavy division, the XVIII Corps is ideally suited to a fast flanking movement. By contrast, the VII Corps has about one thousand tanks (compared to the 363 of the XVIII Corps) and five heavy divisions—ideal for breaking through the heavier Iraqi defenses close to Kuwait and then taking on the elite Republican Guard, which had brought its heavy Hammurabi, Medina, and Tawakalna Divisions into the Kuwaiti theater.

Thus, despite the added distance, taking the XVIII Corps all the way out to the west made sense. But was it feasible?

From the outset, General Schwarzkopf's broad idea was that the start of the ground attack, known as G Day, should come fourteen days after the air attack. G Day, in CentCom parlance, was to be "D + 14"—D Day plus fourteen days. It was a flexible idea, but it had the merit of giving everyone parameters within which to work.

This two-week period, it was hoped, would give the Air Force time to achieve its mission. But this time frame also meant a staggering logistical effort. In effect, General Schwarzkopf was asking the XVIII Corps to move 117,844 personnel, 22,884 wheeled vehicles, and 5,145 tracked vehicles an average of 530 miles down a single road from their defensive to their pre-attack positions in the space of about fourteen days. With the men and women and the vehicles would have to go more than 6 million MREs (meals ready to eat), over 13 million gallons of water, over 23 million gallons of fuel, and over 15,000 short tons of ammunition. No army in the history of warfare had ever moved so much so far so fast.

General Schwarzkopf did not tell his commanders how this or any other aspect of the overall plan was to be effected. Current army doctrine—in contrast to Soviet principles—stresses decentralization. Responsibility is passed on down through the ranks. The CINC gives an overall concept, but nothing more. It is up to the commanders of the various units to work out the details. Thus the general indicated the broad lines of the attack and the targets, or "centers of gravity," he wanted to hit: Kuwait City, the Republican Guard, and lines of communication and supply up the Euphrates Valley. But he went no further.

According to the recollection of Lieutenant General Luck, the commander of the XVIII Corps, General Schwarzkopf summed up the strategy and then declared, "Okay, boys, this is what I wanna do, now you think about this and come back and tell me how I'm gonna do it."

Major General Peay of the 101st Airborne was sitting next to Major General McCaffrey and leaned over to say, "That's it. That's the one. We'll do it!"

Major General McCaffrey summed up the reaction this way: "After the initial shock, there was a tremendous feeling of relief. Instead of fighting some narrowly defined battle with tremendous possibilities of casualties, we would be allowed to overwhelm them at an operational level. It was breathtaking."

The overall confidence with which so ambitious and risky a plan was received is suggestive of the very high degree of confidence that General Schwarzkopf seems to have commanded from the outset of the Gulf operation. Although he was unknown to the public before the start of the war, he was a very well known figure within the Armed Forces. His forthright style was already unusual, and remarked upon, in Vietnam. He had since worked at bases from Germany through Alaska to Hawaii; he had also served several stints at the Pentagon. His humor, big personality, stirring speeches, and, above all, utter commitment to the well-being of the soldiers under his command had become, if not legendary, at least a source of fairly widespread comment within the forces.

This was important. Coming from somebody viewed with any doubt or skepticism by the men and women in his command, his plan could easily have been dismissed as impossibly grandiose. But having commanded units from platoon to corps level, the general showed a touch and an assurance that made everyone from privates to three-star generals ready to believe in him.

The plan reflected Schwarzkopf's study of military history and his determination not to play to Iraq's much-vaunted strengths. A magician himself, he was fascinated by the art of deception. In his childhood, it was the great, orchestrated ploys of victorious generals that had drawn him to the Army. That is why, in a thirty-four-year career, he had never enjoyed the bureaucratic jobs in Washington. The Army, to him, was about soldiering; and soldiering was about the kind of audacity that led Hannibal to bring his elephants over the Alps, Bradley to bring his troops ashore at Omaha Beach on D Day, and Patton to rush to the relief of Bastogne during the Battle of the Bulge.

At West Point, his friends had seen him as a young man who dreamed of taking his place in the history books one day. Schwarzkopf had lost his naïveté since then and had developed a horror of the cruelty of war. But he still saw war as a noble art. He was determined to outfox Saddam through the application of that art—because in so doing he prayed that he could keep casualties to a minimum.

One particular battle came to Schwarzkopf's mind. In 1942 at El Alamein, another desert confrontation, German Field Marshal Erwin Rommel, the "Desert Fox," had known that Lieutenant General Bernard Law Montgomery's Eighth Army was going to attack. So Montgomery went to elaborate lengths to introduce an element of surprise.

He used dummy tanks, trucks, guns, and even a fake oil pipeline to suggest that Allied power was being concentrated to the south when in fact the main assault was to come from the north. Huge dummy staging areas were built in the south at a rate calculated to make Rommel think no attack would come until early November. In fact, Monty moved in late October. In the north, meanwhile, elaborate camouflage was used to disguise the real concentration of Allied forces. The result was that the German Army was caught off-balance even though it knew an attack was coming. Similarly, with his feint at sea and unexpectedly wide flanking maneuver, Schwarzkopf was able to act with devastating surprise despite the fact that for several months more than 1,000,000 troops had stood facing one another. It was as if one football team had been watching another prepare to make a play for six months and was then, despite all its own preparations, caught looking completely in the wrong direction!

Schwarzkopf's plan also reflected the fact that he had come to some firm conclusions about Iraq's weaknesses. As the Iraqis dug their tanks into revetments, immobilizing them as little more than cannons, the general saw clearly that he was facing an enemy preparing itself for a static war. The idea struck him that the Iraqis had had a lot of the *wrong kind of experience*: for eight years, they had faced human-wave Iranian assaults and fought an army with no significant air power. They were very good indeed at World War I, less good at grasping that seventy years and countless generations of weapons and systems had gone by since then. When it came to laying out barbed wire, heavy fortifications, minefields, fire trenches—any kind of defensive emplacement—they were expert; but they lacked mobility, flexibility, and experience in combating air power. Under a three-dimensional attack they might well find themselves in disarray.

They also lacked strategic intelligence: what good was their vaunted artillery without the ability to spot the enemy? Moreover, their logistics—the long supply line from Baghdad to Kuwait—were vulnerable to air attack.

Weighing all this, Schwarzkopf decided on a strategy that would exploit air power, the ability to move at speed, maneuverability, surprise—and massive sudden violence. He also wanted to be sure that the full force of the attack would hit the Republican Guard in southern Iraq. These forces were the core of Saddam's strength, his own hand-picked men. And although the downfall of Saddam was never an explicit goal of the allied assault, Schwarzkopf, Powell, Cheney, and the President were in agreement that any attack should be conducted in a way that would leave the Iraqi dictator very vulnerable. At the end of it all, if possible, the Emperor should have no clothes.

After the Dhahran meeting, there was a mood of exhilaration. Major General McCaffrey went up to Schwarzkopf and said, "General, we were looking for some narrow-minded bureaucratic plan. You have astounded us!"

Schwarzkopf laughed and said, "I beg your pardon, young man!"

The general, as he later told reporters, was ribbed about the plan. There were some in the Pentagon and among the officers in Saudi Arabia who felt it was touch and go. "At first, it all looked about an even bet," said Major Rowe, who worked extensively on planning the flanking maneuver. "It looked ambitious. But the more we studied it, the more confident we became." This confidence developed in part because it became evident that the Iraqi desert terrain out to the west, which initially looked very harsh, could indeed be crossed by an army. Still, questions remained. How would secrecy be maintained with more than 1,500 journalists in Saudi Arabia? Shunting all that POL (petroleum, oil, and lubricants) and armor down a single road, was there not a risk of a major accident? Could so much be shifted in so short a time? Despite such questions, a majority felt the plan was preferable to a frontal assault on Kuwait. Given a choice between moving over tough but empty terrain and moving directly into heavy Iraqi firepower, Schwarzkopf's commanders had few doubts. As for Schwarzkopf himself, he knew his troops and had taken a look at the terrain and was convinced that it could be done.

He had been encouraged in his conviction by reports from fleeing Kuwaitis of Iraqi soldiers begging them for food. Intelligence suggested that morale was not high among the front-line Iraqi troops assembled just over the Kuwaiti border. This, Schwarzkopf knew, could confound straight calculations of numbers. "There is one really fundamental military truth," he said later, "and that's that you can add up the correlation of forces, you can look at the number of tanks, you can look at the number of airplanes, you can look at these factors of military might and put them together. But unless the soldier on the ground, or the airman in the air, has the will to win, has the strength of character to go into battle, believes his cause is just and has the support of his country—unless you have that, all the rest of that stuff is irrelevant. Hannibal never should have crossed the Alps if he'd looked at the correlation of forces!"

Keeping morale up among his own troops was never a major problem for Schwarzkopf. Complaints did not generally go beyond what officers call "the inalienable right of the soldier to bitch." An extraordinary volume of letters poured in expressing support for the troops. The 24th Division alone—reinforced to about 26,000 people—was receiving several tons a day, according to Specialist Uninta Regil. Many soldiers became pen pals with unknown admirers in the United States.

Still, there were highs and lows. The commanders of Desert Storm now knew where they stood. But rumors continued to swirl among General Schwarzkopf's troops. One said that they would be home by Christmas; another insisted that an attack from Saddam could still be imminent. Procedures for getting into protective suits for chemical warfare were repeatedly drummed into the troops, and with that, inevitably, went talk of death.

The worst thing was that the duration of the operation seemed completely unclear. Every day was full of frenetic activity—the only days most soldiers had off in a period of several months were Thanksgiving and Christmas—but where it was all leading was, for some time, uncertain. A phrase became common among the troops to sum up the mood: "Hurry up and wait."

This uncertainty was largely alleviated when, on November 29, the United Nations set a January 15, 1991, deadline for Saddam to leave Kuwait or face war. At that point, soldiers at least felt they had something to set their sights on.

By the time of the UN vote, most of them had moved out into the desert, stationed in camps in a swath running from the port of Jubail on the Gulf coast north to An-Nuayriya and on up the so-called Tapline Road, which runs east–west across the desert south of Kuwait through Hafar al-Batin. In general, the camps were reasonably comfortable, boasting telephones, latrines ("Male urination," "Male defecation," "Female"), sports grounds, and facilities for watching videos. But some were still housed in the notorious camps that greeted the first troops to arrive in Saudi Arabia: places like "Cement City" near Dhahran, a converted cement factory that was home to thousands. Here the ground was so hard, metal stakes had to be used for tents; hot water was unknown; and taking a shower involved standing in line for forty-five minutes.

Schwarzkopf made a point of getting out from his bunker in Riyadh about once a week to see the troops. This lifted his own morale as well as that of the 499,200 U.S. men and 32,000 U.S. women under his command. As CINC, he held the firm belief that his commanding generals should stay close to their troops. He did not want Boomer, Luck, Franks, and others coming to Riyadh to shuffle papers with him: much better, he felt, was to get out in the desert with them on a regular basis. His impact appears to have been inspirational.

He had never liked formality in a general. The dashing or handsome commander, in his view, was more than likely to mask the self-centered preener. He preferred a "muddy-boots" general like General Creighton W. Abrams to Abrams's predecessor in Vietnam, General William Westmoreland.

Like Monty on the eve of El Alamein, Schwarzkopf liked to mingle freely with his men in the desert, shaking their hands, embracing them, chatting with confidence about inevitable victory. As he had in Alaska fifteen years earlier, he reveled in his nickname "the Bear." Only the four stars on his desert cap really set him apart as he strolled around in the same camouflage desert uniforms worn by all the servicemen and -women. "To the younger soldiers particularly, he was inspiring," said Staff Sergeant Justin Smith of the 19th Support Center. "When he came to Dhahran in early December, they just swarmed around him. He was like a father."

One incident in the War Room in Riyadh typified General Schwarzkopf's style of leadership. The room was always filled with generals: his own staff and, often, allied commanders. But there was one very junior soldier who regularly attended meetings. His name was Petty Officer Tom Nichols and his job was not a very demanding one; he had to flip the slides. But when Nichols's birthday came around, General Schwarzkopf made sure that "Happy Birthday" was sung to him. Thus a room full of generals sang "Happy Birthday" to a petty officer.

Out in the field, too, there were small things that made a difference. For example, when more than a thousand ultra-modern M1A1 tanks arrived in December, Schwarzkopf made sure that special steel plates for added protection were welded on the front and that the men of the 24th Division knew about this.

In many ways, Schwarzkopf personified the changes in the concept of leadership that had swept the Armed Forces since Vietnam. That war revealed a terrible crisis of leadership, and the crisis had taken a decade to pass. Countless studies of the qualities essential in officers and the techniques used in assessment of personnel had been made—indeed, Schwarzkopf had co-written one himself when he was at the Army War College in 1973. One aim since then had been to do away with discipline for its own sake and replace it with an intelligent discipline based on mutual trust and shared responsibility between professionals. Another goal was to encourage initiative and get away from the concept, prevalent in Vietnam, that leadership is no more than administration and the avoidance of mistakes. Schwarzkopf, it became clear in the Gulf, led such an army.

For example, one of the major problems in Vietnam was the persistent question in many soldiers' minds: "What the hell are we here for?" In Saudi Arabia, this problem was scarcely encountered. One general said that "my men knew just about everything I knew. That is comforting to a smart person. It's when they are kept in the dark that the trouble begins." Moreover, in one sign of the trust placed in them, soldiers were still free to call home. On the phones, however, there were discreet reminders: "Do not reveal where you are, when the attack will come, or what its purpose is." There were no leaks.

Lieutenant General Luck said, "General Schwarzkopf had a motivated Army because his men generally knew what was going on. They knew it was not about cheaper gasoline. It was about the oil that produced the money that produced the power that threatened our way of life."

The soldiers were patient. But as Christmas approached, their patience was tried. At no time was Schwarzkopf's personal impact on his forces more important than as the holiday season drew near, bringing with it insistent thoughts of home and distant loved ones.

The CINC felt he owed it to his troops to be with them. In the same way, twenty years earlier in Vietnam, the then lieutenant colonel had made a point of going out into the midst of the jungle to eat turkey with his battalion. Such things, he knew, meant a lot more to a soldier than any amount of words.

Shortly before Christmas, he visited the mess hall of a hospital that the 92nd Medical Battalion from Springfield, Illinois, and the 114th Evacuation Hospital from Salt Lake City, Utah, had set up on the outskirts of Riyadh. The mood was fairly grim: there had been talk of as many as 20,000 to 30,000 casualties. Major Karen King watched the general as he strolled around. At one point, he stopped and said to a soldier, "How are you doing?"

The reply was blunt: "I'd like to be home with my family."

"Yeah, so would I," said General Schwarzkopf.

For Major King, this was an arresting moment. "It suddenly brought home to me that General Schwarzkopf was in the same boat as us," she said. "In my twelve years in the military, I had never seen that sort of thing verbalized before by a commander in quite that way. And it was very reassuring to know that we had a leader who was sticking with us and cared about us enough to do so."

Everywhere, soldiers improvised to try and conjure away the loneliness of that time. Out in the desert, Captain Steffan Twitty made a Christmas tree out of a camouflage tent suspended from a pole hung with stick lights of various colors and some Christmas paper. From a distance, it actually looked like a Christmas tree. But that did not help. "Boy, was I homesick," he said. "My family sent me a box of gifts, but I had to throw most of them away because I could not carry them."

Wherever he went, General Schwarzkopf fought back his own emotion. He made a rare appearance in the Joint Operations Center down the corridor from the War Room to wish all his staff a merry Christmas. As usual the room—now hung with models of a C-130 Hercules transporter, an A-10 Warthog, an F-16 Falcon, and an AH-64 Apache helicopter—was buzzing with activity, as the staff processed intelligence on the movements of the Iraqis and the state of readiness of the coalition.

Later Schwarzkopf told Barbara Walters, "When I'm in front of the troops, most of the time, I think that, you know, when I'm with them, they don't want a general to cry and that's very important to me and so therefore I won't. Christmas Eve was tough, I went out to a Christmas Eve service and I was going to take a place way in the back so nobody could see me, so if I did get overcome with emotion, you know, that it would be just me. And I walked into the tent where the service was being held and they had found out that I was coming and, of course, there was a seat reserved absolutely right square in the middle of the tent under all the lights in the front row and so I just had to control it. Because the troops were there and because I owed it to the troops not to do that, then I didn't. So it was a blessing that I was in the very front row in front of everyone where we were in a big U-shaped group where everyone could look right at me."

Mingled with the thoughts of his family were thoughts of an impending war. On December 6, Saddam had announced he would release the foreign hostages he had held in Iraq since August, and by December 14 the last group of American hostages had left Baghdad. President Bush had offered to "go the extra mile for peace," and a diplomatic haggle had developed over whether, when, and where Iraqi Foreign Minister Tariq Aziz and Secretary Baker should meet. But on the central issue there was no sign of progress. In military parlance, Saddam showed no sign that he was about to "unarse" Kuwait. Schwarzkopf knew that the VII Corps was pouring in from Germany and plans for war were proceeding. When Secretary Cheney and General Powell visited Riyadh on December 19, discussion centered on a detailed analysis of the plan to take the war to Saddam.

Thus, at a time of the year whose Christian themes are peace and reconciliation, the general faced the immediate prospect of unleashing violence and destruction. He is a religious man. He does not often attend religious services, and, over the years, the regularity of his appearances in church has been dictated largely by his view of the local pastor in the place he happens to be posted. But he is deeply spiritual; and in Riyadh at this moment his spirit was sorely tested.

It was especially hard because Christmas is a very special time in General Schwarzkopf's family. His father had always built a detailed nativity scene on a big table in the living room at their old house in Lawrenceville, New Jersey. There were shepherds and sheep set in a beautiful mountainous landscape. Outside, the whole house was festooned in lights.

His father felt the occasion to be especially important partly because, for him, it was a tie to the family's heritage and the elaborate Christmas ritual the Schwarzkopfs had maintained since Christian arrived from Germany in 1852. Schwarzkopf Sr. had reveled in the meticulous attention to detail involved in the preparation of the Christmas celebration. In the same way, he adored the details of the electric train set that he had bought for Norman when he was a child. He would spend hours with his son setting out tracks runnning through a landscape dotted with small houses, trees, and animals.

As the father of Cynthia, Jessica, and Christian, General Schwarzkopf joins these two traditions: he builds a model railroad around the Christmas tree. On Christmas mornings, everyone plays with the train, watching it circle the tree while presents are opened. When the tradition began, the general had only an engine and a couple of cars. But over the years the train set has grown more elaborate. Notable acquisitions have included a circus car and a car for transporting logs.

General Schwarzkopf likes to orchestrate the Christmas celebration. He does not dress up, but he does distribute the gifts. On each packet he writes a note or riddle from which his children can guess what is inside. The family eats a special breakfast prepared by Brenda.

A measure of the importance of the occasion to the family is the fact that Brenda and the children kept a few decorated branches of a Christmas tree out for months to await the general's return. His presents were still stacked in what the Schwarzkopfs call the sun room when he finally came home in April. Then Christmas was duly celebrated. This time, however, it was the family that distributed gifts to him. From his sister Sally he received for his train a Beck's beer car, large enough to carry a real bottle. Brenda gave him a dark green hunting jacket.

In December, his sister had also found another gift for him. After buying the Beck's beer car, she was wandering around the Montgomery Mall in Maryland looking for something else to send him. In a shop window she saw two clockwork animals: a pig and a bear. The bear seemed absolutely perfect for Norman.

General Schwarzkopf opened the gift on Christmas Day and, soon afterward, called home. Initially, he seemed in good spirits and said to Sally, "Every day I have a staff meeting in the morning. Everyone is seated. Then my aide enters and announces: 'General H. Norman Schwarzkopf!' Everyone gets up and I walk in. Well, tomorrow I will have my aide announce me, and instead of General H. Norman Schwarzkopf they will see the bear walk in!"

The bear, which came to be known as Burt, took up a permanent place on the table beside General Schwarzkopf in the War Room.

Although he joked about the bear, Sally came away from the conversation believing that her brother saw war as almost inevitable. He sounded discouraged. He had not given up hope of a peaceful resolution, but he was growing despondent. "Time is awfully short," he told his sister.

Referring to the January 15 deadline for Iraq's withdrawal from Kuwait that had been set by the United Nations on November 29, Sally answered, "There are still three weeks left. A lot could happen."

But the general could not hide the way he felt. "Things," he confessed, "are not looking good."

8

Thunder and Lightning

War is the remedy that our enemies have
chosen, and I say let us give them all they
want.
—General William T. Sherman

Arriving in Riyadh on January 10, 1991, Secretary
of State Jim Baker found King Fahd in a relaxed mood,
full of an apparently serene resolve to take on Saddam.
Any hesitations within the Saudi royal family had by now
disappeared. During a fifteen-minute meeting that evening,
the King told the Secretary he was certain that the Iraqi
President would not meet the January 15 deadline for a
withdrawal from Kuwait and that therefore it seemed an
allied attack would have to come. According to one U.S.
official who was at the meeting, the question of the timing
for the beginning of the air assault then came up, and the
King said he did not need to know until a few hours before
the attack started. It was therefore agreed that Secretary
of State Baker would pass the word to Prince Bandar Bin
Sultan, the Saudi Arabian ambassador in Washington,
who would inform the King just a few hours before the
coalition's bombardment of Iraq was set to begin. At the
same time, Ambassador Freeman would inform Prince
Saud al-Faisal, the Saudi Foreign Minister.

The tone of the meeting reflected the fact that, by
January 10, war was all but inevitable, and the Saudis

had developed confidence in the U.S. ability to wage it. Indeed, over a series of meetings, King Fahd had come to respect and like General Schwarzkopf.

Secretary Baker's meeting with Iraqi Foreign Minister Tariq Aziz in Geneva the previous day had been a complete failure. Aziz refused to accept a letter for Saddam from President Bush. Afterward Aziz declared bluntly that Iraq would attack Israel if war broke out. Some time before this meeting, and certainly before the end of December, the President, long torn over the possibility of war, had found equanimity in his determination to fight for the recapture of Kuwait. Bush presented the case as one of good against evil; he rhetorically compared Saddam to Hitler, despite the quiet support that the United States had given the Iraqi ruler over many years in his war against Iran. More to the point, it was a case where appeasement would grant a militarist dictator a degree of oil-based power that would have an incendiary effect on a strategic region and a disruptive one on the entire world economy.

No "new world order," based on a collective commitment to the rule of law, could accept such international thuggery. Indeed, Saddam's invasion directly contravened President Bush's vision, outlined in October 1990, of a "new partnership of nations that transcends the Cold War, a partnership based on consultation and collective action especially through international and regional organizations, a partnership united by principle and the rule of law."

In one reflection of U.S. resolve, a fifty-seven-member task force had started work in Washington on December 1, 1990, to prepare for the reconstruction of Kuwait after it was retaken. Colonel Lester R. Wilson of the 352nd Civil Affairs Command was a member of this group and had no doubts that its establishment reflected a determination to take the war to Saddam if necessary.

General Schwarzkopf was also ready for war. After Vietnam, he had no more illusions about battle. He knew the horrors of warfare. But he remained a military man. That is to say, he continued to believe that some things are worth fighting and dying for; and that, sometimes, war is the only effective means to political ends. For a traditional American such as Schwarzkopf, those ends include the safeguarding of freedom and, where possible, the promotion of democracy; and, more tacitly, the defense of vital U.S. economic interests.

"I am a soldier," Schwarzkopf said. "I took an oath to support and defend the Constitution of the United States of America and to obey the orders of my leaders duly appointed over me, and I did this with the sure knowledge that as a military commander I could be asked to go to battle and protect those things that we Americans believe in."

The German military theorist Karl von Clausewitz, whom Schwarzkopf admired, had stated in 1832 that "war is not merely a political act, but also a real political instrument, a continuation of political commerce, a carrying out of the same by other means." He added sharply that "war is an act of violence to compel the enemy to fulfill our will." By January, with the troops of the VII Corps completing their move from Germany to Saudi Arabia, Schwarzkopf believed he had the means to coerce Saddam into leaving Kuwait and that such coercion was both justified and necessary. It was, in his view, in the long-term best interests of the entire world.

The general's overall strategy, first outlined to his commanders two months earlier, had by now been refined. Broad plans had become precise missions. At endless meetings in the Tactical Air Command Center in the headquarters of the Saudi Royal Air Force, Brigadier General Buster Glosson and Lieutenant General Charles Horner, the two senior U.S. Air Force officers in Riyadh, had mapped the course the air campaign should take.

Iraqi targets for the bombardment—including military depots, a "fertilizer plant" in Al-Qaim apparently used for research on nuclear weapons, the civilian telephone system, chemical-weapons facilities, electrical power grids, Scud missile sites, airfields, gasoline tanks, key bridges both in Baghdad and over the Euphrates, surface-to-air missile systems, command-and-control nodes, and key industrial sites—had been carefully selected. In each case, ordnance and aircraft were matched to the target: for example, the pinpoint accuracy of the F-117 Stealth's laser-guided bombs for the Baghdad telephone exchange; low-flying British Tornadoes to destroy Iraqi runways; the 750-pound bombs of the veteran B-52s for large targets such as military depots; and the Navy's Tomahawk cruise missiles fired from battleships in the Gulf for unprotected sites such as electrical grids.

Extreme precision was possible because of advances in technology. In World War II, the whole city of Dresden was bombed. In the Gulf War, an air shaft in a building could be picked out, although pinpoint accuracy was by no means always achieved.

At the same time, in a drawn-out and sometimes bitterly argued process, the exact shape of the sweeping ground attack had been defined. Because ground troops were going to begin moving into their pre-attack positions at exactly the same time as the air assault started, this maneuver had to be worked out by mid-January. Indeed, although the air and ground attack have been widely viewed as two separate things, they were in fact inextricably intertwined. During the night of January 16–17, as the first aircraft began their bombing missions, the first of more than 100,000 troops of the XVIII Airborne Corps started moving west. In the air and on the ground, the coalition was on the move.

Preparing this had not been a straightforward process. "In the end, it was a lot easier to execute this than it was to plan it," commented Major Richard Rowe of the XVIII Airborne Corps. For one thing, several XVIII Corps staff officers tried in December to persuade General Schwarzkopf that he had to start moving some fuel and soldiers out to the west immediately in preparation for his proposed "left hook" flank attack.

They argued that there was simply no way that the nearly 120,000 men of the XVIII Corps—in addition to their vehicles and a sixty-day supply of food, water, fuel, and ammunition—could all be moved more than five hundred miles inland in the period, initially envisaged as fourteen days, between the launching of the air attack and the start of the ground war. They suggested that some discreet preparatory work on a logistics base to the east of Rafha, about three hundred miles inland, should be done beforehand.

The response from Schwarzkopf was pitiless. According to the recollection of one officer involved in planning meetings, the CINC declared roundly, "There will flat-out be no sign of moving before D Day. I don't give a hoot about the difficulties. You're not going early."

What Schwarzkopf wanted to ensure was that up until the moment the air assault began on D Day, any Iraqi Intelligence officer looking at the array of coalition troops would see *exactly what he expected to see*. That is to say, he would see no troops to the west of Hafar al-Batin, a town about 120 miles inland from the Gulf, roughly in line with a southward prolongation of Kuwait's western border.

The impression would be that an attack would come directly on Kuwait, or that any attempt at a flanking maneuver would be confined to the area close to Kuwait's western frontier, which meets its southern border with Saudi Arabia at a point about 120 miles inland. There would be no indication—none whatsoever—of any possible assault from points between two hundred and three hundred miles inland, which is what the CINC actually planned. Indeed, Schwarzkopf was so insistent on the need for the desert out to the west to remain empty that even the sending of small civilian reconnaissance vehicles to the area around Rafha had to be specifically approved in Riyadh. In a relatively decentralized operation, this was utterly exceptional.

Another point of contention during discussions in December had been just how far into Iraq the attack should go. Initially, commanders favored cutting the Euphrates at As-Samawa, a town about midway between the northern Kuwaiti border and Baghdad. This would have had the advantage of enabling U.S. troops to make some of their advance northward into Iraq along a road, rather than across a tough desert terrain of shale rock and escarpments, and so save much-needed fuel. Moreover, by taking As-Samawa, little more than one hundred miles from the Iraqi capital, Schwarzkopf would have made one of his central tactical aims in the operation highly explicit: that is, the threatening of Baghdad.

It was not that there was ever any thought of going into the Iraqi capital. But Schwarzkopf decided early in his planning that it was essential to pose a *direct psychological threat* to Saddam in order to keep him off balance.

He wanted to plant the insidious thought of a full-scale invasion in the Iraqi leader's mind in order to confine Saddam's response in what the American commander in chief still thought might be a bloody war lasting weeks. Indeed, as the planning for the XVIII Corps' attack went ahead, troops were told they had six essential aims, of which the first five were "rapidly cut lines of communication; assist in the destruction of the Republican Guard; emphasize speed in all operations; emphasize operational security at all echelons; minimize casualties." The sixth was "threaten Baghdad."

Finally, however, Schwarzkopf and his commanders had decided in December that going as far into Iraq as As-Samawa would be a mistake. There was only one causeway into the town, which could easily be blown up, cutting off any coalition troops there. In addition, going into the town would mean risking heavy civilian casualties and getting bogged down in a messy urban fight. Schwarzkopf did not want that.

As intelligence about the desert terrain improved, gathered from sources as various as satellite photographs and the debriefing of Bedouins, it became apparent that it would be possible instead to cut across the desert and block the Euphrates close to An-Nasiriya, about fifty miles nearer Kuwait. It was a gamble—like Rommel's dashes across the desert a half century earlier—but it would save time, avoid the major population center of As-Samawa, and reinforce the element of surprise. Moreover, Schwarzkopf concluded that although his troops would be farther from Baghdad, the psychological threat he wanted to conjure up for Saddam would still exist.

Throughout the planning, Schwarzkopf insisted that the Iraqis never be underestimated. "As a military planner, you always plan for the worst case rather than the best," he said. Colonel John J. Marcellow of the XVIII Corps said, "Every goblin was thrown against our plans: Iraqi chemical attack, tactical, air, helicopter—you name it." Schwarzkopf's men tried repeatedly to convince themselves that what he had proposed was impossible. They tried hard. In military parlance, they "war-gamed his ideas to death." But although it never looked easy, and often looked alarmingly ambitious, the CINC's plan stood the test.

One of the main preoccupations underpinning the plan was Schwarzkopf's obsession with avoiding casualties. He did not want any meat-grinder soldiering. As he would say later, "The loss of one human life is intolerable to any of us who are in the military."

This was one reason for the flanking attack: to avoid what Schwarzkopf called a "slugfest"—the sort of grinding, head-on confrontations that marked World War I and the Iran–Iraq War. The details of the flanking plan were also affected by his concerns. For example, in December, the 101st Airborne Division (Air Assault) contemplated achieving the planned severance of the Euphrates by parachuting soldiers into the river valley. But, in the end, Schwarzkopf would not accept this sort of high-risk air assault operation.

Similarly, although the Marines pressed very hard to make an amphibious landing in Kuwait, Schwarzkopf was determined that the threat from the sea should remain just that: a threat pinning down large numbers of Saddam's troops. He could not imagine how an amphibious landing into heavy Iraqi fire could fail to result in onerous casualties. With the lessons of Vietnam, Grenada, and the aborted Tehran hostage-rescue attempt in his mind, he was not going to do anything merely to accommodate the wishes of one of the services. He was paid to make the best decisions, not to placate people.

By January 11, 1991, when Secretary Baker left Riyadh, all the details for the allied assault were finally in place. According to one senior officer, the plan at that point had been adjusted about forty times in various ways, but never in its overall thrust: deception at sea, rapid flanking movement to the west, and blistering, abrupt firepower from front and rear to free Kuwait City and trap the Republican Guard about one hundred miles farther north, near Basra.

The following day, January 12, Congress authorized war. The main worry in Riyadh had by now come full circle from August. In the place of a fear that Saddam might attack Saudi Arabia, there was concern that Saddam might announce a partial pullout from Kuwait before the January 15 deadline, so perhaps driving a wedge between the ranks of the carefully assembled allied coalition. As a French diplomat commented, "Any announcement of a phased withdrawal on the eve of January 15 would have complicated things enormously." With such a move, Saddam might have contrived to keep his Army intact while achieving his objectives of undermining Kuwait, displaying his might, and destroying Kuwaiti oil production.

But Saddam did nothing, other than rebuff one last-minute attempt at diplomacy by UN Secretary General

Javier Perez de Cuellar, who visited Baghdad and met with the Iraqi leader on January 13, 1991. Yet again, in the words of Lieutenant General Luck, he proved himself "dumber than a stump" when it came to probing the weaknesses of the coalition arrayed against him.

January 15 is an auspicious day in Saudi Arabia. For it was on January 15, 1902, that King Fahd's father, Abdul Aziz Ibn Saud, seized the Mismak fortress in central Riyadh from the rival Rasheed dynasty, so putting an end to the exile of the Saud family and establishing the House of Saud that has ruled Saudi Arabia ever since. In a strange twist, Ibn Saud set out on this conquest of Riyadh from exile in Kuwait City, then a rather miserable port town awash in open sewage. He had been living in Kuwait City, the best natural harbor on the four-thousand-mile Arabian Peninsula, since 1895, plotting revenge on the Rasheeds, who had ousted his family. Eighty-nine years—and a lot of oil—later, an immeasurably larger force was about to move against an occupying army in Kuwait.

The deadline passed. That day, January 15, President Bush signed the National Security Directive authorizing military action. And it was in the early hours of Wednesday, January 16, in Saudi Arabia, that Schwarzkopf received the order from Defense Secretary Dick Cheney and JCS Chairman General Colin Powell to begin the attack. Ambassador Freeman informed Prince Saud al-Faisal that the President's decision had been made. The order went out to the Gulf fleet, from which the first Tomahawk missile was to be fired at Iraq, and to air force bases. Schwarzkopf asked the chaplain, Colonel Carl Peterson, to say a prayer for the safety of U.S. forces. Then, in the bunker below the Defense Ministry where he had spent many of the previous 143 days, he put on one of his favorite songs, Lee Greenwood's "God Bless the U.S.A."

Schwarzkopf's call to battle, conveyed to all his troops, said in part: "I have seen in your eyes a fire of determination to get this job done quickly so we may all return to the shores of our great nation. My confidence in you is total. The President, the Congress, the American people, and indeed the world stand united in their support of your action. Our cause is just! Now you must be the thunder and lightning of Desert Storm. May God be with you, your loved ones at home, and our country."

It was reminiscent of Lieutenant General Bernard Law Montgomery's call to his troops on the eve of another battle, El Alamein, which had influenced Schwarzkopf's planning for the Gulf War. On October 23, 1942, Montgomery, in what he called a personal message to be read to all troops, said in part: "The sooner we win this battle, which will be the turning point of the war, the sooner we shall get back home to our families. Therefore let every officer and man enter the battle with a stout heart, and the determination to do his duty so long as he has breath in his body. *And let no man surrender so long as he is unwounded and can fight.* Let us all pray that 'the Lord mighty in battle' will give us the victory."

Montgomery issued the message in part because he believed that "the morale of the soldier is the greatest single factor in war." It was a belief shared by Schwarzkopf, who was increasingly convinced that the superior morale and stronger will of his forces would be decisive. Referring later to Saddam, he said scathingly, "I have to tell you, a soldier doesn't fight very hard for a leader who is going to shoot him on a whim. That's not what military leadership is all about."

All his professional life, Schwarzkopf had been driven by his love of the soldier. To him it was manifest that love of the soldier was what the Army was all about. Without that, there could be no cohesion, no drive for victory, because the soldier's commitment would be less than absolute. Thus, on the eve of battle, Schwarzkopf declared that "my confidence in you is total." He knew the importance of motivation; and as he ordered more than half a million soldiers into the fight, he emphasized what he saw as the justness of their cause. He also chose to stress the key element in his battle plan: all-enveloping speed. Hence the "thunder and lightning" of the storm descending on the Iraqis from all sides.

Schwarzkopf had elected to call the beginning of the war "D Day." It was just over forty-six years since General Eisenhower had given the order to begin the assault on Nazi forces in Normandy with the most powerful invasion force ever assembled. On D Day in 1944, Allied forces included 11,000 combat aircraft, 39 divisions, and 6,000 warships. Schwarzkopf's firepower was not as extensive—he had just over 2,500 warplanes—but advances in technology made it the most lethal array of military might ever gathered together.

When Eisenhower, on June 5, 1944, despite terrible weather, had uttered the laconic but decisive phrase, "Okay—we'll go," and so launched the Normandy invasion the following day, Schwarzkopf was nine years old. A couple of months later, on his tenth birthday, he had received the extraordinary letter sent from Tehran in which his father expressed his certainty of his son's success in what he called "the battle of life." On January 16, 1991, Schwarzkopf assumed the place in history that letter had portended and he himself had dreamed about at West Point. It was the culminating moment in a life sometimes torn by squalid savagery or held hostage by mediocrity but always steadily directed toward what may only be described as a heroic goal.

The first explosion was that of a Tomahawk cruise missile, launched from a battleship in the Gulf. Then, at about 2:30 a.m. on January 17 (6:30 p.m. on January 16 in Washington), air force Stealth fighters, invisible to Iraqi radar, led the way through an almost moonless night at the head of the coalition's massive air armada.

Over the next five weeks, more than 80,000 air sorties would be flown against the Iraqis. The bombardments would become almost routine. But as the bat-like Stealths made their way through the night toward Baghdad, nervousness in the War Room and the Tactical Air Command Center (TACC) was running high. Iraq was reputed to have powerful anti-aircraft defenses, including artillery and a range of surface-to-air missiles, as well as a redoubtable Air Force.

But the nervousness quickly gave way to relief as the first laser-guided bombs hit communications and air-defense centers in and around the Iraqi capital. Astonishingly, there was little sign of any response from Saddam's Air Force. Even with the months of military buildup in Saudi Arabia and the formal January 15 deadline, the Iraqis appeared to have been taken by surprise.

Lieutenant General Charles Horner had the satisfaction of getting confirmation of a Stealth laser-bomb attack on the main Baghdad telephone exchange when CNN's Bernard Shaw, who had been transmitting live from the Iraqi capital, abruptly went off the air. "When we got through those first ten minutes, we had 'em. It was just a question of time," Horner later exulted to *Newsweek* magazine. The myth of Iraq's awesome power, of the might of the fourth-largest army in the world, had already been punctured.

The success of the first air assault proved the effectiveness of Horner's computerized planning and the correctness of the decision Schwarzkopf had made early on to give Horner sweeping overall control of the air campaign. The U.S. Air Force led the way and performed with great distinction. But aircraft from Britain, Saudi Arabia, France, Italy, and Canada, as well as navy bombers and Marine attack aircraft, also made big contributions.

Their missions were coordinated in a daily Air Tasking Order that could run to as many as 300 pages. So-called strike packages were led by F-14 Wild Weasels and EF-111A Ravens crammed with electronic jamming equipment to knock out Iraqi radar and air-defense missiles.

Behind them came F-15 fighters, British Tornadoes, F-16 fighter bombers, F-111 bombers, navy A-6 bombers, and a host of other aircraft. Airborne warning and control (AWAC) planes coordinated these "packages" of destruction. The combination was so effective that in the first week of the air war the allies lost just ten planes, a fraction of the losses that had been anticipated.

Very quickly, Saddam's ability to command and control his forces in Kuwait and southern Iraq was disrupted because his communications links were damaged. This was an essential goal of Schwarzkopf's in this initial phase of the war. The coalition's aim against the Iraqi Army was straightforward and would be described bluntly by Chairman Powell after six days of bombing: "First we're going to cut it off, and then we're going to kill it."

The CINC watched the progress of the battle from his big black leather chair in the War Room. He now seldom left this bunker. His staff was forever rolling out different maps for him, which he would study intently. Every evening, at 7 p.m., he met with the British commander Lieutenant General de la Billiere, the French commander Lieutenant General Roquejeoffre, and the Saudi commander Lieutenant General Khalid. Respectively, they represented 45,000 British troops, 14,000 French soldiers, and the approximately 60,000-member Saudi Armed Forces. Any news of casualties—seven crewmen were lost in the first forty-eight hours of the war—was accepted with great solemnity. "You felt his compassion for each and every one," said a staff member. "I've worked for some machines. Well, Schwarzkopf had a drive to win the war. But he cared for his people."

It was not just the Air Force that Schwarzkopf ordered into battle on January 17.

At 2:30 a.m., the Army's 1st Battalion of the 101st Aviation Brigade, 101st Airborne Division (Air Assault), under the command of Lieutenant Colonel Dick Cody, attacked Iraq with six AH-64 Apache helicopters and one MH-53 helicopter, in order to destroy three critical ground radar stations inside the country. Special Forces helicopters were also involved in the assault. The secret operation, designed to open up a key western air corridor for the allied air attack, was a success. This was an example of the unusual degree of cooperation between services that Schwarzkopf managed to establish in Saudi Arabia. It also underlines an overlooked fact: in many senses, the "air" and "ground" wars began at the same time.

For, as aircraft screamed overhead and the attention of the media was focused on the bombing of Iraq, Schwarzkopf initiated the key maneuver of Desert Storm. Led by the French Daguet Division, the more than 100,000 troops of the XVIII Airborne Corps started moving toward Rafha, over two hundred miles to the west. It was during the dark night of January 17 that this movement of unprecedented scope began.

Just as Schwarzkopf had hoped, the unrelenting aerial bombardment distracted attention from this massive displacement of people, weapons, fuel, food, tanks, trucks, ammunition, and other supplies.

Over the ensuing days, with the French acting as a screen between them and Iraq, the 3rd Armored Cavalry Regiment, then the 82nd Airborne Division, next the 101st Airborne, and finally the 24th Infantry Division (Mechanized) moved into the wide-open spaces of the desert around Rafha, more than one hundred miles to the west of where Saddam imagined coalition troops to be. Many of these XVIII Corps troops had to move over five hundred miles from their defensive positions near Dhahran. Meanwhile, units of the VII Corps were still arriving from Germany at the port of Jubail and then moving more than one hundred miles out into the desert to bases near Hafar al-Batin. From there, the 1st and 3rd Armored Divisions and 2nd Armored Cavalry Regiment would begin shifting north and west to their pre-attack positions on the eastern flank of the XVIII Corps. One statistic gives an idea of the complexity of these movements: it takes eighteen hours for a single division of 16,000 troops to cross a road!

Moreover, roads do not abound in the Saudi Arabian desert. There is only one going east-west along the Iraqi-Saudi border: the Tapline Road. A section of it was cordoned off to serve as a landing strip for C-130 transport planes carrying troops and equipment into the Rafha area. In the shadow of the air war, no fewer than 1,252 such internal flights were made to transport, among other things, 2,703 wheeled vehicles for the XVIII Corps. Truckers became unsung heroes of the war. They worked day and night to ferry soldiers and logistical supplies westward. In all, 5,476 truck journeys were made on the Tapline Road. A total of 117,844 soldiers were transported. To avoid the bottlenecks on this road, about 30 percent of the troops went via Riyadh and then north, an even longer journey.

This secret maneuver amounted to the equivalent of a force of more than 100,000 soldiers arriving at Norfolk, Virginia, on the Atlantic coast, then moving into pre-attack positions around Cincinnati, Ohio.

The overall commander of this enormous logistical operation was Lieutenant General Pagonis. There was nothing glamorous about it. As one soldier of the 24th Division put it, the logistics people provide "everything from the food that goes in your mouth to what you do with it later." But, as early as the fifth century B.C., the necessity of logistical cohesion had been clear to Clearchus of Sparta, who wrote: "Without supplies, neither a general nor a soldier is good for anything." Pagonis, in effect, through his determination to achieve what some thought was impossible, allowed Schwarzkopf to apply his imaginative strategy.

It did not all go smoothly. In the frenzy to get things to Saudi Arabia, everything had been ordered at what the military call "02" priority, that is, the level immediately below "01," which is a national emergency. Staff Sergeant Justin Smith of the 19th Support Center said he even came across briefcases ordered at "02," and "I must say I downgraded that." As equipment was moved westward after January 17, there was still a shortage of the special, newly designed suede desert boots ordered by Schwarzkopf and of chemical defense suits. All soldiers had two chemical suits, but reserve suits that would have been dropped to them in the event of a protracted war were lacking. The only two sizes available were extra small and extra large. "I felt guilty. There were no mediums," said Sergeant Smith. "I was putting myself in the shoes of these guys and imagining the chaos there might have been. But nobody could do anything about it."

As the westward movement started, Schwarzkopf went to extreme lengths to confound the Iraqis. He ordered an elaborate deception operation from a base code-named "AO Kelty" opposite the "elbow" where Kuwait's border with Saudi Arabia veers northward. This operation, which began five days before the air assault started, and continued well into February, was designed to make the Iraqis think the XVIII Corps was still where it was when the first Stealth bomber unleashed its payload on Baghdad on January 17. About 150 people, using fake, inflatable helicopters and tanks to give the appearance of a real base, kept up a barrage of radio and other signals for Iraqi Intelligence to pick up, so maintaining the illusion that nobody had moved.

This illusion also depended on tight control of the press. Throughout the campaign, Schwarzkopf tried to maintain a balance between his inclination to limit press access strictly and his awareness that a rigid barrier against the media would only arouse resentment. Shortly after arriving in Riyadh, he said, "I ain't no dummy when it comes to dealing with the press. And I fully understand that when you try to stonewall the press, and don't give them anything to do, then before long the press turns ugly, and I would just as soon not have an ugly press."

He was speaking from experience. The complete banishment of the press during the 1983 Grenada invasion had caused an outcry. Schwarzkopf had not made that decision—his commander had—but he was party to it. The very imperfect solution the Pentagon came up with for the Gulf War was a so-called pool system, under which small groups of journalists were generally accompanied by military officials to selected units. Their stories or photographs, after being cleared for security, were then relayed via the Pentagon to the rest of the media. As a result, an overwhelming amount of the coverage came from daily briefings in Riyadh and at the Pentagon.

Schwarzkopf liked to joke with the press. Struck by the number of reporters covering the war, he said, "You've got about two battalions' worth. I'm going to keep that in mind if ever we need you!" But he was touchy on the subject of the pool system: when asked about it at one press conference, he said the rules were set in the Pentagon and "I will refer you to the assistant secretary of Defense for Public Affairs, who makes these policies . . . my job is to follow those policies." This was a strange remark coming from Schwarzkopf: in thirty-four years in the Army he had been conspicuous for his independence, rather than for interpreting his job as one of merely following Pentagon policies.

From his father, who had reason to dislike newspapermen, and from the experience of Vietnam, he had an inclination to regard the media as troublemakers. He dismissed most of the "military experts" paraded on the networks as fools and some of them as irresponsible. He took deep umbrage at what he saw as CNN's readiness to be used by Saddam as a vehicle for propaganda, as when scenes of destruction in Baghdad or battered coalition prisoners of war were shown. On the other hand, he displayed a real talent, and some obvious taste, for dealing with the press; and an apparently sincere concern over the difficult, still-unresolved issue of squaring military security with press freedom in wartime—an old dilemma exacerbated by the worldwide availability of the instant information of CNN. One hundred and twenty-five years earlier, one of Schwarzkopf's heroes, General William T. Sherman, had written of the U.S. Civil War that "newspaper correspondents with an army, as a rule, are mischievous. They are the world's gossips, pick up and retail the camp scandal . . . They are also tempted to prophesy events and state facts which, to an enemy, reveal a purpose in time to guard against it." In the case of the Gulf War, information could be beamed straight to Saddam, an avid CNN watcher, in his Baghdad bunker.

"There needs somehow to be an examination of this phenomenon," Schwarzkopf told Barbara Walters, "and a determination of how do we—I don't want to use the word 'control,' I don't want to use the word 'censorship,' but how do we deal with this situation so that it doesn't cost the lives of American servicemen and -women?"

Pending this examination, Schwarzkopf opted for caution. Major General McCaffrey, the commander of the 24th Division, said that while troops were being moved west after January 17 "we cut off all information, all reporters." Despite the huge number of people moving westward across Saudi Arabia, secrecy was maintained.

When the ground war began on the night of February 23–24, Secretary Cheney initially announced a forty-eight-hour information blackout. But Schwarzkopf objected to this as an excessive measure, and did give a short briefing about five hours after the assault began. Although he said, "I'm not going to discuss in any way the location of any of the forces involved in the battle to date," he did provide reporters with enough information to glean that the attack was going well.

But on the whole the pickings for the media were slim. News organizations were unhappy. While acknowledging the need for security, fifteen major American news organizations, including *The New York Times, Time, Newsweek,*

The Wall Street Journal, The Washington Post, and the *Los Angeles Times*, later complained in a letter to Defense Secretary Cheney that "pools did not work. Stories and pictures were late or lost. Access to the men and women in the field was interfered with by a needless system of military escorts and copy review. The pool system was used in the Persian Gulf War not to facilitate news coverage but to control it."

This control was evident in the way the war was sanitized by the Pentagon. People heard about the great tank battles being fought, but they did not see them. Gun-camera footage of precision bombs was fine when it revealed an Iraqi warehouse being blown up, but not when a bomb went astray, or when real, visible lives were being obliterated. The British did show a bomb that missed; the Pentagon decided against this. After the war, the 24th Infantry Division made a video of the war with a sound track consisting of Bette Midler's "From a Distance" and Bonnie Tyler's "I Want a Hero." Some of the most arresting footage allows the viewer to look down the sights of the laser-guided Hellfire missiles of an AH-64 Apache helicopter as some Iraqi soldiers are quite literally blown away. This sort of thing was certainly available to the Pentagon but was never shown to the American public. Indeed, the only scenes that really jarred with the image of a "clean war" were those of the so-called Turkey Shoot—the wholesale destruction from the air of Iraqis fleeing north from Kuwait City as coalition troops closed in on the town. Here, for once, it was visibly clear that a lot of Iraqis had indeed died.

But General Schwarzkopf did not like to talk about Iraqi casualties. He was in fact very prickly on the subject, refusing to give any assessment of the number of Iraqis dying. "Body count," as he called it, was a festering wound from Vietnam, where he had been obliged to satisfy officers' demands for numbers of Viet Cong dead with estimates that were largely fictitious. For a man of Schwarzkopf's integrity, this was troubling. But during the Gulf War, the mistakes made with body count in Vietnam became the pretext for an obstinate refusal to provide any figures on Iraqi casualties, although the Saudis later estimated that perhaps 100,000 people died in the coalition's air and ground assault and on June 4, 1991, more than three months after the end of the war, the Defense Department estimated that 100,000 Iraqi troops had been killed, or about twice the number of U.S. soldiers lost in Vietnam. On the body-count question, Schwarzkopf showed a raw side.

On January 18, the day after the bombardment began, he set the tone: "I have absolutely no idea what the Iraqi casualties are. I tell you, if I have anything to say about it, we're never going to get into the body-count business. That's nothing more than rough, wild estimates and it's ridiculous to do that." On January 30, he reiterated his stance: "I told you, I'm anti–body count. Body count means absolutely nothing. All it is, is a wild guess that tends to mislead people as to what's going on. That's not the way we do business, so I personally don't like the idea of issuing body counts on a comparative basis. I think it puts undue pressure on commanders to come up with numbers that are unreal."

His point was clear. But it did not address an important issue: whether such stonewalling might also have the effect of misleading those trying to understand the war in a balanced way. The closest Schwarzkopf ever came to publicly hazarding a guess at the toll was to say that there had been "a very, very large number" of Iraqi deaths. In a war where such precision was shown by U.S. forces in so many areas, and intelligence was generally sophisticated, this analysis was almost absurdly vague.

Saddam's attempts to inflict casualties came principally through his Scud missiles. On January 18, he fired seven Scuds at Israel and one at Saudi Arabia. They were the first of the eighty-one he would fire. This was the beginning of the Scud-against-Patriot battle, which pitted the previously untried U.S. Patriot anti-missile system against the Scuds—and soon produced a rash of Scud-versus-Patriot T-shirts in the boutiques of Riyadh and Dhahran.

The Scud, a NATO code name for the Soviet SS-1 surface-to-surface missile, is, as Schwarzkopf liked to point out, a very inaccurate, militarily insignificant weapon. But fired into a populated area, it can be a very nasty device; indeed, on February 25, a stray Scud warhead would fall on a barracks near Dhahran, killing twenty-eight Americans in what, for the U.S. forces, was the bloodiest single episode of the war.

Moreover, whatever its failings as a missile, fired against Israel it was politically explosive. For Schwarzkopf, the questions were: Would Israel respond? And would his coalition, with its several Arab members, hold together in the event of such a retaliation?

This was a difficult moment for both the CINC and the U.S. Administration. Schwarzkopf had expected the attack on Israel, but this did not make controlling the Israeli reaction any easier. The modern state of Israel has since its foundation in 1948 lived by the code of "an eye for an eye." As Israeli governments see it, to do otherwise would be eventually to risk another Holocaust. Defense Secretary Cheney and President Bush had to show great diplomatic skill in persuading Israeli Defense Minister Moshe Arens and Prime Minister Yitzhak Shamir that it would only play into Saddam's hands for Israel to launch its own proposed air and commando operation against Iraq. This outcome was achieved in telephone conversations with the Israeli officials shortly after the Iraqi attack on January 18. Bush and Cheney also had to promise that the hunt for Scud missile launchers would become a top priority of the air campaign. Meanwhile, the Patriot systems, which proved very effective, were immediately rushed to Israel; and Under Secretary of State Lawrence S. Eagleburger was sent to Jerusalem on a conciliatory mission.

If the Israelis had attacked, Schwarzkopf said later, he did not believe the coalition would have held. "We could not have held it together and it certainly would have made our task much, much more difficult in the long run."

So the Scud hunt was energetically pursued. Finding fixed missile launchers is not that difficult. But as Schwarzkopf commented, "Finding the mobile launchers is like finding a needle in a haystack." Moreover, there were some intelligence failures. In general, the CIA and the code-breaking National Security Agency provided commanders with a steady flow of timely information. Spy satellite photographs and intercepted Iraqi military communications, as well as a host of other data, were rapidly processed in the Joint Operations Center. Forwarded to Schwarzkopf in the War Room, they gave him the information essential for the deep and disruptive strikes that are at the heart of the AirLand Battle doctrine. Later, CIA director William H. Webster told *The Wall Street Journal*: "I believe that intelligence was right on the spot," and it is clear that vastly superior intelligence was one of the keys to Schwarzkopf's victory. He could see and see deep; Saddam knew next to nothing of coalition movements.

But on the question of Scud launchers, intelligence agencies gravely underestimated the Iraqi numbers. Schwarzkopf said, "I would tell you that we went into this with some intelligence estimates that I think I have since come to believe were either grossly inaccurate or our pilots are lying through their teeth!"

Over the ensuing weeks, a lot of allied air power was diverted to hunting out the Scud launchers. Apart from anything else, this was essential to placate Israel. Meanwhile, the Scuds provided the first real sense of war for many of Schwarzkopf's soldiers. "Putting on those charcoal-lined chemical suits with the first Scud alerts, you'd see your whole life pass before you," said Major Charlie Wright of the 92nd Medical Battalion out of Springfield, Illinois.

With time, however, they became routine. "You'd put on your mask and go back to sleep," Wright said. Some troops even took to sitting out and taking pictures of the firework display provided by the violent encounter of Scuds and Patriots—a practice they abandoned when the murderous Scud warhead falling on the barracks at Dhahran reminded them this was a real war, after all.

Many Saudis panicked. A mass exodus began from Riyadh to Jidda, out of range of the Scuds, on the Red Sea coast. The 550-mile highway across the desert between the two cities was jammed. Prices for housing in Jidda soared. Rumors swirled that—in this country, of all places—there would be no gas on the highway. So Saudi families piled containers of gas into their Chevrolets and their Mitsubishis. In fact, there was plenty of gas. The Jidda end of the highway was littered with discarded jerry cans.

Schwarzkopf was in fact never seriously worried that the Scuds might be fitted with chemical warheads. Since becoming CentCom's commander in chief in November 1988, he had been studying Iraq's military capability closely, and U.S. Intelligence had reported that the relatively complicated technology needed to add the chemical warhead to the missiles had not been mastered by Saddam. Still, the CINC was taking no chances; he, too, would clamber into a chemical suit when the Scud alerts sounded.

The Scuds had another effect on Schwarzkopf: they increased his contempt for Saddam. As he would say later, "Unfortunately, war is not a clean business." But mistakes are one thing, random potshots at civilians another. These were the actions of a killer, not a commander. Even amid carnage, war has its codes. But Saddam fired Scuds at Tel Aviv and Riyadh. He paraded battered prisoners of war, such as Lieutenant Jeffrey N. Zaun, a naval flight officer, on television; and he said on January 21, 1991, that he would use them as human shields at strategic sites. He released a massive quantity of Kuwaiti oil into the Gulf on January 25 in an act of so-called eco-terrorism. In an even more bizarre and treacherous act, he sent one battalion into the deserted Saudi border town of Khafji on January 30, and as the Iraqi tanks advanced, they had their turrets pointing backward. This is a universal sign of surrender. But then the turrets swung around, the tanks started firing, and eleven Marines were killed in a battle Schwarzkopf described as "about as significant as a mosquito on an elephant." With all of this, Saddam gave Schwarzkopf the clear impression of a desperate man who had no idea of what he was up against.

War, Clausewitz said, "is nothing more than a duel on an extensive scale." It is a battle of temperament, in which one commander in chief is pitted against another, as well as a battle of numbers and firepower. Schwarzkopf conceded on January 18, "I've been trying to psychologically intimidate him [Saddam] from long before the beginning of this conflict." By the end of January, in the light of all he had learned in five months in Riyadh, Schwarzkopf was convinced that his own will was the more resolute, his aim more focused, his military skill greater.

After two weeks of bombing, he also felt that a first phase of the war was over. On January 28, the Pentagon announced that more than eighty Iraqi aircraft had fled to Iran in a clear sign there was no longer any contest over control of the skies. At least twenty-nine Iraqi aircraft had been destroyed, and the coalition had not lost a single plane in air-to-air combat. Iraq's centralized air-defense command and control had been largely dismembered. The country's nuclear, biological, and chemical storage and production capabilities had been damaged. Direct attack had begun on the elite Republican Guard close to the Kuwaiti border in southern Iraq. More than thirty bridges had been demolished to sever supply lines to Kuwait. Schwarzkopf estimated that if Saddam needed 20,000 tons per day of supplies to support his troops, he was now getting only 2,000 tons to them. "We get many, many reports out of Kuwait that Iraqi soldiers are begging for food from Kuwaiti civilians," he said.

But the conundrum remained: When to attack on the ground? Although a debate continued in the press over *whether* a ground war would be necessary, Schwarzkopf never had any doubt. He is an infantryman; and he has always believed that, however great the transformations of warfare caused by new technology, a basic fact remains: nobody, in the end, can substitute for the action of the infantryman closing on the enemy and seizing the ground. Other units all support that essential role. Hence his battle strategy, from the outset, involved a combination of air and ground power. One secret purpose of the air campaign had been precisely to give his ground troops time to complete the big move into their pre-attack positions. It was always an air-ground war.

He remembered Vietnam. There, as in the Gulf, U.S. forces were dominant in the air. As the commander of an infantry battalion, he had sat and waited outside Vietnamese villages while they were pounded from the air and with artillery. It seemed nothing and nobody could survive through the onslaught. Then he would lead his infantry into the villages, and, from holes and shelters, the Viet Cong would emerge and give his men a tremendous fight.

So going in on the ground was essential. But timing remained an open question. Schwarzkopf had at first thought of an interval of about fourteen days between the beginning of the bombing and a ground attack, and Washington tended to favor moving as fast as possible because it was worried that cracks might appear in the coalition. Indeed, back in December, Schwarzkopf's deputy, Lieutenant General Calvin Waller, had publicly urged President Bush to wait until February, because there was concern in Riyadh that political pressure might build to act faster. There was such pressure. But, as January ended, Schwarzkopf was still not satisfied that the Iraqis had been softened up enough. He was, of course, supported by the Air Force, which kept nudging him to press ahead with the air campaign alone.

Military strategy comprises three essential considerations: where to attack, with what force, and when. By the end of January, Schwarzkopf knew the exact number of troops he was going to send against the Iraqis, and exactly where each unit was going to launch its attack. But he had still not answered the third part of the equation.

"We're going to do it as rapidly as we possibly can," he said on January 18, "but we're also going to do it in such a way that we try to minimize casualties. We don't want to have to pay a terrible price to get it over with quickly." For weeks, he grappled with that dilemma.

By the end of January, preparations for his flanking assault were virtually completed, and there was no sign of any Iraqi awareness of the huge move to the west. The last of his VII Corps forces were arriving from Germany and then moving into the desert northwest of Hafar al-Batin. The Iraqi desert terrain opposite the VII Corps and the XVIII Corps to its west remained largely unguarded. Instead, Iraqi troops massed on the seafront of Kuwait City, expecting an amphibious attack; and Schwarzkopf kept drumming home the false message that it was coming. For example, on January 30, he declared, "I would be remiss if I didn't mention the readiness of our amphibious force. We have very large amphibious forces . . . and they are continually training and ready to do the job when called upon to do so." He knew that Saddam would be watching this on CNN.

Military doctrine holds that an attacking force should enjoy an advantage of three-to-one against a well-entrenched enemy. Schwarzkopf had about 530,000 U.S. troops and 200,000 other forces against an estimated 540,000 Iraqi troops in the Kuwaiti theater. Moreover, the Iraqis had 4,700 tanks against Schwarzkopf's 3,500; they had more artillery; and they were renowned for their tenacity in a defensive war. The commander was haunted by the specter of massive casualties and did not want to take any chances.

Other commanders shared his concern. On January 28, after a long and wearying day, the deputy commander of the French forces, Brigadier General Daniel Gazeau, had made this entry in his journal: "Strange day. Meeting with the doctor and other officials. I have to make sure everything is prepared if we incur losses. For an hour and a half, we talked as if we were a *firm of undertakers*. Not amusing, but you have to be ready for the worst." The meeting, Brigadier General Gazeau said, was based on the assumption that hundreds of coffins might be needed.

The following day, January 29, the French Defense Minister, Jean-Pierre Chevènement, resigned. Long a promoter of French-Iraqi military ties and an opponent of confrontation, he made the decision because it was now clear to him that a ground war was inevitable.

Schwarzkopf was determined not to be hurried. War is a gamble. No plan survives the impact of hundreds of thousands of armed men. That is why war is regarded as an art, not a science. As Clausewitz wrote, war "has to deal with living and moral forces, the consequence of which is that it can never attain the absolute and positive. There is therefore everywhere a margin for the accidental, and just as much in the greatest things as in the smallest." But Schwarzkopf wanted to do everything to keep the number of lives gambled to a minimum.

In calculating the right moment, a commander, in the final analysis, has to trust his gut feeling. There can be no scientific justification for something like Eisenhower's decision to go on D Day despite the unfavorable weather. For Schwarzkopf, at the end of January, it did not feel right yet.

In the end, he was prepared to take the political risk of waiting in order to minimize casualties. The politicians were worried: how long would it be before television images of suffering Iraqis brought changes in the public mood, a fracturing of the Arab countries in the coalition, and Soviet restiveness? "The assumption in Washington was that the air campaign would be two weeks at the most," said one senior official. But Schwarzkopf took his time. His complete control of the air dramatically diminished the tactical risk of waiting and possibly losing the crucial element of surprise. By now he knew that Saddam was completely blinded.

On Monday, February 4, 1991, Sally Schwarzkopf was in her home in Bethesda, Maryland, when the telephone rang at about 1:00 p.m. She picked up the receiver and was greeted by the sound of a lot of static. Then, through the crackling line of a bad long-distance connection, she heard a familiar voice singing "Happy Birthday to You."

Her brother sounded in good spirits. He said, "I was looking at the calendar, and I thought of all the important people that were born on February 4. Charles Lindbergh came to mind. And then Sally Schwarzkopf!" Fifty-nine years earlier, this shared birthday had been one of the things that contributed to the friendship that developed between Schwarzkopf's father and the famous aviator.

The general's good mood turned out to be rather shallow. As the conversation turned to the war, Sally felt her brother's humor darkening and had the impression that his voice was a little shaky. She said, "I know it is hard and awful, but I am glad it is you that is down there, because you care so much about the soldiers." This comment seemed to make the general even more emotional.

A couple of days earlier, General Schwarzkopf had gone north to the area near Rafha where the XVIII Corps had now completed its enormous move to the west. He wanted to know how many days' advance warning of G Day— the launch of the ground assault—commanders felt they needed in order to complete their preparations. The reply was seven days: enough time for a series of so-called deep operations designed to soften up the enemy before the invasion. These operations were to include sixteen Special Forces missions to destroy Scud launcher sites, artillery attacks on border posts, helicopter strikes to scatter Iraqi forces, and armed air reconnaissance. Although he had been somewhat skeptical of the Special Forces' usefulness at the outset of the campaign, Schwarzkopf ended by using them extensively in the deep, disruptive strikes, aimed at destroying the military cohesion of the enemy, that are stressed in the AirLand Battle doctrine.

Schwarzkopf, who was briefed during his visit by Major Richard Rowe of the XVIII Corps, said that he would provide seven days' advance warning of G Day. At the time of this visit, and right up until the ground attack, the XVIII Corps was expecting no fewer than 5,400 casualties, and no more than 7,700, according to Major Charles Lane Toomey.

A few weeks earlier, before the move west, Schwarzkopf had visited the XVIII Corps' 24th Infantry Division commander, Major General McCaffrey, and asked him to predict the number of casualties among his 26,000 troops. "I said, sir, I don't think the Iraqis are very good," McCaffrey recalled. "So I would say not more than 300 to 500 killed or wounded. If they do fight effectively, it could go as high as 2,000 in the 24th Division."

It was against this sort of grim backdrop that the general weighed his decision on when to move. He agonized over it and had nightmares over some incident, such as a chemical attack on troops stuck in a minefield, that could cause heavy casualties. He told reporters his decision would be "a compendium of actual results, measurable results, estimated results, anecdotal reports, and gut feel." And he said the single most important thing was "minimum loss of life."

"He would not go until he knew every possible step had been made to reduce losses," said Lieutenant General Roquejeoffre, the French commander. "He would be urged by Washington to move ahead. They felt the air phase was going on too long. But no, no, not yet, he would insist. He would say the Iraqis were not sufficiently diminished yet."

On February 8, Chairman Powell and Defense Secretary Cheney arrived in Riyadh to discuss the timing of the assault. The meeting was attended by about twenty of the coalition's top commanders. According to one general present, the consensus among the commanders was that the ground campaign, once started, would probably take between ten days and four weeks. There was a sense that the air campaign had become one of diminishing returns and that a move should be made soon. All the ground troops, at this point, were locked in and ready at their appointed positions in a 350-mile sweep from the coast to beyond Rafha. Cheney and Powell listened and probed. By the end of their visit, a G Day of 4 a.m. on February 22, local time (8 p.m. of February 21 in Washington), had been tentatively set.

Because of the need to complete pre-attack operations to soften up and scatter Iraqi forces, it was agreed that the countdown to the attack should start on February 15. This was referred to as "G – 7," or seven days before G Day. On February 13, in Baghdad, at least two hundred Iraqi civilians died in an allied air attack on what the coalition said was a command-and-control bunker and the Iraqis said was a civilian shelter. This increased pressure to move ahead before opinion turned against the bombing campaign.

In a message bearing the date of February 15, the day the countdown started, Major General McCaffrey gave his order to attack to the 24th Division. The written order was conveyed to all his troops. The message began: "Soldiers of the Victory Division, we now begin a great battle to destroy an aggressor army and free two million Kuwaiti people. We will fight under the American flag and with the authority of the United Nations. By force of arms we will make the Iraqi war machine surrender the country they hold prisoner. The 26,000 soldiers of the reinforced 24th Infantry Division will be the First to Fight. Our mission is to attack 300 kilometers into Iraq to block the Euphrates River valley. Our objective is to close the escape route for 500,000 enemy soldiers in Kuwait."

From this date, February 15, the day after Valentine's Day, allied efforts built to a crescendo. There was a massive B-52 bombing of Republican Guard positions. So-called deep operations by the Army, well inside Iraqi territory, began. Engineers started to clear minefields through the use of mine-clearing line charges, or MICLICs—small rockets that leave a trail of charges whose explosion clears a path wide enough for a tank. Ducts to bring oil into the trenches Saddam's forces had dug were destroyed, so preventing the use of fire trenches. Apache helicopters flew up to one hundred miles into Iraq to reconnoiter and to attack isolated Iraqi positions in the desert. In a sign of the sagging morale of the Iraqis, an entire infantry battalion surrendered to two Apaches of the 101st Airborne Division near the air base of As-Salman during one such raid. Despite all the warnings about Saddam's equipment, this battalion had no shoulder-fired surface-to-air missiles, essential weapons for modern warfare. Here, as elsewhere, the Iraqis were simply not prepared to fight in three dimensions.

With Schwarzkopf watching for any sign of a last-minute shift to the west by Iraqi forces, the countdown continued: G – 6, G – 5, G – 4. By February 19, G – 3, Schwarzkopf was convinced the Iraqis were crumbling beneath the redoubled air assault. "Iraq's military is hurting and hurting very badly," he told *The Washington Post*. "Our assessment of them is that they are on the verge of collapse." But on G – 3, the countdown stalled.

This was the day on which Soviet diplomacy clicked into high gear. Ever since Soviet envoy Yevgeny M. Primakov visited Baghdad on February 12, there had been rumblings of a Soviet attempt to resolve the conflict before the ground attack. On February 18, Iraqi Foreign Minister Tariq Aziz went to Moscow, and the following day, Iraq indicated it would accept a Soviet peace proposal. By February 22, with the countdown still holding, this plan had been made public. It called for a cease-fire and said Iraq had agreed "to withdraw its forces immediately and unconditionally" from Kuwait, and to complete this operation within twenty-one days. The withdrawal from Kuwait City was to be completed within four days, and the release of all prisoners of war within three days. In all, it satisfied many of the coalition's demands. But the plan was made conditional on a cease-fire—and so was not in accordance with UN Resolution 660, which said the withdrawal must be unconditional—and it stated unilaterally that all UN resolutions, such as the trade embargo on Iraq or call for reparations to Kuwait, must lapse once the Iraqi withdrawal was completed.

By this time, neither President Bush nor Defense Secretary Cheney nor Secretary Baker nor Chairman Powell nor Schwarzkopf had much appetite for procrastination. They felt Saddam had been given ample warning already. Tens of billions of dollars and an immense amount of preparation had gone into laying the groundwork for war; soldiers were straining at the leash. An Iraqi scorched-earth policy had begun in Kuwait, involving the destruction of oil wells. On February 22, the President gave his final, almost impossible, ultimatum to Saddam: start large-scale withdrawal from Kuwait by noon the next day and complete it within a week, or face a ground war. When the President spoke, the countdown resumed, this time irrevocably. It was G – 2.

The next day, G – 1, impromptu chapels along the 350-mile length of the front were packed with soldiers. Troops swallowed nerve-agent antidotes and anthrax inhibitors to protect themselves from expected chemical or biological attack. Tension ran very high. "Until we crossed the border," said Major Rowe of the XVIII Corps, "nobody had concluded that this guy would not fight." The fact that there was sixty days' worth of logistical support for the troops reflected enduring fears that the battle might be protracted. Lieutenant General Luck, the commander of the XVIII Corps, said, "You always pray, but more often than not there are casualties."

Throughout the forces, from Schwarzkopf down, there was the knowledge that this was a pivotal moment: after the defeat in Vietnam, the humiliation of the 1980 Tehran raid, the embarrassments of Grenada, the enormous military spending of the Reagan years, and the heavy-handedness of the 1989 Panama invasion, the reputation of the military hung in the balance.

A message from Major General McCaffrey to his troops on the eve of battle reflected all these concerns. Among his instructions were: "Protect your HONOR—civilians and enemy prisoners of war." He also urged "safety" and said "RISK—work, work, work to reduce." The last of the ten instructions was very simple: "Pray."

With the long-awaited battle set to begin, Schwarzkopf had two targets: the recapture of Kuwait and the destruction of the Republican Guard. The former justified the war; the latter was the only means to achieve its less explicit objective of eliminating Saddam as a potentially aggressive force in the Gulf area and, if possible, eliminating him completely.

At the core of Clausewitzian military theory lies the notion of the center of gravity. In his treatise *On War*, he wrote that in any enemy force "a certain center of gravity, a center of power and movement, will form itself, on which everything depends: and against this center of gravity of the enemy, the concentrated blow of all the forces must be directed." This idea was broadly incorporated into the AirLand Battle doctrine, which espouses the notion of deep attacks aimed at essential targets that destroy the enemy's ability to fight cohesively. In the Gulf, this "heart of the hostile power" was the Republican Guard, Saddam's hand-picked elite force.

Although, when asked on January 18 if Saddam was a target, Schwarzkopf said, "We're not trying to kill any particular person," several senior officials said that planning for the aftermath of the war was based on the assumption that a humiliating defeat would swiftly lead to Saddam's downfall. The Iraqi leader was not directly targeted. But Schwarzkopf made his plans in the knowledge that the key to undermining the man who had invaded Kuwait was the destruction of the Republican Guard.

His military plan was thus based on a direct attack on Kuwait City combined with a massive pincer movement to trap the Republican Guard.

The 1st and 2nd Marine Divisions, the U.S. Army Tiger Brigade of the 2nd Armored Division, and Saudi and other Arab forces were to breach Saddam's mine barriers and make for Kuwait City. Meanwhile, the approximately 250,000 troops of the VII Corps and XVIII Corps, closing in from the southwest and the northwest respectively, were to trap and destroy the approximately 130,000 Republican Guard gathered in northern Kuwait and southern Iraq. A major part of the armed effort was therefore not aimed directly at Kuwait at all but at the Republican Guard, the military cornerstone of Saddam's regime.

In the mission statement he gave to his troops, Lieutenant General Luck, the commander of the XVIII Corps, was explicit in this targeting of the Republican Guard. The mission of the corps in its sweeping flanking movement to the Euphrates River was "to prevent the reinforcement of and escape from the Kuwaiti theater of operations by Iraqi forces; on order, continue the attack east to assist *the destruction of the Republican Guard forces command.*"

In origin, the Republican Guard bore some resemblance to Hitler's SS. The guard was conceived as the dictator's personal paramilitary force—well equipped, devoted, and politically committed to the ruling Baath ("Renaissance")

Party. Under Saddam, several brigades were recruited from his hometown of Tikrit; in a country where successions have tended to be determined by coups and murders, they were seen as an essential bulwark against the unexpected. After 1986, however, they were expanded into a major combat force, better paid, better fed, and better armed than the regular Army. Most of the Soviet T72 and T62 battle tanks and the Soviet BMP fighting vehicles were provided to the Republican Guard. Their artillery and machine guns were all of superior quality. The August 2 invasion of Kuwait was largely their work.

In the end, while a couple of divisions remained near Baghdad throughout the war, Saddam committed six Republican Guard divisions to the Kuwaiti theater: the Hammurabi, Medina, and Tawalkana heavy divisions, and the Al Faw, Nebuchadnezzar, and Adnan infantry divisions. But while he placed his conscripts as virtual cannon fodder close to the Saudi border, he had, by February 24, pulled the Republican Guard back to positions south and west of the second Iraqi city of Basra.

Schwarzkopf planned a phased attack, spread over two days, in part to see which way the Republican Guard would move. He wanted to prompt some sort of reaction before committing all his troops.

According to his original plan, much of the VII Corps and the XVIII Corps were not supposed to move until G + 1, the day after the start of the assault. But when there was no Iraqi reaction in the early hours of fighting, and extraordinarily little resistance, his plans changed. If possible, he wanted to achieve the maximum impact of what the Army today calls an "exploitation attack" and what in other times has been called the blitzkrieg: swift, unrelenting violence, by day and night, to keep the enemy forces off balance and destroy them.

The 1st and 2nd Marine Divisions were the first to attack, at 4 a.m. on Sunday, February 24 (8 p.m., February 23, in Washington). They wore chemical suits inside their

M60 tanks and armored troop carriers as they cut through paths cleared by engineers in the feared minefields laid just inside Kuwait. Two Saudi task forces also breached the minefields. As the Marines advanced into Kuwait, AH-1 Cobra helicopter gunships and A-6 attack planes fired on beleaguered Iraqi troops, who quickly began to surrender en masse. As U.S. missiles and artillery fire spread across the featureless, flat terrain, hundreds of Iraqis waving anything they could find as a token of surrender gave themselves up. Later, Schwarzkopf called this rapid minefield breach by the Marines "a textbook operation" that would "be studied for many years to come as the way to do it." His praise was surely heartfelt, but may also have been aimed in part at allaying the fury of the 17,000 other Marines out in the Persian Gulf who were denied the amphibious landing they had wanted.

At the same time, more than three hundred miles out on the far western flank of the coalition (Schwarzkopf's front was much wider than the distance between New York and Washington), the 6th French Armored Division, accompanied by a brigade of the U.S. 82nd Airborne Division, moved rapidly forward toward the target of the As-Salman airfield. Here, about a hundred miles inside Iraq, two Iraqi infantry divisions collapsed. More than three thousand prisoners were taken. The 82nd Airborne promptly moved forward to take control of handling the prisoners and cleaning up—actions known in the military as "following and supporting operations." Once the airfield was taken, the French would ensure the protection of the western flank of the coalition's operation.

To the east of the French and the 82nd Airborne Division was the 101st Airborne Division (Air Assault), which, at 7:30 a.m., airlifted about seventy miles into Iraq to set up a vital forward base for fuel and supplies, which they named Cobra. This base alone, with its roughly three hundred helicopters, was larger than the division's Stateside home, Fort Campbell, Kentucky.

All these initial moves brought far less response from the Iraqis than had been expected. They had little will to fight. Everywhere, Schwarzkopf ordered his so-called PsyOps units, specialized in psychological warfare, to drop leaflets explaining how to surrender. Accompanied by diagrams of smiling U.S. soldiers accepting the surrender of relieved-looking Iraqis dreaming of their wives and children, these leaflets said: "To seek refuge safely, the bearer must strictly adhere to the following procedures: (1) Remove the magazine from your weapon. (2) Sling your weapon over your left shoulder, muzzle down. (3) Have both arms raised above your head. (4) Approach your multinational forces' positions slowly, with the lead soldier holding this document above his head. (5) IF YOU DO THIS, YOU WILL NOT DIE." Thousands of Iraqis followed the instructions, printed in English and Arabic.

By midmorning on Sunday, it was already clear to Schwarzkopf that the Iraqis were in disarray. As one of his operational planners commented, "The Iraqis were not capable of figuring out what was going on and telling someone. We fight fast and in three dimensions, and they were stalled at fighting World War I again." From the very early hours of that first day of fighting, it started to become clear that a rout was on. Within ten hours, 5,500 prisoners had been taken.

Every battle has a crisis, a moment at which its outcome is decided. That does not mean the fighting ceases then and there. But the course of events is set. For Schwarzkopf, the crisis came within hours of the outset; knowing this, he determined that all his forces should be used immediately to push home the advantage.

Around 10 a.m., Sunday, he called the commander of the XVIII Corps and asked, "How soon can you go?" Part of the corps—the French, the 82nd, and the 101st—had already attacked. But the 24th Division of over 20,000 soldiers and the 3rd Armored Cavalry Regiment of about 6,000 troops had not been due to attack until the following day, Monday. The reply was that the rest of the corps could attack in five hours, at 3 p.m., Sunday—more than twelve hours ahead of schedule.

"Fine, go," said Schwarzkopf.

Similarly, he ordered the VII Corps, sweeping around inside and to the east of the XVIII Corps, to move on Sunday afternoon rather than in the early hours of Monday, as had been originally planned. Here again, the CINC accelerated schedules by more than twelve hours in order to achieve the maximum disorienting impact on the enemy that AirLand Battle envisages. Reinforced with the 1st British Armored Division and the U.S. 1st Infantry Division (Mechanized), the VII Corps contained the main thrust of Schwarzkopf's attack, with some 140,000 troops and about 1,200 tanks. It was directed against what Schwarzkopf called Saddam's center of gravity: the Republican Guard on the northern fringes of Kuwait and in southern Iraq.

The 1st Infantry Division out of Fort Riley, Kansas, led the way for the VII Corps. It breached a minefield on the Saudi-Iraqi border about eighty miles west of Kuwait and surged into Iraq. Alongside it came the 2nd Armored Cavalry Regiment. Behind them, the massed tanks of the 1st British Armored Division and the U.S. 1st and 3rd Armored Divisions rolled into Iraq in a swath stretching westward from the Wadi al-Batin ravine along Kuwait's western border with Iraq. They plunged northward into Iraq, meeting more resistance than the XVIII Corps but still advancing faster than had been expected, in preparation for a wheeling movement east into Kuwait and against the Republican Guard the following day.

Throughout the front, Schwarzkopf's troops acted with the force of devastating surprise. The 24th Division, for example, raced more than sixty miles into Iraq before meeting a single enemy soldier. Even then, the enemy was always looking the wrong way. "Never once did we attack an enemy force that saw us coming or was dug in prepared to defend against our attack," said Major General

The Ground War

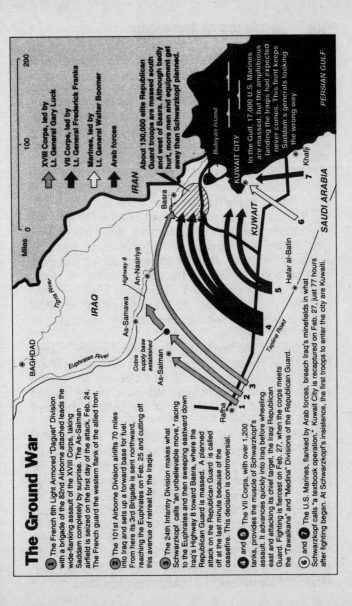

1 The French 6th Light Armored "Daguer" Division with a brigade of the 82nd Airborne attached leads the wide-flanking assault of the XVIII Corps, taking Saddam completely by surprise. The As-Salman airfield is seized on the first day of the attack, Feb. 24. The French guard the western flank of the allied front.

2 The 101st Airborne Division airlifts 70 miles into Iraq and sets up a forward base for fuel. From here its 3rd Brigade is sent northward, reaching the Euphrates on Feb. 25 and cutting off this avenue of retreat for the Iraqis.

3 The 24th Infantry Division makes what Schwarzkopf calls "an unbelievable move," racing to the Euphrates and then sweeping eastward down Iraq's Highway 8 toward Basra, where the Republican Guard is massed. A planned attack on the Republican Guard is called off at the last minute because of the ceasefire. This decision is controversial.

4 and **5** The VII Corps, with over 1,200 tanks, provides the muscle of Schwarzkopf's assault. It advances quickly into Iraq before wheeling east and attacking its chief target, the Iraqi Republican Guard. Fighting is fiercest on Feb. 27, when the corps meets the "Tawalkana" and "Medina" Divisions of the Republican Guard.

6 and **7** The U.S. Marines, flanked by Arab forces, breach Iraq's minefields in what Schwarzkopf calls "a textbook operation." Kuwait City is recaptured on Feb. 27, just 77 hours after fighting began. At Schwarzkopf's insistence, the first troops to enter the city are Kuwaiti.

XVIII Corps, led by Lt. General Gary Luck

VII Corps, led by Lt. General Frederick Franks

Marines, led by Lt. General Walter Boomer

Arab forces

About 130,000 elite Republican Guard troops are massed south and west of Basra. Although badly hurt, more men and equipment get away than Schwarzkopf planned.

In the Gulf, 17,000 U.S. Marines are massed, but the amphibious landing the Iraqis had expected never comes. This feint keeps Saddam's generals looking the wrong way.

BAGHDAD

Tigris River

Euphrates River

IRAQ

As-Samawa

An-Nasiriya

Highway 8

Basra

IRAN

Cobra supply base established

As-Salman

Rafha

Tapline Road

Hafar al-Batin

Bubiyan Island

KUWAIT

KUWAIT CITY

Khafji

SAUDI ARABIA

PERSIAN GULF

Miles

0   100   200

McCaffrey. "They were unaware we were there and they were looking the wrong way."

This element of surprise was compounded on the second day of the war by an appalling sandstorm that reduced visibility to less than a hundred feet. The storm created problems for the coalition. For example, some aerial resupply missions had to be stopped. But it created far more problems for the disoriented Iraqis. Once again, superior technology aided Schwarzkopf's forces. Using the navigation devices called global positioning systems, they always knew exactly where they were and where they were heading. These high-tech gadgets, based on digital coordinates of positions and satellite connections, could tell soldiers how far they were from pre-set targets even as sand blew sideways into their faces. Rampaging out of whipping sand on Iraqis looking in the other direction, or, later, out of the night on soldiers who did not even know the coalition was inside Iraq, the allied forces had an effect that was indeed as sudden, dramatic, and enveloping as thunder and lightning.

By contrast, the Iraqis fired thousands of artillery rounds but seldom appeared to have any means of knowing where the coalition troops were. If they had any fire-control systems, it was not obvious. Moreover, to the general surprise of U.S. forces, none of the artillery delivered chemical weapons.

On the second day, Monday, February 25, the XVIII Corps' 101st Airborne Division sent its 3rd Brigade up into the Euphrates Valley, where it cut this avenue of retreat for the Iraqis at two points between An-Nasiriya and As-Samawa and established a base named Eagle. With this central mission accomplished, the corps commander, Lieutenant General Luck, called General Schwarzkopf in the War Room in Riyadh. He told him that all missions up to that point had been swiftly and successfully accomplished and the Euphrates Valley was now blocked. General Schwarzkopf then asked about casualties.

"Sir, to my knowledge, our casualties at this point are very low," said Luck.

"How low are they, Gary?"

"One report of one wounded soldier, sir."

There was a pause.

"Gary," said General Schwarzkopf, his voice bursting with emotion, "that's *great*."

This trend continued. On all fronts, the second and third days saw rapid progress with remarkably light casualties. Troops scarcely slept as they pressed to push home the advantage without delay—a basic tenet of current military doctrine.

The Marines raced toward Kuwait City, where the 1st Division took the international airport after a fight with the Iraqi 3rd Division. They could have moved into Kuwait City on the third day of ground fighting, Tuesday, but, for diplomatic reasons, Schwarzkopf wanted the Arab forces to do that.

The XVIII Corps moved in force into the Euphrates Valley. There the 24th Infantry Division, moving with remarkable speed, took the key targets of the Tallil and Jaliba air bases in tough fights with the Iraqi 49th Division. Around Tallil, there were some extraordinary scenes with the maintenance people, electronics repairmen, and engineers of a logistics support unit attacking Iraqi commando bunkers in the dark using night-vision goggles, machine guns, and hand grenades. These logistics specialists had stumbled upon the bunkers, which had been bypassed by troops up ahead, and had no alternative but themselves to fight. This sort of thing was indicative of the general spirit and flexibility of Schwarzkopf's army.

At Tallil, which the XVIII Corps renamed the Bragg base, there was a remarkable find: hundreds of thousands of tons of munitions that appeared to commanders to have been put there at the time of the Iran-Iraq War. The 82nd Airborne Division moved in to perform the task of destroying these—and were still at it a couple of weeks later when the order came to withdraw. Some of their work led to explosions lasting about ten hours, and debris was thrown over a radius of three miles. "We could have stayed longer. It was quite a rush destroying this," said Colonel John Marcellow of the XVIII Corps. At Jaliba, meanwhile, at least twenty Iraqi aircraft were also destroyed, as well as numerous anti-aircraft guns and tanks.

Even at this front on the Euphrates, mail and its effect on morale were not forgotten. Specialist Uninta Regil would ride up from the base in Saudi Arabia on a CH-47 Chinook helicopter. M60 machine guns were pointed out on either side for protection. "I loved the ride," she said; "the pilots played good rock 'n' roll." When they got to the Euphrates, bags of mail were dropped to the troops.

After taking Tallil and Jaliba, the 24th Division veered east down the ten-lane Highway 8 toward Basra. Even at this stage, commanders had the impression that Saddam did not yet know they were in the Euphrates Valley. As they headed east, they fought Republican Guard elements, particularly infantry units from the Al Faw, Adnan, and Nebuchadnezzar Divisions.

Farther south, the VII Corps also pivoted east into Kuwait, now moving shoulder to shoulder with the XVIII Corps to their north and beginning the assault on the Republican Guard. Their massive tank attack caused extensive damage to two heavy Republican Guard divisions, the Tawalkana and the Medina. Hundreds of Iraqi tanks were destroyed.

Schwarzkopf's was an enormous army moving at unprecedented speed. According to commanders, it was the fastest, deepest attack in U.S. military history. The army moved well over two hundred miles in one hundred hours. Some of the M2 and M3 Bradley fighting vehicles recorded speeds of just under fifty miles per hour; M1A1 Abrams tanks went even faster. In a reflection of Schwarzkopf's experiences in Vietnam of losing men to friendly fire, elaborate so-called anti-fratricide steps were taken to prevent coalition aircraft from firing on this onrushing army. All ground vehicles were marked with an inverted V in fluorescent paint, and extensive vehicle recognition training preceded the invasion. Still, mistakes were inevitable, particularly with ground being covered so fast. In the worst of them, on February 26, nine British soldiers were killed when their armored scout cars came under fire from A-10 aircraft. Schwarzkopf, who had himself been mistakenly bombed by U.S. B-52s in Vietnam, said later, "It's a terrible tragedy and I'm sorry that it happened."

On Wednesday, February 27, seventy-seven hours after the fighting started, Kuwaiti forces, followed by a Saudi brigade and then U.S. troops, finally entered Kuwait City. Schwarzkopf, in a typically deferential gesture, had been insistent that the formal act of retaking Kuwait City be led by the Arabs. It was not quite August 25, 1944, in Paris, but it was a time of elation. In a series of wars since World War II, American soldiers had not known anything quite like it. Kuwaitis, who had faced a long and harrowing occupation, feted the troops wildly. At the moment of the recapture, Schwarzkopf had been in the Gulf for almost exactly six months.

It was a few hours after this, at 1 p.m. on Wednesday, that an exultant General Schwarzkopf decided to explain his flanking strategy to the world in a press conference which—in mocking reference to Saddam's vow to wage the "mother of all battles"—would become known as the "mother of all briefings." It was an extraordinary performance, brisk, articulate, convincing, overpowering. Quickly packaged on videocassette, without any editing or alteration, it became an instant best-seller in the United States.

Here Schwarzkopf likened his plan to the Hail Mary play in football, where the quarterback, desperate for a touchdown at the very end, sends every receiver way out on one flank and lobs the ball, accompanied by a prayer, in their direction. The simile was colorful and will no doubt go into the history books; but it does not bear much analysis. If anyone was desperate on the eve of the attack, it was the Iraqis and not the coalition troops. Moreover, although the XVIII Corps did make a massive and devastatingly surprising move way out on the flank, an awful lot of Schwarzkopf's "team" attacked in other directions. In military terms, his front was quite simply huge, and by no means concentrated in one corner.

The impact of this front on the Iraqis, as Schwarzkopf explained, had been devastating. Kuwait City was retaken and all avenues out of it blocked. Of an estimated 42 Iraqi divisions in the Kuwaiti theater, he said, over 29 had been "rendered completely ineffective." Of Iraq's more than 4,000 tanks, he suggested, 3,700 had been destroyed. There were already about 50,000 prisoners of war—a total that would rise to 71,000. "We've almost completely destroyed the offensive capability of the Iraqi forces in the Kuwaiti theater," he said.

The CINC clearly relished an opportunity to give his scathing assessment of Saddam: "As far as Saddam Hussein being a great military strategist, he is neither a strategist, nor is he schooled in the operational arts, nor is he a tactician, nor is he a general, nor is he a soldier. Other than that, he's a great military man." Of all these criticisms, the strongest, coming from Schwarzkopf, was also the simplest: that Saddam was not a "soldier." For the CINC, this one word embraces a code of honor, dignity, honesty, and discipline that is the framework around which he has built his life. Having so conspicuously trampled on these traditions, Saddam was beneath contempt.

Schwarzkopf also heaped criticism on the Iraqi generals: "I attribute a great deal of the failure of the Iraqi Army to their own leadership. They committed them to a cause that they did not believe in. They are all saying they didn't want to be there, they didn't want to fight their fellow Arabs, they were lied to when they went into Kuwait, and then after they got there, they had a leadership that was so uncaring that they didn't properly feed them, didn't properly give them water, and in the end, kept them there only at the point of a gun." All this amounted to the antithesis of the treatment of soldiers to which Schwarzkopf had devoted much of his energies over the previous two decades in a bid to build a professional and motivated U.S. Army.

In Kuwait, as opposed to Vietnam, the Army had been allowed to fight, and Schwarzkopf underscored the point: "I'm very thankful for the fact that the President of the United States has allowed the United States military and the coalition military to fight this war exactly as it should have been fought. The President in every case has taken our guidance and our recommendations to heart and has acted superbly as the Commander in Chief of the United States."

Amid all the bravura at the press conference, however, a key point tended to get obscured. This was that while one part of the mission Schwarzkopf had set himself— the recapture of Kuwait—was completed, the other—the destruction of the Republican Guard—was not. Although the XVIII and VII Corps had engaged large elements of the Republican Guard as they swept east, some of the force remained, and was now huddled in a twenty-mile box around Basra. At this point, the coherence existing until then between political direction and military force faltered.

Schwarzkopf said that the "gates are closed." And he described how his troops were closing in: "To accomplish the mission that I was given, I have to make sure that the Republican Guard is rendered incapable of conducting the type of heinous acts that they've conducted so often in the past. *What has to be done is for these forces to continue to attack across here and put the Republican Guard out of business*. We're not in the business of killing them. We have PsyOps aircraft up. We're telling them over and over again, all you've got to do is get out of your tanks and you will not be killed. But they're continuing to fight, and as long as they do, we're going to continue to fight with them."

As Schwarzkopf uttered those words, it was around dawn on the twenty-seventh in Washington. By the end of the Washington workday, the decision had been made to cease fighting unilaterally at midnight because Kuwait had been recaptured. Conveniently, this gave the hostilities a name: the "hundred-hour war." It was a good, "mediagenic" label, even if it was inaccurate. It had been a forty-three-day war and a hundred-hour battle.

But calling off the hostilities after one hundred hours did change the precise nature of the coalition's mission. If indeed the object was the "destruction" of the Republican Guard—and these were the words used in Lieutenant General Luck's mission statement—then that object was by no means wholly achieved when the cease-fire was imposed. It was largely accomplished, but not entirely. Some of the Republican Guard—how many is still unclear, but perhaps as many as two scarred divisions—were allowed to limp away northward toward Baghdad out of Basra.

Major General McCaffrey's 24th Division had a close-up view of this process. He was closing in from the west on precisely these remaining Republican Guard forces around Basra when he was told to call off the fight. Meanwhile, precisely as planned in Schwarzkopf's original "pincer" strategy, the 1st Infantry Division was closing in from the south. Having swept east down the Euphrates, McCaffrey's division was no more than twenty miles from Basra facing the Hammurabi Heavy Division, probably the most powerful single force in the Republican Guard. After an initial exchange of artillery fire, the Hammurabi, he said, "started to break and to stream to the rear."

McCaffrey planned his attack for 4 a.m. on January 28 (8 p.m. on the twenty-seventh in Washington). But half an hour before he was set to go, he said, the assault was called off because of the impending cease-fire, which was to come into effect at midnight Washington time.

"Going to Basra," he said, "was easily within our grasp the next day, and we had plans to do so. The Republican Guard was crumbling. Any one piece was too much for them. All of our forces together were crushing them." Because the attack was called off, however, thousands of people and some equipment got away. The Hammurabi was damaged but by no means destroyed. Still, McCaffrey added, "We had accomplished our mission, destroyed the Iraqi armed forces as an offensive force for at least the next five years."

Another member of the 24th Division, Brigadier General Joe N. Frazar, offered this account: "The Republican Guard was dissolving in front of us. I don't know if we were surprised by the cease-fire, but maybe we had a question in our minds as to why we were stopping. From our perspective it seemed premature, but we did not have the whole picture. We had plenty of supplies and a good plan to get into Basra. We would have taken it. The 1st Infantry Division was closing in from the south. Two divisions were therefore poised and we were ready to go. We had a detailed plan for the capture of Basra, down to brigade and battalion level. We were going to cut it off, and leave the 101st and the 82nd Airborne to sweep through the town. There were a couple of bridges to the north of Basra over which the Republican Guard were escaping. They were all boxed around Basra. As we had planned, we were pushing the battle in to the enemy. Then it was called off. Obviously, if we had taken Iraq's second city, Basra, it would have had a significant impact."

Just how significant is very hard to judge. But it is clear that a 124-hour war would have led to a more complete destruction of the Republican Guard—in line with the original mission—and the occupation of Iraq's second city. What effect this in turn would have had on Saddam's hold on power, and so on the underlying mission of forcing his departure, is unclear. The pressure on Saddam would certainly have been turned up a notch. But, given the closed nature of the Iraqi regime, it is impossible to estimate whether this might have been decisive. It was never likely that some external force, such as a Kurdish or Shiite rebellion, could topple him. But might an even greater humiliation and the loss of Basra have goaded a group of officers to oust him? Again, there is no knowing. It is also difficult to judge the degree to which further destruction of tanks and other military equipment would have hampered Saddam in putting down the subsequent Kurdish and Shiite revolts in the north and south of the country. He would certainly have had less firepower. But would the difference have been a decisive one?

What is clear is that more equipment got away than was thought at the time of the cease-fire. Defense Intelligence Agency and CIA estimates reported in *The New York Times* suggest that about 1,430 of Iraq's armored personnel carriers got away, where originally it was believed that no more than 500 did. Similarly about 700 of Iraq's estimated 4,550 tanks in southern Iraq escaped, against an earlier estimate of between 500 and 600.

It is also clear, however, that going into Basra could have been problematic. A fight for the town might have been extremely messy, and its occupation could have created a situation from which it was not easy for Schwarzkopf and his army to extricate themselves. "Had we captured Basra, it would have been a disaster," argued Colonel Ralph Cossa, an expert on Iraq at the National Defense University in Washington who assisted the Joint Chiefs of Staff in planning for the war's aftermath. "What would we have done with it? We would have passed to the fully fledged status of an occupying power, and there would have been no logical way out of it."

Lieutenant General Luck, the commander of the XVIII Corps, saw the cease-fire this way: "Our mission was to occupy the Euphrates River valley, attack east, and destroy the Republican Guard . . . We were ready, as any good military force, to do the next thing. We felt like we were ahead 66–0 in the fourth quarter and prepared to score another touchdown or a field goal. People were still psyched to go on. But the President probably made the right decision. In fact, not probably: I know he did."

Although he accepted the cease-fire, and had no argument with it in the end, General Schwarzkopf clearly felt some uneasiness and ambivalence, according to officials close to him. It was the general's role, not to make the decision, but merely to place the options before the military leadership. When Chairman Powell called him after the press conference on February 27 to discuss what to do, the general's response, in the words of one official he later discussed it with, could be summed up as: "I am prepared to stop. But with time, I could do more."

What might have been done was in fact illustrated two days *after* the cease-fire, on March 2, when a patrol made up of the 1st Brigade of the 24th Division came under fire from Iraqi Republican Guard troops of the Hammurabi Division that were trying to withdraw up the Euphrates. A major battle, approved by Schwarzkopf, ensued. In the fight, which lasted several hours, the 24th Division destroyed 81 Iraqi tanks, 95 armored personnel carriers, 11 battlefield missile systems, and 23 trucks. "We brought the sky in on the Iraqis," said Major Rowe of the XVIII Corps.

Later, General Schwarzkopf explained his view on the cease-fire to the British television interviewer David Frost:

> We were driving into their [the Republican Guard's] flank now, with two corps completely intact, and they were in a complete rout. And I reported that situation to General Powell. And he and I discussed, have we accomplished

our military objectives? The campaign objectives. And the answer was "Yes." There was no question about the fact that the campaign objectives that we established for ourselves were accomplished. The enemy was being kicked out of Kuwait, was going to be gone from Kuwait; we had destroyed the Republican Guard as a militarily effective force . . . I mean, it is a question of how do you define the word "destroy"? The Republican Guard was a militarily ineffective force. And we had inflicted great damage upon them and they had been routed. Now, I obviously—you know we didn't destroy them to the very last tank. And again, this is a point that I think may be lost on a lot of people. That was a very courageous decision on the part of the President to also stop the offensive. You know, we didn't declare a cease-fire. What we did is, we suspended offensive operations. Frankly, my recommendation had been, you know, continue the march. I mean, we had them in a rout and we could have continued to wreak great destruction upon them. We could have completely closed the doors and made it in fact a battle of annihilation. And the President made the decision that we should stop at a given time, at a given place, that did leave some escape routes open for them to get back out, and I think that was a very humane decision and a very courageous decision on his part also. Because it's one of those ones that historians are going to second-guess forever . . . There were obviously a lot of people who escaped who wouldn't have escaped if the decision hadn't been made to stop where we were at that time. But again, I think that was a very courageous decision on the part of the President.

These remarks were seized upon in Washington as evidence of a rift at the end of the war between President Bush and the general. Schwarzkopf later apologized to the President for what he called "a poor choice of words." But he was also intensely angered by what he saw as press exaggeration and distortion of the incident. There was no rift. Schwarzkopf never discussed the timing of the cease-fire directly with the President, according to officials close to him. But on the twenty-seventh, as his commanders prepared for their assault on the remaining Republican Guard around Basra, the general did lay out the options to Chairman Powell and indicate his own preference for proceeding.

After some discussion, however, he acquiesced in Washington's desire to end the war. The decision was not made over the general's objections. It was a slight modification of the original plan because some of the Republican Guard were going to be allowed out. But it was not so dramatic a change that the general was prepared to argue forcibly for continuing with the attack against the Republican Guard.

The war had clearly been won, and the manner of its winning was little short of miraculous. Certainly, there had been exaggerated estimates of the Iraqi Army. As it transpired, the Iraqis were inept at putting their various systems together into any cohesive force. They lacked experience in fighting air power, and were incapable of responding to an army, such as Schwarzkopf's, trained to exploit mobility, speed, and deep strikes into the enemy rear. The anxiety over chemical attack also proved unfounded. A combination of fear, lack of coordination, and basic inability to handle some of the technology appeared to explain the Iraqi decision not to employ its chemical arsenal.

But the Iraqis were still a potent army. The war was won by brilliant generalship, not lost by sheer Iraqi incompetence. If victory was always likely for the coalition because it was applying overwhelming force to an isolated enemy, it was by no means inevitable that its victory would come at such light cost to its troops.

This was ensured only by Schwarzkopf's remarkable exploitation of surprise, deception, and speed; his unerring sense of timing; his diplomatic skill in welding one force from several; his ability to make tough decisions such as ruling out an amphibious Marine landing; and, not least, his capacity to inspire his troops through his own example. Air Vice Marshal Ian Macfadyen, the chief of staff of the British forces, said, "He must go down in history as one of the great commanders. What he achieved is unique in military history. To bring together so disparate a force and then fight a battle involving one million men with such tiny losses is unprecedented."

The victory also reflected the dramatic transformation of the U.S. Armed Forces over the two decades since Vietnam. Not many Americans had paid attention. But the Armed Forces had become a highly flexible, more racially integrated, motivated, and professional group of men and women applying a doctrine, the AirLand Battle, suited to the remarkable technology in their possession. They were trained to fight the Russians in Europe, striking fast and deep to disrupt the enemy, and they fought this way in the desert. Brigadier Saheb Mohammed Alaw, the commander of the Iraqi 48th Division, said, "You attacked us with the same NATO force that was designated to attack the entire Warsaw Pact, and the entire earth shook."

During the whole hundred-hour campaign, 155 U.S. military men and women were killed, or 0.03 percent of the total U.S. force in the Gulf. (Another 108 were killed during the Desert Shield phase, according to the Pentagon.) As Schwarzkopf said, this was "almost miraculous, even though it will never be miraculous to the families of those people." The XVIII Airborne Corps of 117,844 soldiers lost 21 soldiers killed in action, or 0.02 percent of its troops. Another 62 soldiers in the corps were wounded, for a total of 83 casualties. This compared with a pre-assault estimate, based on months of intelligence and analysis, of minimum casualties of 5,400 troops in the corps. No military expert in the United States had come out with a prediction of fewer than 3,000 casualties. Former National Security Adviser Zbigniew Brzezinski predicted 20,000, and he was by no means exceptionally pessimistic.

Schwarzkopf's achievement thus lay outside the bounds of anybody's analysis or imagination inside or outside the Armed Forces.

On the outskirts of Riyadh, before the war, the 92nd Medical Battalion and the 144th Evacuation Hospital had set up a tent hospital with 400 beds. They expected to have to deal with about 1,200 patients a day; they were certain that all the 400 beds would be filled. They never had more than 76 patients. By the end of the war, many people were sitting around playing chess or cards, and the 26 surgeons were keeping their hands in by removing moles or performing vasectomies. The standing joke was that it had been a terrible war because the soldiers had been obliged to do without dessert for two nights when their civilian caterers disappeared after a Scud attack on Riyadh! In one room, the staff had taken a gurney—the padded, wheeled stretcher usually used for rushing patients into the operating room—and placed a piece of plywood on top of it. Across the plywood they had placed a net. In Schwarzkopf's war, on his army's side, stretchers ended up serving as makeshift Ping-Pong tables.

9

A Time of Reckoning

Heroism has no model.
—Louis de Saint-Just

As one approaches Kuwait from Saudi Arabia the sky grows darker, threatening rain that never comes. The gathering gloom does not portend a storm; it is the product of the black smoke billowing from the more than five hundred oil fires started by Saddam's troops before they fled, helter-skelter, northward to their ravaged home. Even in midmorning the darkness deepens near Kuwait City to the point that visibility is no greater than fifty yards. Night, it seems, has fallen before noon. But this is no ordinary night: it is a palpable and chilling obscurity, as if thick fog and moonless gloom have come together. Darkness visible. Along the road, looming like jagged shadows, lie smashed tanks, crumpled trailers, severed electricity cables, and upturned vehicles. Amid all the wreckage a solitary sign is still standing. It states that "it is one of the principles of Islam not to throw waste in the road."

There is very little besides waste, scrupulously guarded by Kuwaiti soldiers manning checkpoints in the midst of a country that has been eviscerated. They are proud of their rudimentary English. "Welcome to Kuwait," they say, and

"Have a nice day." But there is nothing nice to do or to behold in the aftermath of war.

When the smoke lifts a little, it is only to reveal a flat, gray terrain full of the twisted metal carcasses of war. The horizon, which is not distant, is lit at regular intervals with flames. Kuwait City—and there was never much more to this country than oil and the port town that administered the resultant revenue—exists in little more than name. The once-proud corniche, where tens of thousands of Iraqi soldiers dug in to face an amphibious U.S. Marine landing that never came, has been reduced to rubble. Stores, restaurants, and museums have been plundered. An eerie silence prevails. The only signs of activity in the days following the war are the lines of Kuwaitis waiting outside reopened banks to withdraw money. Otherwise, just rubble, pockmarked buildings, and silence. And the graffiti somebody has scrawled on a wall: "Free Kuwait/Bush did it/I love CNN."

This was the desolate scene that greeted General H. Norman Schwarzkopf when, on Sunday, March 3, 1991, he flew to Kuwait's devastated airport on his way to a meeting with Iraqi generals aimed at formalizing an end to hostilities. Five days had passed since the end of the war, but the general had not yet come face-to-face with its ravages. From his past, he knew something of what he might find. "War," he had said, "is a profanity because, let's face it, you've got two opposing sides trying to settle their differences by killing as many of each other as they can, and that is sort of a profane thing when you get right down to it."

But this particular profanity, even by war's abject standards, was exceptional. Oil fueled it. Coming in to land, Schwarzkopf was astonished by the nightmarish vision of fires, smoke, and destruction. He later declared, "I was totally unprepared for the scene, and the first thing that flashed through my mind was that if I ever visualized what hell would look like, this was it. It was so senseless, absolutely senseless destruction, because by every definition it would accomplish nothing." On his return to Riyadh, he confided to U.S. Ambassador Freeman that "if hell had a national park, Kuwait right now is what it would look like!"

Schwarzkopf was angered by what he saw. It confirmed all his contempt for Saddam: this was the work not of an army but of a marauding band of armed looters in uniform. He was by now convinced that the Iraqi leader was, as he later put it, a "war criminal"; and when asked if he thought Saddam would get off scot-free, he predicted, "He's not going to get off." In the days after the war, according to officials close to Schwarzkopf, there was a sense that the humiliation of Saddam had been so dramatic that his days were probably numbered.

At the airport, Schwarzkopf boarded a helicopter for the short flight to Safwan in southern Iraq where the meeting was to be held. When the two Iraqi lieutenant generals and eight officers arrived, they were searched with a metal-detection scanner before entering the tent set up for the talks. Despite his anger, Schwarzkopf refused to allow photographs of this procedure because he did not want to humiliate the Iraqis. The senior Iraqi general, who was wearing winter-dress uniform, did not initially recognize Schwarzkopf, perhaps because he was, as usual, dressed in the same desert battle fatigues as the rest of his troops.

The Allied delegation led by Schwarzkopf included the Saudi commander, General Khalid Bin Sultan; the British commander, Lieutenant General Sir Peter de la Billiere; the French commander, Lieutenant General Michel Roquejeoffre; and representatives of several co-alition countries. The Iraqi generals were Sultan Hasheem Ahmad, Saddam's deputy chief of staff, and Salah Abbud Mahmud, commander of the 3rd Corps. At the main table, Schwarzkopf and Khalid sat opposite the two Iraqis. Tension was considerable. It mounted when, in response to a statement from the Iraqis that they held 41 prisoners of war, Schwarzkopf said, "As of last night we had 60,000, but we're still counting."

The main purposes of the meeting were to arrange for the swift release of these prisoners, to agree on procedures for avoiding accidental engagements between coalition and Iraqi forces, to exchange information about soldiers missing in action, and to identify the locations of Iraqi-laid minefields. After a two-hour meeting, Schwarzkopf and Khalid announced that agreement had been reached.

But it later transpired that, on one extremely important detail, Schwarzkopf felt that he was deceived. This was the question of whether the Iraqis should be allowed to use helicopters in the war's aftermath.

Until the March 3 meeting, Schwarzkopf had issued a standing order that anything flying in Iraqi airspace was to be shot down. This order was confirmed during the talks. But at the end of the meeting, the Iraqi generals pleaded with Schwarzkopf to allow the use of helicopters alone, and the CINC acceded to their request.

"I think they suckered me," he later told David Frost. "I think when they asked me to use helicopters—at that time, you see, nothing was flying over Iraq. And we had said, 'You will not fly over Iraq.' And they looked me straight in the eye and said, 'Well, you know, you have destroyed all our bridges, you have destroyed all our roads, and therefore it is hard to get around the country. We would like to fly our helicopters. And the purpose of flying those helicopters will be for transportation of government officials.' " Given his priorities, which were to get back prisoners of war and to set up demarcation lines to stop further conflict, Schwarzkopf said this seemed acceptable.

He continued, "So, when they said to me, you know, 'We would like to fly helicopters,' I said, 'Not over our forces.' 'Oh no, definitely not over your forces, just over Iraq, for the transportation of government officials.' That seemed like a reasonable request. And, within my charter, I felt that was something that it was perfectly all right to grant. I think I was *suckered because I think they intended—right then, when they asked that question—to use those helicopters against the insurrections that were going on.* I think that absolutely was their intention—again, a personal opinion—but as I just said, they suckered me."

This was a typically frank assessment by Schwarzkopf of the way his instinctive inclination to trust an officer in uniform served him badly.

At the time of the meeting, a Shiite-led rebellion in Basra was already gaining momentum. Within days, a burgeoning Kurdish uprising in the north of Iraq had also spread to at least seven towns. It immediately became clear that Saddam was using helicopter gunships as one means to suppress these insurrections. Thus Schwarzkopf's decision to allow the Iraqis the use of helicopters made Saddam more able to confront the uprisings. Whether the difference it made to Saddam was decisive is hard to assess: certainly, his forces would have been a lot less mobile without the helicopters.

The United States did not respond, although the vague and contradictory nature of officials' comments suggested some uneasiness within the Administration. On March 13, ten days after the Safwan cease-fire meeting, at a time when Kurdish rebels claimed they controlled 75 percent of northern Iraq, President Bush said, "These helicopters should not be used for combat purposes inside Iraq." The next day, he declared, "I want to bring them [U.S. troops] home, but I'd like to have some security arrangement in place and . . . using helicopters . . . to put down one's own people does not add to the stability in the area." A day later, on March 15, Schwarzkopf reiterated that fixed-wing aircraft would "be subject to being shot down." But he did not mention helicopters, whose use he had, after all, permitted. A few days later, Pentagon spokesman Pete Williams confirmed that Iraq was using "dozens" of helicopters against the rebellions and asked, "Is our policy somewhat ambiguous?" The reply he gave to his own question was "Yes."

Schwarzkopf was not formulating that postwar policy. The conflict had clearly passed out of its military and into its political phase. But according to officials close to him, he understood the thinking behind the hands-off approach: concern over the United States getting enmeshed in what could only be a highly risky, probably fruitless, attempt to resolve the age-old internal conflicts of Iraq; and skepticism over the possibility of identifying any coherent opposition force to put in Saddam's place. Nobody wanted another quagmire like Vietnam.

There was also fear of a "Lebanonization" of Iraq, which might leave a Shiite entity in the south and a Kurdish enclave in the north. This proposition was unattractive to two key U.S. allies: Saudi Arabia (a conservative Sunni power always alert to possible disruptive influence from the Shiite fundamentalism of Iran) and Turkey (whose suspicion of Kurdish nationalism is decades old). It was one thing to have proceeded with the war while it was still on, and Schwarzkopf had suggested that more could be done before stopping the fighting; it was another to reopen it with murky political objectives, no UN mandate, and a great deal of regional uneasiness.

Iraq was an arbitrary creation. It had been carved by Western powers out of the vestiges of the Ottoman Empire at the end of World War I. An agglomeration of Kurds, Sunnis, and Shiites, it has never been held together by the religious or cultural identity of its population; indeed, over the past two decades, its status as a nation state has been guaranteed primarily by the terror, discipline, and ruthlessness of Saddam and his Arab Nationalist Baath Party. The party's credo was once defined as "Unity, Freedom, Socialism," but Baath leaders have come to concentrate, through the use of force, on the first of these goals exclusively. Because of the party's stranglehold on the country, there was a broad consensus among senior U.S. officials in the war's aftermath that Saddam's depar-ture could come only from within; in other words, that his end, if it came, would be Shakespearean—the unexpected shot from somebody he trusts—rather than the result of any mass protest movement. President Bush did not want to get involved any more than was absolutely necessary. Schwarzkopf, too, was realistic about the political ends to which military force could be applied once the battle he had engineered over several months had been stopped at one hundred hours.

This was not an easy time for the general. With the war over, fatigue inevitably set in. The exhilarating planning of a battle was replaced by the dispiriting planning of a protracted withdrawal, complicated by the fact that the punctiliousness of U.S. Customs makes bringing any dusty or sandy equipment back into the country virtually impossible. "It was a lot easier to get the stuff over here than it is getting it back," commented one weary logistics officer.

The Kuwaitis' procrastination in moving to rebuild their country was also a source of some irritation. After the end of the war, Sheik Jabir al-Ahmad al-Jabir al-Sabah, the Kuwaiti ruler, took more than two weeks to return from his comfortable exile in Taif, Saudi Arabia, arriving in Kuwait City only on March 14. Until then, it seems, the conditions were a little too unkempt for his taste. The U.S. Army found that delays, bickering, and disarray were the main characteristics of the country in the weeks after the war. Schwarzkopf visited Kuwait City on March 12, when he took a vial of sand from the city's beach and, according to one State Department official, exhorted the country's rulers, in no uncertain terms, to get down to work. On the same day, the port was finally reopened and a big ceremony organized. Schwarzkopf was invited. But he insisted on maintaining a low profile, and declined to attend.

Referring to General Douglas MacArthur, who fashioned the rebuilding of Japan after World War II, one official who spent a lot of time with Schwarzkopf in Riyadh said, "The tragedy is Schwarzkopf would have made a wonderful MacArthur without the hubris. He was exceedingly well equipped to coordinate the reconstruction of Kuwait. But Kuwait, unlike Japan, was not the enemy. It was the object of a liberation effort."

Colonel Lester Wilson of the 352nd Civil Affairs Command, who had been working for several months to prepare the reconstruction effort, said the U.S. Army "had a terrible time with the Kuwaitis trying to get things restarted. We had a unit of the Army standing by at the port for days ready to offload cargo, but the Kuwaitis could not organize any shipments. The port needed cranes and stevedores, but for weeks nothing happened. Many of the ministers remained in Taif, so we were having to deal with second-or third-level guys, and they liked to talk rather than do things. There was a lot of haggling over contracts, but very little action."

Consequently, the morale of Schwarzkopf's troops sagged. When would they get home? Like them, the CINC longed to return to his family. But he was determined to stay with his soldiers until after formal cease-fire terms were worked out by the United Nations—something not finally accomplished until April 6, 1991, when Iraq agreed to the establishment of a UN peacekeeping force in the Kuwaiti border area; the destruction of its biological and chemical weapons and long-range missiles; and the payment of reparations to Kuwait. All sales to Iraq of weapons of mass destruction and long-range ballistic missiles were also banned indefinitely.

The general was disturbed by the violent upheaval in Iraq and the sense that the order and cohesion of the buildup to war had been replaced by tumult and disarray. The press images of smiling U.S. soldiers had now given way to frenzied scenes of fleeing, bedraggled Kurdish refugees. By the end of March, Saddam had effectively quashed the uprisings in the north and south, sending more than half a million Kurds into refugee camps in southeastern Turkey and Iran.

But far outweighing this unease was Schwarzkopf's irritation at what he saw as the fickle, revisionist thinking of some commentators. Even within the coalition, he had, according to one well-placed official, to listen to the gripes of the Syrians and Egyptians, who now argued that the coalition should have gone into Baghdad. But the outside experts were worse. As all the erroneous prewar commentary had shown, armchair opinion is a facile commodity. It was so easy to question what a war costing billions of dollars had achieved: to say that Saddam was still there, Kuwait destroyed, the Kurds under attack and scattered, the Israeli-Palestinian conflict unresolved, and hundreds of thousands of U.S. troops still stuck in the desert.

But Schwarzkopf, according to those close to him, still had a clear sense of mission accomplished. As a soldier, he had done his duty, with the loss of an extraordinarily small number of American lives. Certainly, he had hoped for Saddam's downfall. But as the UN cease-fire terms made clear, Iraq was no longer a threat to any of the surrounding countries. Its nuclear, chemical, and biological warfare programs had been virtually shut down, its army shattered, its huge arsenal of armaments largely destroyed. The conservative Gulf states, with their immense oil reserves and equally immense strategic importance to the United States, were safe for the foreseeable future.

Moreover, Kuwait had been recaptured, a stand made in the name of the rule of law. This, for Schwarzkopf, was significant. He considers himself an idealist—he is certainly in no way a cynic—and he believes his idealism is directed toward the making of a better world. In Kuwait, the Iraqis had indulged in an orgy of butchery, killing those who resisted, terrorizing others. It was a ruthless occupation. "None of us wants to die," Schwarzkopf said, "but there are certain things out there worth fighting for. I would die for my family tomorrow, to protect my family, and I think most people would. And I think freedom, liberty . . . are some things that you have to be willing to die for."

On March 8, 1991, as he addressed troops of the XVIII Airborne Corps departing from Dhahran, Schwarzkopf made his position clear: "Despite the fact you were badly outnumbered, you were determined to show petty dictators that they just can't get away with bullying their neighbors and taking what they want because they think they are so tough. I think you not only proved that to one petty dictator but to any petty dictator anywhere in the world that should choose to try to pull the same stunt either in the near or the far future."

He went on to conjure up a vision of the military heroism whose pursuit had lain at the heart of his life's effort. Referring to the conduct of the Gulf War, he said, "Valiant charges by courageous men over 250 kilometers of enemy territory. Along with a force of over 1,500 tanks, almost 250 attack helicopters, over 48,500 pieces of military equipment moving around, behind, and into the enemy and totally breaking his back and defeating him in 100 hours. It's a war story worth telling, and every one of you deserves to tell it."

This, too, had been accomplished: pride had been restored in the Armed Forces. Sitting in Dhahran a couple of weeks after the war, Staff Sergeant James L. Washington of the 598th Maintenance Company out of Fort Benning, Georgia, said, "This uniform feels different now. It has more of a sense of pride. There's more . . . I feel more of a distinction as opposed to before." To an almost incredulous U.S. public, many of them used, since Vietnam, to thinking about the military in generally negative terms, a highly professional, motivated, and competent institution had suddenly been revealed. Men and women worked together harmoniously within it; so, too, did blacks and whites; and leaders led with a courage and articulateness that surprised people. Schwarzkopf had watched, from the inside, the slow transformation that led to this point; and now he had the immense satisfaction of seeing his work vindicated and appreciated by the public.

Moreover, this new U.S. Army had also been revealed to other countries in which, after Schwarzkopf's war, the glib assertions of American decline slipped less easily from people's tongues.

As important as anything to Schwarzkopf was the fact that the effort he had led was an international one, in which Americans were exposed to, and worked with, a wide range of nationalities. With his eclectic upbringing and wide traveling during his military career, he had long been concerned by what he saw as the parochialism betrayed by American youth.

He was thus particularly touched when he was invited to the French embassy in Riyadh in March to receive a general's sword and the French Foreign Legion's white kepi, with its distinctive flat circular top and almost horizontal visor. These were presented by General Maurice Schmitt, the chief of staff of the French Army, who came from Paris for the occasion. Schwarzkopf's French, although extremely rusty, was up to saying: "Merci beaucoup, mon général." He then made everyone laugh by revealing that Barbara Bush had been quite charmed by Brigadier General Daniel Gazeau, the second-in-command of the French forces, who, as the man conducting the French press briefings, had been appearing on U.S. television. "The President's wife asked me to find out who that man with the Maurice Chevalier accent is!" Schwarzkopf said.

Lieutenant General Roquejeoffre, the commander of the French forces in Saudi Arabia, explained his country's fascination with Schwarzkopf. "He appeared at first as something of a brute. But then people realized that he was in fact extraordinarily sensitive, with an unusual ability to listen to others and put them at their ease. There have been so many great generals for whom human life does not count that much. But he came across as a man who cared about each individual life. Moreover, he was a diplomat and a politician as well as a military man."

Schwarzkopf was determined to stress the international character of his victory to his troops. "You're going to take back the fact that the word 'Arab' isn't a bad word," Schwarzkopf told them, "that you don't judge all Arabs by the actions of a few."

He added, "You're going to take back the fact that there are many soldiers in this world and you worry about them and greatly respect them. And you are going to take back the fact that Islam is not a religion to be feared, it's a religion to be respected just as we respect all other religions; that's the American way." After all, he reminded them, their attack had been flanked by an Egyptian corps, by Kuwaitis and Omanis and Saudi Arabians.

In the name of the integration of the forces for which he had worked tirelessly, Schwarzkopf also told his army soldiers not to forget the "great Air Force that prepared the way for you," "the great Navy pilots that were there and the great ships that were at sea," and the "two divisions of Marines out there making a hard push into Kuwait City."

As he worked out all the details of getting his troops home—more than 200,000 of them would leave before he did—Schwarzkopf began to consider his own future. He was swamped by letters, teddy bears, and commercial as well as a few romantic propositions. He knew that he was a hero: a treacherous thing to be. Above all, he felt that he needed time—to be with his family and to reflect. Like any good general, he needed to gauge the lay of the land.

But one decision had to be made immediately. His retirement, after thirty-five years in the Army, was due in August. But, according to two people close to him, in the weeks after the war he was offered the post of chief of staff of the Army, replacing the retiring General Carl E. Vuono. The post was offered to him by Chairman Powell.

General Schwarzkopf declined. He had never particularly enjoyed life at the Pentagon; and the years after 1991 promised to be particularly grim, with the basic task at hand for the forces being the creation of the so-called peace dividend: that is, the reduction of budgets, closing of bases, and a 25 percent cut in troops over five years, decided by the Pentagon as the logical response to the winding down of the cold war. Indeed, within a couple of months of talking about cutting off and killing the Iraqi Army, Chairman Powell was talking about another kind of "viciousness"—this time in the closure of forty-three bases by 1997. "We must be vicious with this process," he told the Defense Base Closure and Realignment Commission on April 26, 1991.

Rather than administer this thankless process, Schwarzkopf decided to retire as planned. After his feat of soldiering in the Gulf, what greater challenge could he hope for? "Nothing he can do in the military," said his old friend Leroy Suddath, "would match what he had already done."

Slowly, the preparations for departure proceeded. By mid-April, nearly two months after the end of the war, Schwarzkopf was almost ready to leave, along with a party of about three hundred members of his CentCom staff. For a few weeks already, this staff had been allowed one twelve-hour shift off a week, in a break with the seven-days-a-week schedule they had followed since arriving. Most people were tired, reflective, and anxious to get home.

With soldiers at last getting some free time, they were able to see a little of Saudi Arabia. Up until then, most of them either had been out in the desert, or had shuttled between their rooms and work in Riyadh. One site they visited during this recreation time was the ruin of Dar'iyah, the town that, during the eighteenth century, had been the stronghold of the first empire of the House of Saud. Situated a few miles from the modern capital of Riyadh, Dar'iyah once stood at the center of a million-square-mile desert empire. But today it consists of no more than roofless homes of mud brick, the jagged vestiges of towers, and empty palaces where details such as an intricately painted wooden door suggest the past splendor of the walled city. From the surrounding desert comes a warm wind redolent only of a great and soothing emptiness.

Dar'iyah was destroyed in 1819 by an invading Turkish army led by Ibrahim Pasha. The Turks' superior technology quashed any Saudi resistance. With guns and howitzers that appeared as terrifying inventions to the desert people, they blasted the eighteenth-century capital of the House of Saud until there was nothing left. For the Saud family, it was a lesson they did not forget in the power of superior technology and the vulnerability of their desert civilization.

One hundred and seventy-one years later, they had another civilization to protect. In one way, it was similar to their first empire: it was built around a fiercely rigorous interpretation of Islam. In another, it was utterly different: it hinged on the enormous wealth produced by the oil reserves discovered by an American engineer in the 1930s. Oil money changed almost everything. As one looks out from Dar'iyah, some of its fruits are clear: the spaghetti junctions of massive, largely empty highways; countless electricity transmission towers striding across the desert; modern minarets and mosques; high-rise buildings and cranes lurking over a multitude of building sites. To conserve this second empire, the House of Saud did not hesitate to put technology on its side. In calling on the United States, King Fahd unleashed on the Iraqis the awful destructive power of "smart" bombs and cruise missiles, weapons as terrifying and startling to the Iraqis as the howitzer was to the Saudis in 1819.

General Schwarzkopf had hoped to avoid this onslaught. But once he felt compelled to fight, he followed the example of the Civil War generals he admired, and waged war ferociously. Seldom has any victory been so overwhelming.

On the day of his departure, Saturday, April 20, the Saudis rewarded him. At a ceremony in Riyadh, they presented him with the Order of King Abdul Aziz, First Class. No foreigner had received this decoration before. Presenting the award, Lieutenant General Khalid Bin Sultan said, "The American troops who came to Saudi Arabia were inspired by General Schwarzkopf's example and by their own instincts for fairness. They did indeed respect the values of this host nation. I have often said that if the world is to have a superpower, thank God it is the United States!"

This, the general later told his family, was a particularly moving moment for him. Initially, Lieutenant General Khalid had been suspicious of the American presence in Saudi Arabia and of General Schwarzkopf's role. But over time, the two men's relationship had improved to the point where they became real friends.

Khalid's glowing reference to the United States was a measure of the political distance traveled in the previous months. After he became the CINC at Central Command in November 1988, Schwarzkopf had found in his travels in the Middle East that there was a widespread suspicion of U.S. commitment to the region. Arms were being bought elsewhere, and, with them, political alliances being made, because the U.S. resolve was no longer credible to many Middle Eastern leaders. In six months, this tendency had been dramatically reversed. The general left Riyadh confident that lasting alliances and military arrangements would grow out of the coalition's victory. Because of the amount of oil in the Gulf, this was clearly a development of substantial political significance to Washington.

Accepting the award, Schwarzkopf in turn presented Lieutenant General Khalid with the Legion of Merit, the seventh-highest decoration in the U.S. military. Then, answering questions, he underlined his belief in the overwhelming success of his mission.

Referring to the Kurdish uprising, he said, "It's important to remember that this rebellion has been going on for many, many years. There's no question about the fact that the Kurds probably saw an opportunity to take advantage of a major defeat of the Iraqis to continue with their rebellion. But to somehow imply that because we did not continue for one more day the attack, that the rebellion did not succeed, is bogus." He went on, "I don't think that we should ever say that . . . what's happening to the Kurds now means that our mission failed. It's exactly the same thing that happened to the Kurds a few years ago at the end of the Iran-Iraq War. It's exactly the same thing that's happened to the Kurds for many years. Yes, we are disappointed that that has happened. But it does not affect the accomplishment of our mission one way or another."

Nine days before Schwarzkopf said this, on April 11, President Bush had announced a major U.S. relief effort for the more than 500,000 Iraqi Kurds fleeing into Turkey. This effort would involve sending over 10,000 American troops into northern Iraq to secure zones to which the Kurds could return in safety.

After the ceremony, Schwarzkopf said his last farewells. He had been offered the opportunity to return to a formal ceremony and parade in Washington, but had rejected this. He wanted to go directly to his family, whom he had not seen for almost eight months. Moreover, he told officials in Washington that he did not want soldiers to have to march on a Sunday.

It was a bright, blustery April day. In the early morning soldiers jogged along the beach at Tampa Bay. The lush golf course, with its palm trees and abundant azaleas, and its members in their electric buggies, seemed an image of the good life in America. MacDill Air Force Base, the home of Central Command, awaited General Schwarzkopf. Signs made by the expectant crowd said things like "Welcome Back," "Job Well Done," or "Dad Come Home And Get Your Hug."

General Schwarzkopf had wanted to come home as discreetly as possible. He said initially that he wanted to be met only by the personnel at the base and his family. But a few days before he was due to arrive, Brenda had heard some bitter comments on the radio about the general not allowing the people of Tampa to welcome him. She felt that he was being misinterpreted and called him in Riyadh to express her concerns. In the end, he said, "Let them open the post, so long as there is no big ceremony." He had one other specific request: that his black Labrador, Bear, be present for the occasion.

For several days before his arrival on April 28, 1991, volunteers had been blowing up red, white, and blue balloons to assemble into a huge balloon flag. But the spring day was so windy that the idea had to be abandoned at the last moment.

Nonetheless, the occasion, if not grand, was extremely festive. A sign, strung across one building, said: "MacDill AFB welcomes General Schwarzkopf and the CentCom staff." Despite the wind, a big American flag was maneuvered into place behind the podium set up for the general, his family, his dog, and various dignitaries. A military band played. Hundreds of people, waving flags, pennants, and yellow ribbons, stood in the early morning sunshine to greet the man who, over the previous six months, had stirred an American imagination deadened by sound-bite politics and savings-and-loan scandals.

The first to arrive, in his Lear jet, was the Kuwaiti ambassador to the United States, Sheik Saud Nasir al-Sabah, and members of his family. His presence had not been expected until a few hours before the ceremony. But the ambassador heard about General Schwarzkopf's arrival, canceled a previous engagement, and flew down.

Shortly afterward, with the same precision timing shown throughout his mission, General Schwarzkopf's white-and-gray Boeing 707 United States of America jet appeared in the clear sky above the palm trees of MacDill and landed at the appointed hour of 9 a.m. A small U.S. flag fluttered above the cockpit as the plane slowly taxied toward the waiting crowd. As the boarding ramp was pushed up to the main door, the General's wife, Brenda, sister Sally, children, Cynthia, Jessica, and Christian, and dog, Bear, moved to positions immediately below the aircraft.

When the door opened, General Schwarzkopf briskly saluted, staring straight ahead of him into the assembled crowd and the clear American day. Cheers greeted him. Exactly a quarter century had passed since he returned for the first time from Vietnam to encounter an indifference that shocked him.

After his salute, Schwarzkopf quickly abandoned any trace of military formality. He threw open his arms and, beaming with happiness, hurried down the ramp to embrace his family. Slowly he made his way through the crowd toward the podium, pausing to shake people's hands and kiss a multitude of babies. Although he was still dressed in desert fatigues and suede desert boots, it did not take an enormous effort of the imagination to visualize this big, smiling 240-pound man, at some future date, displaying this feel for the people in a political role, glad-handing admirers and pausing to listen to one and all. "We love you, General Schwarzkopf!" one woman yelled.

As he approached the podium, Schwarzkopf caught sight of a Vietnam veteran wearing a conspicuous badge saying: "In memory of the 58,044 brothers who never returned from Vietnam." He immediately turned to him and warmly grasped his hand. "Hi ya, buddy," he said, clapping an arm around the man's shoulder.

The general did not know it, but this man was Warren J. Stines, Jr., a former radio operator in the 3rd Marine Division who had been in Vietnam at the time of Schwarzkopf's second tour in 1970. Stines came home after a nervous breakdown and was a hundred percent disabled for several years. He returned strapped to a stretcher in a jet full of the maimed and disabled. They were piled in four stretchers high. There were people with chest wounds and double amputations, and the journey was punctuated with the cries of men under restraints screaming from pain or screaming to be released. When the plane at last arrived, a young woman from the Red Cross came aboard and gave everyone a bag containing stationery, envelopes, and some change to make telephone calls. At the bottom of the bag was a medal produced by the Veterans of Foreign Wars; it said: "Welcome home. Your country is grateful."

By no means did all Vietnam veterans receive such medals. Stines was at MacDill to present to Schwarzkopf a petition with 10,435 signatures requesting that the medal be reproduced and given to all veterans of the Gulf and Vietnam Wars.

"We had the same capacity, the same ability as those guys in the Gulf," Stines said, "but the only difference is the government would not allow us to do it in Vietnam. They were given the green light and we were put on hold. But *erase all that*. That's erased now. The people in the Gulf made us proud. I came here to thank Schwarzkopf for giving me back my pride. I came here to thank him for changing things because that's what America is all about— change, progress, the ability to overcome. We were asleep for a few years."

Within Schwarzkopf's family, too, a wound had been healed. At the airport, his sister Sally was conspicuous for the yellow sash she wore. The sash had been made by the general's other sister, Ruth, from whom he had been estranged after Vietnam. Ruth had kept a vigil for her brother throughout the months that he was in Saudi Arabia. An electric candle was lit in her home in Vermont. This war, she believed, was just in that it was necessary that Saddam Hussein be stopped. Thus, where Vietnam had driven the siblings apart, the Gulf War brought them closer. One of the first calls Schwarzkopf made on his return was to Ruth.

Schwarzkopf, flanked by his family, took up his appointed position on the podium, and the military band began to play "The Star-Spangled Banner." Tears welled in the general's eyes. He seemed to wage an enormous internal battle to hold back the emotion about to burst inside him: the joy of homecoming, the lingering tension of his mission, the pride of having served his country well as a soldier.

When the anthem was over, Brigadier General William M. Boice, who had remained at MacDill as CentCom's chief of staff during the war, pronounced "those two words that every warrior loves to hear: 'Welcome Home.' "

Schwarzkopf gave the thumbs-up sign. "It's great to be home," he said. "I can't describe to you the emotion in all our hearts to be back in this great free nation . . . and to hear this great national anthem. It's an emotion I will never forget." He then turned to the Kuwaiti ambassador and said, "Mr. Ambassador, I'm proud to report to you that Kuwait is free!"

The general's thoughts then turned to others. He urged the crowd not to leave with him but to wait for the three hundred members of his CentCom staff arriving a half hour later. And he reminded them that although more than 50 percent of the troops were home, "there are still over 200,000 troops there, and I urge you all to continue the great support until the last American is home."

He concluded with some very simple words. "It's a great day," he said. "A great day to be a husband"—and he turned to Brenda—"a great day to be a father"—and he turned to his children—"a great day to be a brother"—and he turned to Sally—"a great day to be a master of a great dog"—and Bear was straining at the leash—"a great day to be a soldier"—and he looked straight out at the crowd—"and a great day to be an American."

The United States had changed in Schwarzkopf's absence. It had not solved any of its problems. The federal deficit, the recession, the widening gap between rich and poor, the problems of inner cities, of education, of the banking system, of drugs and AIDS and violence and ailing industries from Detroit to Texas—all this and more remained. But the country looked at itself a little differently; and in this changed attitude some saw at least the opportunity to tackle the ills of America with a new vigor.

In an age where political discourse, and so the practice of leadership, appeared to have been reduced to the management of fleeting appearances on television, Schwarzkopf was unmistakably a man who could not be packaged. He was, in every sense, too big for that. His attraction lay in his being a whole man, comfortable enough with his emotions to know that he did not have to hide them in order to lead. He wore a uniform but also, as he said, wore his heart on his sleeve; he was unafraid to talk about liberty, ideals, and dying for one's beliefs; he commanded more than half a million men and women with an absolute authority but without hesitating to mingle and show that he was one of them. In many ways he was old-fashioned, but to most American people it was reassuring that old-fashioned virtues could indeed win the day.

Above all, perhaps, he had the courage of his own convictions. In the words of Richard Daft, a professor of management at Vanderbilt University, "Schwarzkopf works from the inside out. He takes what is inside himself and convinces the world to accept it, instead of looking to what the world wants and trying to provide it." This quality had emerged in him many years earlier. For example, in Vietnam in 1970, Schwarzkopf found a group of officers whose main concern had become that of avoiding mistakes—an attitude not uncommon among corporate officers today. Instead of joining the fold, he chose to impose his own aggressive vision on his battalion, revolutionizing the lives of his men in a way that was painful but that many of them came to appreciate. Later, in posts from Alaska to Germany to Georgia, he was never afraid to break the mold: not for the sake of being different, but for the sake of motivating the men and women in his command to do better and feel fulfilled by working toward an ideal. He was never interested in the status quo or in leading by merely accepting what he was told. In the Gulf, too, he did not hesitate to assert his own view—as in his firm insistence that he needed 500,000 men, not half that, to attack the Iraqis.

Where did this gift for leadership come from? From a very early age, Schwarzkopf was clearly pushed by his parents to set himself the highest ideals. When he was only ten, his father was concerned to impress upon him that childhood was giving way to youth and that he was well equipped for the great challenges of life. But the family's unusually lofty standards—of honor, duty, and endeavor—were not set with a cool and distant severity. On the contrary, Schwarzkopf appears to have been encouraged by a father who was both emotional and idealistic and by a loving mother with a strong streak of independence. He grew up in an atmosphere of exceptional warmth. Both his parents were unafraid of change and going it alone: his father founded the New Jersey State Police and then forged an effective gendarmerie in Iran; his mother, before her marriage, was a single working woman in New York, living far from her divorced parents, at a time when this was most unusual. Together, they moved around the world for many years, adapting to a host of new challenges and providing their children with an eclectic culture.

By the time he was thirteen, Schwarzkopf's parents had sown the seeds that were to burgeon into his capacity for rapport with those who served under him. Three children, reared in homey circumstances in small-town America, were suddenly transported to a palace in Persia where they were surrounded by servants. But at the first hint of grandiose illusions, they were rapidly and firmly brought to earth by a parental edict forbidding them from giving orders to the servants and by repeated reminders that they were *ordinary Americans*. Hence it was natural that the general should show an affinity for other ordinary Americans decades later; a similar respect for other nationalities was drilled into him by a father who insisted that he eat a sheep's eyeball rather than give offense to his Iranian hosts.

All this clearly contributed to Schwarzkopf's character. But Jay Conger, a professor of management at McGill University and author of two books on charismatic leadership, suggested that "the family sets the tone for a true leader, but that is not enough. After the family provides the desire to succeed, the motivation and the confidence, a challenging mission as a young adult is often very important in the development of a charismatic leader."

For Schwarzkopf, this "mission" was Vietnam. There—in unnecessary deaths, lies, and failure—he saw the costs of bad leadership. At the same time, he was able to develop his own ideas about leading men and put them into practice in grim circumstances. By the time he was thirty-five, he already had what amounted to a philosophy of leadership forged in the face of life-and-death challenges. This philosophy involved an unusual mix of discipline, love, courage, iconoclasm, and leading by example. It was an outlook that still retained at its heart the dreams of glory he had revealed at West Point when he talked of wanting to emulate the great commanders of history; but it was now tempered with a new realism.

For two decades, these qualities were known only within the Army. Then, just a year from what would have been an anonymous retirement, fate intervened in the form of Saddam Hussein's invasion of Kuwait. Abruptly, Schwarzkopf stood center-stage for the world to judge how his upbringing, his education, his subsequent experience of peaks and troughs, and, most of all, his innermost character would be put to the test. It was a test of the heroic dimensions he had dreamed of thirty-five years earlier. He was not found wanting.

America, or at least a very large part of it, was entranced. Schwarzkopf came home to something approaching Schwarzkopfmania. By turns curt, humorous, explosive, desolate, and icily determined, he had become, despite himself, the world's first truly "telegenic" general. There were bubble-gum cards, "Stormin' Norman" sandwiches, and suggestions that he become a football coach, a business leader, or a university chancellor.

In corporate America, there was even talk of a new Gulf School of Management, stressing the importance of managers mingling with employees, of motivation talks, of intelligence on the competition, of surprise schemes, and the need to really blitz a new market rather than coming at it in a half-hearted way. Schwarzkopf's press conferences on the war became instant manuals of management style. Above all, Schwarzkopf was being looked to by corporate America as an example of leadership through vision and optimism, in contrast to the defensive style of management that hides behind bureaucratic rules and seeks above all to avoid mistakes.

He seemed to have engendered some hope in what had seemed a generally dispirited country. Where America was talking itself into a recession, it appeared, on Schwarzkopf's return, to be talking itself out of one. "There was a malaise that I trace all the way back to Vietnam," said Adrian Cronauer, a Washington lawyer who, as a military broadcaster in Vietnam, was the model for the *Good Morning, Vietnam* movie. "It was a sense of being unable to do anything worthwhile or laudatory. Now I sense a revival of confidence, a can-do attitude that I have not seen for many years, an interest in the rest of the world that was not there before, and more optimism. People are looking for new opportunities."

Whether this attitude amounted to something substantial and lasting, or a mere fleeting whim, was hard to judge in the immediate aftermath of the war. With Saddam still in power and the Kurds suffering greatly, some argued that the war had merely been a colossal waste of money. Others saw a danger that the braggadocio and bluster of victory would only distract a society whose problems remained as widespread as ever. Even within the Armed Forces, there were misgivings. "People said they were proud of me, they sent me food, toys, greetings," said Air Force Staff Sergeant Julio Rios on his return to New York. "But what really got to me is we did not need that stuff over there, we had plenty of everything. They should have sent it right here, to our cities, where we have people who are starving." He went on, "We did not have to go that far, we could have avoided the war. We have not accomplished anything. Saddam is still in power killing people. We had him on the ropes, and once we had started, we should have gone all the way. I think the war could have been avoided, but once we were fighting, we should not have stopped when we did."

Most Americans, however, were satisfied. Indeed, Schwarzkopf's popularity was such that there were insistent calls for him to enter politics. Florida Republicans were eager to draft him for the 1992 legislative elections, or even for the presidential campaign. While not ruling out a possible political foray at some future date, Schwarzkopf appeared to harbor serious misgivings.

It seemed that Schwarzkopf was in fact being tugged two ways. In the general's family, politics has always been viewed with deep suspicion. His father's loathing of the former New Jersey governor Hoffman was passed on to the children in the form of a contempt for the deal-making and unscrupulousness of the political world. The military was sacred because of its identification with certain immovable values. By contrast, politics was entirely fluid, devoid of fixed principle. "Norm hates politics," according to his sister Sally. "My father was the same. He couldn't stand politics. They were begging him to run for the Senate, but he always refused."

Still, Schwarzkopf's potential gift for politics is clear to everyone—and certainly to himself. He has the popular touch. He appears to like the limelight and to enjoy "working" a crowd. He dominates but is capable of being deferential; he is strong-willed but diplomatic; he speaks a language that everyone understands. His temper, most of the time, is now under control. He clearly enjoys leadership and performing on a large stage; at this point, a quiet retirement for him seems inconceivable. Moreover, his hold on the imagination of the American public is a phenomenon that has not been seen in U.S. society for many years.

In public, he has said that he is an "independent." But, according to his family, he has voted Republican in the past three elections—twice for Reagan and then for Bush—essentially because of his firm belief in the need for a strong defense policy. It would thus seem more natural, but by no means inevitable, that he would, like Eisenhower, emerge on a Republican ticket.

But if he did enter politics, Schwarzkopf might find the endless need for compromise hard to accept. He is naturally uncompromising. Even in his statements since the war, he has shocked—and irked—some retired officers, including old friends, with his forthrightness.

For example, by stating outright that officers, himself included, were made to lie about body count in Vietnam, he amazed his old friend from West Point Leroy Suddath. "Schwarzie never lied. I never lied. *No officer would do that*," Suddath insisted. "I was shocked at that and think there must be a misunderstanding. I doubt seriously if anybody ever told anybody to inflate numbers. That was a great shock to me, and I hope the remark is clarified."

General William C. Westmoreland was outraged. "I was surprised by what Schwarzkopf said about Vietnam," he said. "I can't conceive of anybody encouraging a lie or his lying even if encouraged to do so. The remark showed a side of his personality I was not aware of. A vindictive side. What a shocking statement. I can't imagine that. I can't conceive of it happening. I was amazed that he would make such a broad uncomplimentary statement that I am sure an awful lot of people would disagree with. I deplore the thought of there being on the scene an internal conflict and animosity between Desert Storm and Vietnam. What a disservice that would be. It is unconscionable. The soldiers in Vietnam did the job given them by politicans well. Schwarzkopf's words were so imprudent. They set the stage for this conflict I am describing between veterans of the two wars. I mean, this was a four-day war! Skillfully done, yes, but with all the advantages."

Schwarzkopf also stumbled into a brief but awkward misunderstanding with the President when he stated publicly that his advice had been to "continue the march" rather than call a cease-fire. His inclination is to speak out, and he may find that in the political arena a lot of people do not appreciate that. Still, Schwarzkopf told *Time* magazine: "That's a sad commentary, when we say that the representatives of the American people can't say what they believe."

On balance, it seems likely that he will bide his time. During the Gulf campaign, he told *The New York Times* that he was neither a hawk nor a dove; rather, he was an owl, one who hopes "to watch, to learn and be wise." He has expressed a special interest in education and might be drawn to being a university dean or chancellor if such an opportunity arose. The environment is another cause to which he would like to contribute.

But in the end the pressure to try politics may just be too tempting to resist. To an American public tired of the style of its politicians, he has suggested the possibility of renewal. That will not be quickly forgotten. Eisenhower was fifty-five at the end of World War II in 1945, rejected an invitation to be a presidential candidate in 1948, and ultimately ran and won in 1952. Schwarzkopf was fifty-six at the end of the Gulf War. He has time.

• • •

Schwarzkopf came home to an astonishing array of gifts. There were his Christmas presents from his family arranged beneath the branches of a tree that had been painted silver. But far outnumbering these were the gifts sent by admirers throughout the country and piled in the dining room and the garage. He began opening these on the Sunday of his return; but most had to be left for the following day.

All of Monday, April 29, 1991, was spent going through them. Schwarzkopf and his daughter Cynthia opened the presents in the garage. There were hundreds of different kinds of teddy bears, ranging from small creatures to five-foot giants. They were all stacked in the sun room of the house. There was also a big bronze sculpture of a bear fishing. Although the children kept exclaiming, "I want this" and "I want that," Schwarzkopf decided to give most of the presents to hospitals and orphanages.

His sister Sally said Schwarzkopf seemed little changed. "The one thing that seemed different in those first few days," she remarked, "is that he was not interested in watching the television news. Before going to Saudi Arabia, he would always come home and switch it on. I wanted to watch the arrival ceremony on the local news on Sunday. But he was not interested."

Schwarzkopf did remark how much his son Christian, aged thirteen, had grown up in his absence. His voice had deepened and he had become a young man. "And I missed that," the general commented with regret.

On Tuesday, April 30, Schwarzkopf went to Washington and lunched with the President. On his return, he said that it had been wonderful and that the President had asked him more questions about skeet shooting than about the war. His only regret concerned the food. In Saudi Arabia, Schwarzkopf had conceived a passion for lamb. The filet mignon at the White House was very small, so Schwarzkopf was delighted when some lamb chops were also offered. But at that moment the President engaged him in conversation and by the time the general had finished talking, the lamb chops were gone!

By the end of the week, after a day of skeet shooting and a day back at work at MacDill, Schwarzkopf was relaxed enough to consider watching a movie. After dinner, he looked through the videotapes and asked Sally if she would prefer to watch a documentary about an Indian chief or *Dear America: Letters from Vietnam*—a movie produced by the Vietnam Veterans Ensemble Theater Company and the Couturie Company about Vietnam. It is based on letters sent from soldiers there. Sally said she did not mind which video they watched. Schwarzkopf chose the Vietnam movie.

Sally was worried. "That's a very sad movie," she warned him. But Schwarzkopf put it on, and brother and sister sat watching it from beginning to end in silence.

They watched President Lyndon Johnson saying, "I cannot promise you the end will come this year or even next year." They watched soldiers with legs blown away, their buddies carrying them through elephant grass. They heard one G.I. say, "Anyone who walks more than fifty feet through elephant grass in this place should get a Purple Heart." They listened: "The nights are pure hell"; "You kill because that little son of a bitch is doing his best to kill you"; "Better to fight and die for freedom than to live under oppression and fear"; "Just hope to stay alive day to day and get back home and go to school." The statistics kept flashing up on the screen. December 1966: 385,600 soldiers in Vietnam and 6,644 dead. December 1967: 485,600 soldiers in Vietnam and 16,021 dead. December 1968: 536,100 soldiers in Vietnam and 31,160 dead. December 1969: 475,200 soldiers in Vietnam and 40,024 dead. And so on until there were more than 58,000 American soldiers dead. They saw a sad Christmas service, soldiers in tears, and soldiers scarcely able to talk. And there was General Westmoreland, crisply dressed, asking a "lad" how he was doing. They heard the agony of a mother asking questions forever unanswerable about her lost son. They watched the fear and the hopelessness. They saw a soldier, angry over the outcry of the 1970 Kent State University killings of four students, asking, "So why don't they cry out over the more than 40,000 red-blooded Americans who have already given their lives in Vietnam? *Damn it.* Help *us*." And they listened to one nineteen-year-old soldier writing to his parents and saying, "I can't believe half the shit I've seen here so far. It's not that I can't understand this war. *It's that I can't understand war. Period.*"

The movie ended at 11:15 p.m. on Friday, May 3, 1991. Schwarzkopf had watched with an expression of deep intensity. Sally, worried, kept glancing over at him. It was just over two decades since he had been in Vietnam, a week since his return from the Gulf. When it was over, she broke the long silence by saying, "That stuff is hard to take. Isn't it?"

Schwarzkopf did not reply. He removed the cassette, placed it back in its case, and, in silence, went to bed.

Acknowledgments

We are deeply grateful to General H. Norman Schwarzkopf's sister Sally, whose kindness and consistent support were uniquely helpful in revealing the character of her brother and the salient events that shaped him. Without her unfailing enthusiasm and insight, it would have been impossible to draw this portrait.

Our thanks also to the following people for their valuable help: Colonel Paul Cullinane for sharing his precious Super 8 footage and his memories with a stranger; Paul "Buck" Deer for devoting much time to reliving the difficult days of Vietnam and for evoking the war in an extraordinarily vivid way; Lieutenant Colonel Faris R. Kirkland for his insights into the psychology of military leadership; Colonel Tom Cameron for sharing his recollections of Vietnam; Professor Mark Gasiorowski for his expertise on Iran and particularly the CIA-instigated coup of 1953; Leroy Suddath, Dave Horton, John McGuinn, Ward Le Hardy, and Charles Prather, West Point cadets of the class of 1956, for their memories of the Academy; General Richard E. Cavazos for his help in understanding Schwarzkopf's style of leadership and soft spot for hunting dogs; Vice Admiral John Metcalf III for his assessment of Operation Urgent Fury in Grenada; Sergeant Thomas De Feo of the New Jersey State Police Museum for sharing information on H. Norman Schwarzkopf, Sr.; and Walter Unger for his research into the background of the Schwarzkopf family.

For their unstinting help in revealing the details of Desert Shield and Desert Storm, we are also grateful to retired

General George B. Crist, who provided a frank assessment of Central Command; Major Tom O'Brien, who circumvented military bureaucracy in Saudi Arabia with charm and skill; Major General Barry R. McCaffrey, who conveyed what it is to be a warrior; Lieutenant General Gary E. Luck, who recounted how he led his XVIII Corps on one of the fastest and most remarkable flanking attacks in military history; Colonel John Marcellow, Major Richard Rowe, and Major Charles Lane Toomey, who were patient in their detailed explanations; Brigadier General Joe N. Frazar, who provided many insights on Schwarzkopf's style of leadership; and Lieutenant General Michel Roquejeoffre, the commander of the French forces in Saudi Arabia, who offered an intriguing assessment of Schwarzkopf as diplomat.

Colonel James L. Anderson, Brigadier General John "Doc" Bahnsen, Bill Chupp, Colonel David Crotty, Mike Filben, David Means, Lieutenant General Harold Moore, Ted Regan, Kermit Roosevelt, Bill Savage, Colonel Ned V. J. Longsworth, Brigadier General Daniel Gazeau, General William C. Westmoreland, General Michael J. Dugan, John S. Kincannon, and Richard W. Murphy were all most helpful and we thank them for their guidance. We also thank the several government officials, both U.S. and European, who offered their insights but preferred to remain anonymous.

This book is based on more than one hundred interviews conducted in the United States, Saudi Arabia, and Kuwait.

In addition, we are indebted to the fine Gulf War reporting of *The New York Times, The Wall Street Journal, The Washington Post*, the *Los Angeles Times, Newsweek*, and *Time* magazine. Often the correspondents of these publications were obliged to circumvent the obstacles posed in their path by restrictive military regulations; only through their remarkable efforts was a truthful picture painted of the war.

General Schwarzkopf's interviews with Barbara Walters

of ABC Television and David Frost of public television constituted an invaluable source. So, too, did interviews with General Schwarzkopf published in *The New York Times, The Washington Post*, the *Los Angeles Times, Life, The New Republic*, the *Atlanta Journal-Constitution, Newsweek, U.S. News & World Report*, and *Time*. Rather than resort to footnotes in a book that owes as much to journalistic techniques as to the more distanced scholarship of biographical research, we have chosen to identify sources in the body of the text.

The following books provided particularly useful background: *Friendly Fire* by C. D. B. Bryan (G. P. Putnam's Sons); *The Lindbergh Case* by Jim Fisher (Rutgers University Press); *The Airman and the Carpenter: The Lindbergh Kidnapping and the Framing of Richard Hauptmann* by Ludovic Kennedy (Viking Press); *The Kingdom: Arabia and The House of Sa'ud* by Robert Lacey (Harcourt Brace Jovanovich); *The Seven Pillars of Wisdom* by T. E. Lawrence (Doubleday & Company); *On War* by Karl von Clausewitz (Penguin Books); *The Art of War* by Sun Tzu (Shambhala Dragon Editions); and *Saddam Hussein and the Crisis in the Gulf* by Judith Miller and Laurie Mylroie (Times Books).

The pressures in writing a book quickly are enormous. We thank our superb agent, Amanda Urban, whose swift effectiveness is unrivaled and whose upbeat inspiration helped us get the job done. Anne Marie Somma and Tamara Grobovsky did much painstaking research that was essential to this book. Our thanks also to Martin Arnold for his consummate navigational skills, developed in more than thirty years on the waters of *The New York Times*. Jan Benzel, Bill Carter, Edwin McDowell, Alex S. Jones, Randall Rothenberg, and Deirdre Carmody of *The New York Times* picked up the slack and offered tremendous encouragement. Barbara Williams of *The New York Times* unraveled XyWrite: many thanks. Rachel Powell of *The New York Times* conceived and drew the wonderful maps:

we are most grateful to her. Susan Di Sesa was a true friend to us in this enterprise. At Farrar, Straus & Giroux, we are indebted to Jennifer Trone and Elaine Chubb for their assistance, and especially to Linda Healey, our discerning editor, for her wise guidance and her support.

We are grateful to Professor Sydney Cohen and June Cohen for constant encouragement, to Robin and Jennifer Walden for the calls that kept us sane, and to Jessica, Daniel, and Aaron for their tolerance of their dads' constant "typing."

Professor Bert Cohen offered much excellent advice; the final shape of this work owes a great deal to his help. Martine Benatar Cohen, whose understanding made this book possible, was a constant inspiration. Above all, we wish to thank Gail Hammer, whose help, both in editorial contributions and in moral support, was immeasurable: this book could not have been written without her.

Index

357

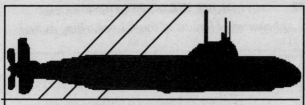

Tom Clancy's

#1 *New York Times* Bestsellers

_THE SUM OF ALL FEARS 0-425-13354-0/$6.99
"Vivid...engrossing...a whiz-bang page-turner!"
—The New York Times Book Review

_CLEAR AND PRESENT DANGER 0-425-12212-3/$5.99
"Clancy's best work since *The Hunt For Red October.*"
—Publishers Weekly

_THE CARDINAL OF THE KREMLIN 0-425-11684-0/$5.99
"The best of the Jack Ryan series!"*—The New York Times*

_PATRIOT GAMES 0-425-13435-0/$5.99
"Marvelously tense . . . He is a master of the genre he seems
to have created."*—Publishers Weekly*

_RED STORM RISING 0-425-10107-X/$5.99
"Brilliant . . . Staccato suspense."*—Newsweek*

_THE HUNT FOR RED OCTOBER 0-425-13351-6/$5.99
"Flawless authenticity, frighteningly genuine."
—The Wall Street Journal